CW00471695

Imprisonment:
European perspectives

Imprisonment: European perspectives

Edited by
John Muncie and **Richard Sparks**

 Published in association
with The Open University

New York London Toronto Sydney Tokyo Singapore

First published 1991 by
Harvester Wheatsheaf,
66 Wood Lane End, Hemel Hempstead,
Hertfordshire, HP2 4RG
A division of
Simon & Schuster International Group

Typeset in 10/12 pt Times
by Photoprint, Torquay, Devon

Printed and bound in Great Britain

British Library Cataloguing in Publication Data

Imprisonment: European perspectives.
 I. Muncie, John II. Sparks, Richard
 364.6
 ISBN 0–7450–1127–6
 ISBN 0–7450–1128–4 pbk

1 2 3 4 5   95 94 93 92 91

Contents

Editors' Introduction

This volume of contributions to the study of European prisons and penal systems appears at a time when, perhaps more than ever before, problems of imprisonment are at the forefront of public consciousness and debate. In the United Kingdom, the penal system has broken out of its traditional invisibility, through a succession of prison disturbances, industrial disputes and increasingly spectacular riots and roof-top protests and subsequent judicial enquiries. In attempts to understand and come to terms with a penal system that is commonly regarded as 'in crisis', academic commentators and newspaper editors have begun to look elsewhere – notably other European countries – in what can only be described as a desperate search for instances of good practice which could help politicians and penal administrators find a solution to current ills. A desire and energy to reform the penal system is arguably greater now than at any time since the rehabilitative vision of the Gladstone report of 1895.

This volume is intended as a timely contribution towards enhancing the quality of such debates. It underlines the importance of comparative study at a time when the economic, legal and political integration of all European nations is high on the political agenda. It does so firstly by reminding us that a willingness and desire to learn from the practices and policies of other countries has strong historical precedents dating back at least to the sixteenth century, and reaching its apogee in the work of John

Howard at the end of the eighteenth century. Secondly, this volume explores contemporary penal policies in a number of European countries – particularly England and Wales, Scotland, Germany, Holland and France – with a view to highlighting the *diversity* of practice that can, and does, exist within roughly comparable industrial societies. Thirdly, the final section of this volume considers the possibilities for the future *convergence* of policy and practice under the auspices of the 1987 European Prison Rules as well as the influence of the European Convention on Human Rights, especially via its judicial arm, the Court of Human Rights at Strasbourg.

Writers on crime and punishment have often alluded to the need for comparative study. However, the promised comparisons have, with one or two notable exceptions, rarely been forthcoming. Criminology and penology (these 'bastard' disciplines as Herman Mannheim called them) are necessarily affected by changing local penal climates and the press of immediate, and often parochial, concerns and political battles. Under such circumstances it is only too easy to mistakenly regard the contingencies of one's own national situation, for example its accustomed judicial reasoning or the size of its prison population, as unavoidable and necessary things.

This position has now begun to change. The trickle of prisoners' cases heard before the European Court of Human Rights; the incipient influence of the European Prison Rules; the regular publication by the Council of Europe of the respective rates of imprisonment in member states: developments such as these have begun to demonstrate to reformers, academics, lawyers and administrators that a comparative awareness is both possible and beneficial.

There are several reasons why we think it important that the analysis of prisons and penal systems should now assume a comparative form. Comparison works against taken-for-grantedness, whether that takes the form of complacency or of pessimistic fatalism. The depth of penal problems in the United Kingdom and United States of America, two countries which do look at one another a good deal, can encourage resignation. Examples from the Netherlands and Scandinavia show the Anglo-American audience that it is possible for industrial societies, with moderate crime rates, to reduce their reliance on imprisonment without grievous consequences. In this sense comparison is about identifying difference and using it as a spur to action.

On the other hand, comparison is also about more than simply discovering that the grass is greener, or less green, on the other side of the prison fence. Indeed, in a wider theoretical and historical sense the similarities and connections between national systems may be equally or more important. As Foucault comments on the emergence of new models of incarceration during the eighteenth century, it is a phenomenon which 'has European dimensions'. At this level the questions which arise include: how did it come about that at particular stages of their development *all* European nation-states adopted the 'prison solution'; how have their paths subsequently diverged such that not only the level but also the character of imprisonment now varies markedly; and what does this suggest about the future of imprisonment?

It is worth remembering that amongst the differing historical sources represented here both the work of Howard and of Rusche and Kirchheimer were in their different ways pan-European in scope. Howard was in a very clear sense the first comparative penologist, and the breadth of knowledge which he acquired on his prodigious journeys contributed greatly to the authority of his work and the extent of his influence. Equally, Rusche and Kirchheimer's account of the rise of the prison in the context of the development of industrial society reminds us that the very existence of contemporary modes of punishment is only really intelligible in relation to upheavals and forces which were continental in scale.

Whether contemporary economic and political changes in Europe will prove as momentous for the future of punishment as those which Rusche and Kirchheimer detail cannot be foretold. What is certain, however, is that the analysis of modern penality in Europe must now take account not only of differences between practices in particular countries but also of social, legal and administrative processes which exceed the former boundaries of the nation-state.

This book is intended to begin the process of opening up our understanding of different penal systems and enhancing our assessment of the possible impact European integration could have on each nation-state's legal and penal strategies. It is, of course, only a partial survey of the many issues, concerns and

debates which are pertinent to the study of diversity and convergence in European penality. No single volume can hope to be fully
comprehensive in geographical scope or thematic coverage. In
large measure we have been restricted by the availability of
information with which to work. For example, this book does not
include chapters on the differential treatment of women and ethnic
minorities in different jurisdictions. To the best of our knowledge,
after wide consultation, library and computer searches, such work
has yet to be undertaken or is in its infancy. We can only hope
that the current interest in establishing a European dialogue will
eventually produce the necessary enthusiasm and resources to
enable such projects to come to fruition.

The volume is also designed as an integral part of the Open
University post-graduate course *Doing Prison Research* offered by
the Faculty of Social Sciences. The course forms part of the Open
University's *Advanced Diploma in Criminology*. Whilst the contents of this volume have been chosen and are best understood in
the light of the teaching objectives and contents of the course, they
will be of interest to all those policy makers, practitioners and
students of criminology and penology who recognise that the final
decade of the twentieth century will be increasingly dominated by
the influence of pan-European decisions on how we define, treat
and punish the 'imprisoned citizen'.

Richard Sparks
John Muncie

March 1991

Acknowledgements

The editors and publisher wish to thank the following who have kindly given permission for the use of copyright material:

Michael Adler and Brian Longhurst for extracts from *The Scottish Government Yearbook*, 1990 and 1991 volumes.

Columbia University Press for extracts from *Punishment and Social Structure* by G. Rusche and O. Kircheimer, Columbia University Press, 1939.

The Council of Europe for the European Prison Rules.

Macmillan Press for D. Melossi, *The Establishment of Modern Prison Practice in Continental Europe* in D. Melossi and M. Pavarini (eds), *The Prison and the Factory*, Macmillan Press, 1981.

Oxford University Press for the article *The Origins and Consequences of Dutch Penal Policy* by David Downes, *British Journal of Criminology*, Volume 22, No. 4, October 1982.

While every attempt has been made where appropriate to trace the copyright holders of the extracts included in this volume, the editors and publishers would be pleased to hear from any interested parties.

PART 1

The origins of penal systems

Introduction

The first part of this book concerns the social history of imprisonment. In doing so it reflects our acknowledgement that debates and issues surrounding the proper role of prison in contemporary society can only be enhanced through a close examination of why such institutions were originally constructed and with what purpose.

The particular readings have been selected because collectively they illustrate four main themes:

Firstly by locating specific forms of imprisonment in their precise socio-historical contexts we can note how the role and purpose of incarceration changes according to economic and ideological circumstances.

Secondly the readings begin to open up the benefits of an approach which is comparative on both historical and international dimensions. Throughout, we have been keen to illustrate the correspondences and divergencies between different forms of punishment by contrasting European countries. The readings deal primarily with the seventeenth and eighteenth centuries and in particular with the ways in which the shift from houses of correction to the 'modern' prison was established, not only in England, but in comparable European countries. Our comparative material, in the main, comes from such northern European countries as France, Germany and Holland.

Thirdly the readings illustrate current debates between historians about the explanation for the chronology of the development of modern systems of punishment. For some the origins of imprisonment lie in the rehabilitative ethos of the houses of correction first established in England in 1557. For others, the birth of the modern prison coincides with the beginnings of an industrialised urban society or with the emergence of a capitalist mode of production. The readings also reflect the continuing debate between liberal or humanitarian readings of the history of imprisonment and those emanating from a more radical or revisionist position. The debate here, in essence, is concerned with the degree to which penal reform was instigated by key philanthropic individuals or driven by a wider set of economic and political imperatives. Commentators likewise differ on the question of what counts as 'progress' in the matter of penal reform and penal politics. Historical research, then, is not a simple matter of telling the facts in an unproblematic fashion. Rather history is a profoundly political subject which is underwritten by the ideological concerns of its author. These readings should be studied with this warning in mind.

Finally, a historical perspective guards against the impression that modes of punishment are either entirely new or unchanging. We find that disillusionment with a purely coercive function of prisons surfaces as early as the sixteenth century. Already debates had begun about the best means by which the incarcerated could perform some contemporarily defined positive role and go on to lead what came later to be termed a 'good and useful life'. Similarly, a historical perspective helps to make us aware that questions of penal conditions and the rights of prisoners, far from being just contemporary issues, have been a major topic of disagreement almost since the first forms of incarceration were established.

We begin with John Howard's account of the condition of prisons in England, Germany, Holland, Austrian Flanders and France in the late eighteenth century. Taken from his renowned work *The State of the Prisons* first published in 1777, these extracts not only mark the work of the first comparative penologist, but, in their attention to detail, the first systematic attempt to provide a complete account of prison regimes. Howard travelled widely throughout Europe and witnessed prison conditions at first hand. His graphic descriptions of distress in English prisons and his more favourable response to the organisation and conditions in some European prisons, such as the rasp-houses in Holland, provided the impetus for his drafting of a Bill to be considered by the English Parliament and which in part laid the foundation for reform of the prison system at the turn of the century.

The reading from Austin van der Slice marks the first attempt from within modern criminology to account for and assess the nature and effects of the sixteenth-century houses of correction; the forebears of those Dutch prisons for which Howard reserved so much praise. Van der Slice establishes how the use of imprisonment for 'reformatory' purposes marked a radical departure from previous practice where coercive or purely custodial principles were paramount. As a result the house of correction is frequently cited as the first example of modern imprisonment. In accordance with the traditions of a humanitarian history, van der Slice emphasises the positive and progressive aspects of such regimes as the rasp-houses in Amsterdam and the Bridewells in London. Their rise is attributed in the main to the enlightened vision of aldermen, justices of the peace and other public officials.

Georg Rusche and Otto Kirchheimer provide us with a competing interpretation of the origins of houses of correction. By establishing a relationship between social structural variables, such as the state of the labour market and changing forms of punishment over time, their work represented a powerful challenge to orthodox histories. It began to call into question both the humanitarianism of penal reform and also the legitimation of the State's power to punish. Drawing freely from examples across Europe, but in the main Germany and England, Rusche and Kirchheimer argue that the origins of forced labour in the houses of correction lie in the population decline and shortages of labour in the seventeenth century, whilst later prisons, which they identify as having a more repressive function, were born from a period of over-population and large-scale unemployment instigated by the advent of industrialisation and factory production.

Their pioneering work of 1939 has provided a starting point for numerous subsequent histories of imprisonment (for example, Foucault, *Discipline and Punish*, 1979; Ignatieff, *A Just Measure of Pain*, 1978; Melossi and Pavarini, *The Prison and the Factory*, 1981) and also for current debates concerning the relationship between imprisonment, economy, unemployment and a reserve army of labour (for example, Box and Hale, 'Economic Crisis and the rising prison population' *Crime and Social Justice*, 1982; Jankovic, 'Labour market and imprisonment' *Crime and Social Justice*, 1977).

Rusche and Kirchheimer's influence is clear in the article by Dario Melossi taken from his co-authored work, *The Prison and the Factory*, published originally in Italian in 1977. Melossi's views are indicative of a revitalised interest in the social history of imprisonment which burgeoned within the broader agenda of critical criminology during the late 1970s and early 1980s. The piece reproduced here illustrates how the centrality of prison labour shifts according to wider economic imperatives and how as a result the birth of the modern prison in different European countries was contingent on their relative development of capitalist modes of production. In particular, Melossi develops Rusche and Kirchheimer's thesis by situating the austere and highly regulated regimes of the newly constituted prison within the same bourgeois impulse to establish discipline and regulation in industrial factories and other institutions of the early nineteenth century.

Collectively these readings mark a recurring (though hardly continuous) interest in comparative penology. It is of note though that the breadth of such work rarely stretches further than recording the cross-fertilisation of reformist notions or economic variables between different jurisdictions. A fully systematic, historical and comparative penology, which is alive to the relative influence of economic structures, reform ideologies, political movements and individual initiatives within particular localities, remains something for the future.

1

The state of the prisons

John Howard

The general view of distress in prisons

There are prisons, into which whoever looks will, at first sight of
the people confined, be convinced, that there is some great error
in the management of them: their sallow meagre countenances
declare, without words, that they are very miserable. Many who
went in healthy, are in a few months changed to emaciated
dejected objects. Some are seen pining under diseases, 'sick, and
in prison'; expiring on the floors, in loathsome cells, of pestilential
fevers, and the confluent smallpox; victims, I must not say to the
cruelty, but I will say to the inattention, of sheriffs, and gentlemen
in the commission of the peace.

The cause of this distress is that many prisons are scantily
supplied, and some almost totally destitute of the necessaries of
life.

There are several bridewells (to begin with them) in which
prisoners have no allowance of food at all. In some, the keeper
farms what little is allowed them: and where he engages to supply
each prisoner with one or two pennyworth of bread a day, I have

Source: Extracts from pp. 1–10 and 46–136 of Howard, J. *The State of the Prisons
and an Account of the Principal Lazarettos in Europe*. First published 1777. Reprint
of abridged 3rd edition 1929, London, J. M. Dent and Sons Ltd.

known this shrunk to half, sometimes less than half the quantity, cut or broken from his own loaf.

It will perhaps be asked, does not their work maintain them? for every one knows that those offenders are committed to hard labour. The answer to that question, though true, will hardly be believed. There are few bridewells in which any work is done, or can be done. The prisoners have neither tools, nor materials of any kind: but spend their time in sloth, profaneness and debauchery, to a degree which, in some of those houses that I have seen, is extremely shocking.

Some keepers of these houses, who have represented to the magistrates the wants of their prisoners, and desired for them necessary food, have been silenced with these inconsiderate words, 'Let them work or starve.' When those gentlemen know the former is impossible, do they not by that thoughtless sentence, inevitably doom poor creatures to the latter?

I have asked some keepers, since the late act for preserving the health of prisoners, why no care is taken of their sick: and have been answered, that the magistrates tell them the act does not extend to bridewells.

In consequence of this, at the quarter sessions you see prisoners covered (hardly covered) with rags; almost famished; and sick of diseases, which the discharged spread where they go; and with which those who are sent to the county goals infect these prisons.

The same complaint, want of food, is to be found in many county gaols. In above half these, debtors have no bread; although it is granted to the highwayman, the house-breaker, and the murderer: and medical assistance, which is provided for the latter, is withheld from the former. In many of these goals, debtors who would work are not permitted to have any tools, lest they should furnish felons with them for escape or other mischief. I have often seen these prisoners eating their water-soup (bread boiled in mere water) and heard them say, 'We are locked up and almost starved to death.'

As to the relief provided for debtors by the benevolent act, thirty-second of George II (commonly called the Lords Act, because it originated in their house) I did not find in all England and Wales (except the counties of Middlesex and Surrey) twelve debtors who had obtained from their creditors the fourpence a day, to which they had a right by that act. The means of procuring it were out of their reach. In one of my journeys I found near six hundred prisoners, whose debts were under twenty pounds each: some of them did not owe above three or four pounds: and the expense of suing for the aliment is in many places equal to the small debts; for which some of these prisoners had been confined several months.

At Carlisle but one debtor of the forty-nine whom I saw there in 1774, had obtained his groats: and the gaoler told me that during the time he had held that office, which was fourteen years, no more than four or five had received it; and that they were soon discharged by their creditors neglecting to pay it. Not one debtor had the aliment in York Castle, Devon, Cheshire, Kent, and many other counties. The truth is, some debtors are the most pitiable objects in our goals.

To their wanting necessary food, I must add not only the demands of gaolers, etc. for fees; but also the extortion of bailiffs. These detain in their houses (properly enough denominated spunging-houses), at an enormous expense, prisoners who have money. I know there is a legal provision against this oppression; but the mode of obtaining redress (like that of recovering the groats) is attended with difficulty: and the abuse continues. The rapine of these extortioners needs some more effectual and easy check: no bailiff should be suffered to keep a public house; the mischiefs occasioned by their so doing, are complained of in many parts of the kingdom.

Here I beg leave to mention the hard case of prisoners confined on exchequer processes; and those from the ecclesiastical courts: the latter are excluded from the privilege of bail; and the former, generally, from the benefit of insolvent acts.

Felons have in some gaols two pennyworth of bread a day; in some three halfpennyworth; in some a pennyworth; in some none: the particulars will be seen hereafter in their proper places. I often weighed the bread in different prisons, and found the penny loaf seven ounces and a half to eight ounces, the other loaves in proportion. It is probable that when this allowance was fixed by its value, near double the quantity that the money will now purchase, might be bought for it: yet the allowance continues unaltered: and it is not uncommon to see the whole purchase, especially of the smaller sums, eaten at breakfast; which is sometimes the case when they receive their pittance but once in two days: and then on the following day they must fast.

This allowance being so far short of the cravings of nature, and in some prisons lessened by farming to the gaoler, many criminals are half starved: such of them as at their commitment were in health, come out almost famished, scarce able to move, and for weeks incapable of any labour.

Many prisons have no water. This defect is frequent in bride-wells, and town gaols. In the felons' courts of some county gaols there is no water: in some places where there is water, prisoners are always locked up within doors, and have no more than the keeper or his servants think fit to bring them: in one place they were limited to three pints a day each: a scanty provision for drink and cleanliness!

And as to air, which is no less necessary than either of the two preceding articles, and given us by Providence quite gratis, without any care or labour of our own; yet, as if the bounteous goodness of Heaven excited our envy, methods are contrived to rob prisoners of this genuine cordial of life, as Dr. Hales very properly calls it: I mean by preventing that circulation and change of the salutiferous fluid, without which animals cannot live and thrive. It is well known that air which has performed its office in the lungs, is feculent and noxious. Writers upon the subject show, that a hogshead of air will last a man only an hour: but those who do not choose to consult philosophers may judge from a notorious fact. In 1756, at Calcutta in Bengal, out of a hundred and seventy persons who were confined in a hole there one night, a hundred and fifty-four were taken out dead. The few survivors ascribed the mortality to their want of fresh air, and called the place Hell in miniature.

Air which has been breathed, is made poisonous to a more intense degree, by the effluvia from the sick, and what else in prisons is offensive. My reader will judge of its malignity, when I assure him, that my clothes were in my first journeys so offensive, that in a post-chaise I could not bear the windows drawn up; and was therefore obliged to travel commonly on horseback. The leaves of my memorandum-book were often so tainted, that I could not use it till after spreading it an hour or two before the fire: and even my antidote, a vial of vinegar, has, after using it in a few prisons, become intolerably disagreeable. I did not wonder that in those journeys many gaolers made excuses; and did not go with me into the felons' wards.

I learn from a letter to Sir Robert Ladbroke, printed in 1771, page 11, that 'Dr Hales, Sir John Pringle, and others have observed, that air, corrupted and putrified, is of such a subtile and powerful nature, as to rot and dissolve heart of oak; and that the walls of buildings have been impregnated with this poisonous matter for years together.'

From hence any one may judge of the probability there is against the health, and life, of prisoners crowded in close rooms, cells, and subterraneous dungeons, for fourteen or fifteen hours out of the four and twenty. In some of those caverns the floor is very damp: in others there is sometimes an inch or two of water: and the straw, or bedding is laid on such floors; seldom on barrack-bedsteads. Where prisoners were not kept in underground cells, they are often confined to their rooms, because there is no court belonging to the prison, which is the case in many city and town gaols: or because the walls round the yard are ruinous, or too low for safety: or because the gaoler has the ground for his own use. Prisoners confined in this manner, are generally unhealthy. Some gaols have no sewers or vaults; and in those that have, if they be not properly attended to, they are, even to a visitant, offensive beyond expression: how noxious then to people constantly confined in those prisons.

One cause why the rooms in some prisons are so close, is the window-tax which the gaolers have to pay: this tempts them to stop the windows, and stifle their prisoners.[1]

In many gaols, and in most bridewells, there is no allowance of bedding or straw for prisoners to sleep on; and if by any means they get a little, it is not changed for months together, so that it is offensive and almost worn to dust. Some lie upon rags, others upon the bare floors. When I have complained of this to the keepers, their justification has been 'The county allows no straw; the prisoners have none but at my cost.'

The evils mentioned hitherto affect the health and life of prisoners. I have now to complain of what is pernicious to their morals; and that is, the confining all sorts of prisoners together: debtors and felons, men and women, the young beginner and the old offender; and with all these, in some counties, such as are guilty of misdemeanors only; who should have been committed to bridewell to be corrected, by diligence and labour; but for want of food, and the means of procuring it in those prisons, are in pity sent to such county gaols as afford these offenders prison-allowance.

Few prisons separate men and women in the daytime. In some counties the gaol is also the bridewell: in others those prisons are contiguous, and the courtyard common. There the petty offender is committed for instruction to the most profligate. In some gaols you see (and who can see it without sorrow) boys of twelve or fourteen eagerly listening to the stories told by practised and experienced criminals, of their adventures, successes, stratagems, and escapes.

'I must here add, that in some few gaols are confined idiots and lunatics. These serve for sport to idle visitants at assizes, and other times of general resort. Many of the bridewells are crowded and offensive, because the rooms which were designed for prisoners are occupied by the insane. Where these are not kept separate, they disturb and terrify other prisoners. No care is taken of them, although it is probable that by medicines, and proper regimen, some of them might be restored to their senses, and to usefulness in life.

I am ready to think, that none who give credit to what is contained in the foregoing pages, will wonder at the havoc made by the gaol-fever. From my own observations in 1773, 1774, and 1775, I was fully convinced that many more prisoners were destroyed by it, than were put to death by all the public executions in the kingdom. This frequent effect of confinement in prison seems generally understood, and shows how full of emphatical meaning is the curse of a severe creditor, who pronounces his debtor's doom to rot in gaol. I believe I have learned the full import of this sentence, from the vast numbers who, to my certain knowledge, and some of them before my eyes, have perished by the gaol-fever.

But the mischief is not confined to prisons. Not to mention now the number of sailors, and of families in America, that have been infected by transports; multitudes caught the distemper by going to their relatives and acquaintance in the gaols: many others from prisoners discharged; and not a few in the courts of judicature.

The general prevalence and spread of wickedness in prisons, and abroad by the discharged prisoners, will now be as easily accounted for, as the propagation of disease. It is often said, 'A prison pays no debts'; I am sure it may be added, that a prison mends no morals. Sir John Fielding observes, that 'a criminal discharged – generally by the next sessions, after the execution of his comrades, becomes the head of a gang of his own raising': improved, no doubt, in skill by the company he kept in gaol. And petty offenders who are committed to bridewell for a year or two, and spend that time, not in hard labour, but in idleness and wicked company, or are sent for that time to county gaols, generally grow desperate, and come out fitted for the perpetration of any villainy. Half the robberies committed in and about London, are planned in the prisons, by that dreadful assemblage of criminals, and the number of idle people who visit them. How contrary this to the intention of our laws with regard to petty offenders; which certainly is to correct and reform them! Instead of which, their confinement doth notoriously promote and increase the very vices it was designed to suppress. Multitudes of young creatures, committed for some trifling offence, are totally ruined there. I make no scruple to affirm, that if it were the wish and aim of magistrates to effect the destruction present and future of young delinquents, they could not devise a more effectual method, than to confine them so long in our prisons, those seats and seminaries (as they have been very properly called) of idleness and every vice.

[. . .]

Those gentlemen who, when they are told of the misery which our prisoners suffer, content themselves with saying, 'Let them take care to keep out', prefaced perhaps, with an angry prayer; seem not duly sensible of the favour of Providence which distinguishes them from the sufferers: they do not remember that we are required to imitate our gracious Heavenly Parent, who is kind to the unthankful, and to the evil: they also forget the vicissitudes of human affairs; the unexpected changes to which all men are liable: and that those whose circumstances are affluent, may in time be reduced to indigence, and become debtors and prisoners. And as to criminality, it is possible, that a man who has often shuddered at hearing the account of a murder, may on a sudden temptation commit that very crime. Let him that thinks he standeth take heed lest he fall, and commiserate those that are fallen.

[. . .]

An account of foreign prisons

I designed to publish the account of our prisons in the spring 1775, after I returned from Scotland and Ireland. But conjecturing that something useful to my purpose might be collected abroad; I laid aside my papers, and travelled into France, Flanders, Holland, and Germany. I flattered myself that my labour was not quite fruitless; and repeated my visit to these countries, and went also to Switzerland, in 1776.

In the conclusion of my first edition, I made a promise, if the legislature should seriously engage in the reformation of our prisons, to take a third journey, through the Prussian and Austrian dominions, and the free cities of Germany. This I accomplished in 1778, and likewise extended my tour through Italy, and revisited some of the countries I had before seen in pursuit of my object. These observations were published in a second edition in 1780. But before the publication of another edition, I wished to acquire some further knowledge on the subject. For this purpose in 1781 I again revisited Holland, and some cities in Germany. I visited also the capitals of Denmark, Sweden, Russia, and Poland; and in 1783 some cities in Portugal and Spain, and returned through France, Flanders, and Holland. The substance of all these travels is now thrown into one narrative. I have only to add, that, fully sensible of the imperfection that must attend the cursory survey of a traveller, it was my study to remedy that defect by confining my attention to the one object of my pursuit, during the whole of my journeys abroad.

Holland

Prisons in the United Provinces are so quiet, and most of them so clean, that a visitor can hardly believe he is in a gaol. They are commonly (except the rasp-houses) whitewashed once or twice a year: and prisoners observed to me how refreshing it was to come into the rooms after they had been so thoroughly cleaned. A physician and surgeon is appointed to every prison; and prisoners are in general healthy.

In most of the prisons for criminals there are so many rooms that each prisoner is kept separate. They never go out of their rooms: each has a bedstead, straw mat, and coverlet. But there are few criminals, except those in the rasp-houses and spin-houses. Of late, in all the seven provinces, seldom more executions in a year than from four to six. One reason of this, I believe, is the awful solemnity of executions, which are performed in presence of the magistrates, with great order and seriousness, and great effect on the spectators. I did not see the process in Holland; but it was particularly described to me, and was similar to what I had been witness of in another place abroad.

The common method of execution for unpremeditated murder, is decollation by a broadsword. Robberies are generally punished by the halter. For the more atrocious crimes, such as premeditated murder, etc., the malefactor is broken on the wheel; or rather on a cross laid flat upon the scaffold. But a description of the manner of this execution, which is finished by a *coup de grâce* on the breast, would not be agreeable to any of my readers.

Debtors also are but few. The magistrates do not approve of confining in idleness any that may be usefully employed. And when one is imprisoned, the creditor must pay the gaoler for his maintenance, from five and a half to eighteen stivers a day, according to the debtor's former condition in life. The aliment must be paid every week: in default whereof, the gaoler gives eight days' notice; and if within that time, the money, or security for it, be not brought, the debtor is discharged.

Another reason is, that the situation is very disgraceful. But, perhaps, the principal cause that debtors, as well as capital offenders, are few, is the great care that is taken to train up the children of the poor, and indeed of all others, to industry. No debtors have their wives and children living with them in prison: but occasional visits in the daytime are not forbidden. You do not hear in the streets as you pass by a prison, what I have been rallied for abroad, the cry of poor hungry starving debtors.

The States do not transport convicts: but men are put to labour in the rasp-houses, and women to proper work in the spin-houses: upon this professed maxim, Make them diligent, and they will be honest. The rasping logwood, which was formerly the principal work done by the male convicts, is now in many places performed at the mills, much cheaper: and the Dutch, finding woollen manufacturers more profitable, have lately set up several of them in those houses of correction. In some, the work of the robust prisoners does not only support them; but they have a little extra time to earn somewhat for their better living in prison, or for their benefit afterwards.

Great care is taken to give them moral and religious instruction, and reform their manners, for their own and the public good. The chaplain (such there is in every house of correction) does not only perform public worship, but privately instructs the prisoners, catechises them every week, etc., and I am well informed that many come out sober and honest. Some have even chosen to continue and work in the house after their discharge.

Offenders are sentenced to these houses, according to their crimes, for seven, ten, fifteen, and even to ninety-nine years: but, to prevent despair, seldom for life. As an encouragement to sobriety and industry, those who distinguish themselves by such behaviour, are discharged before the expiration of their term. And the prisoner who gives information of an intended escape is greatly favoured in this respect: his term is shortened, and sometimes he gains his liberty. A little before the election of new magistrates, those who are in office inspect these prisons; and inquire of the keeper which prisoners, of those who have been confined a few years, have been diligent and orderly; and of the minister, which of them have been most attentive to public and private instructions. According to the accounts, they abridge the appointed time of punishment: so that fourteen years will sometimes be reduced to eight or ten; and twelve years to six or seven. This practice is in every view wise and beneficial. Indeed, I have some reason to think that criminals are often doomed to a longer term, with an intention to make such deductions upon their amendment.

I was informed that the produce of the work does not maintain these houses: though the men that are robust earn from eight to ten stivers a day; and healthy women by spinning, etc., from four to six. But some earn less; and those that are infirm, very little: none however are quite idle, unless sick. This is surely excellent policy; for besides guarding against the pernicious effects of idleness in a prison, and breaking criminals to habits of industry, if work so constant does not support the houses, how much heavier would be the public burden, maintaining the numerous offenders in these prisons, if, as in many of our bridewells, no work at all were done there?

[. . .]

Germany

The Germans, well aware of the necessity of cleanliness in prisons, have very judiciously chosen to build them in situations most conducive to it; that is, near rivers: as at Hanover, Zell, Hamburg, Berlin, Bremen, Cologne, Mentz, and many other places.

In the gaols that I first saw, there were but few prisoners, except those called, improperly, galley-slaves. One cause of this, is a speedy trial after commitment.

The galley-slaves have everywhere in prison to themselves. They work on the roads, the fortifications, chalk-hills, and other public service; for four, seven, ten, fifteen, twenty years, according to their crimes: and are clothed, as well as fed, by the government. At Wesel, which belongs to the King of Prussia, there were ninety-eight of these slaves: they have two pounds of bread a day, and the value of three halfpence every day they work.

I saw but a very few underground dungeons in any new prisons abroad; in Germany none, except at Liege. At Lunenburg the dungeons are disused: and instead of them are built additional rooms upstairs; one for each prisoner. And in many of the gaols each criminal is alone in his room; which is more or less strong, lightsome, and airy, as the crime he is charged with is more or less atrocious.

One often sees the doors of sundry rooms marked Ethiopia, India, Italy, France, England, etc. In those rooms, parents, by the authority of the magistrates, confine for a certain term dissolute children: and if they are inquired after, the answer is, they are gone to Italy, England, etc.

I do not remember any prison in Germany (nor elsewhere abroad) in which felons have not, either from the public allowance, or from charities, somewhat more to live on than bread and water. In some places a person goes on market-days with a basket for prisoners: and I have seen him bring them a comfortable meal of fresh vegetables. But there are separate prisons, in which confinement for a week or two on bread and water is all the punishment for some petty offences. Perhaps when a condemned criminal is only to live a day or two, such diet may be more proper than the indulgence with which the Germans, and other foreigners treat prisoners after sentence of death, which is commonly executed within forty-eight hours. The malefactor has then his choice of food, and wine, in a commodious room, into which his friends are admitted; and a minister attends him during almost all his remaining hours.

I went into Germany in June 1778, by Osnabrug and Hanover. The prison at Osnabrug I should entirely omit, did I not entertain a hope, that the account of it may possibly engage the notice of an amiable prince who is the present bishop, and so be the means of alleviating the sufferings of the miserable prisoners. The prison and the house of correction is one large building, situated in an airy part of the suburbs, near a brook. A Latin inscription over the gate implies, that it was erected 'at the public expense, in 1756, for the purposes of public justice and utility, by confining and punishing the wicked'. There are seventeen chambers for criminals, which have no light but by a small aperture over each door. I was happy to find here no more than one prisoner. He had been confined three years, and had survived the cruelty of the torture. In another part of the house I found many miserable and sickly objects, men, women, and children, almost all without shoes and stockings. They were spinning in different rooms, which were dirty beyond description. These rooms open into an offensive passage, which a gentleman in office in the city, to whom I was recommended, durst not enter. I inquired of the keeper concerning several particulars in the diet, etc., but the misery expressed in the countenances of the prisoners, made me totally disregard the information given me by words.

BREMEN. The gaol is a tower at one of the gates. In the lower part there are four strong rooms (or cells) about thirteen feet four inches by six feet eight, and six feet high. The doors are four feet ten inches high and five inches thick, with iron plates between the boards. The windows are only small apertures (fourteen inches by nine). I found a prisoner in the same cell in which I had seen him five years before. He had made his escape, but had been retaken. There has been no execution in this city for twenty-six years.

In another prison down ten steps from the street, there are six rooms for criminals without windows. One was six feet nine inches by four feet and a half, and seven feet high: another was ten feet by five and a half, and six feet high. The allowance is six sous (3¼d.) a day, but there were no prisoners. In this dismal abode, one had lately beaten himself to death against the wall, which was stained with his blood.

I sat an afternoon with Dr. Duntze of Bremen, who told me he was in London in 1753 and 54, with an inquisitive friend, a

German. They went into Newgate to observe the effects of the ventilator; and were struck with an offensive smell in one of the rooms. Next day they were both indisposed. The doctor's complaint turned out a kind of jaundice. After a few days' confinement he visited his friend, and found him excessively low; and in a short time he died with every symptom of the gaol-fever.

[. . .]

French Flanders and France

The French provinces in Flanders and the Netherlands, are chiefly governed by the same *arrêt de parlement* as the provinces in France.

LILLE. The Tour de St. Pierre at Lille is an old building. There were in it, 24 May, 1783, three debtors, five smugglers, and four vagrants. Five were sick in a very offensive room, with only one bed. Allowance is one pound and a half of bread. The small and dark dungeons down fifteen steps, I was glad to find unoccupied.

I have reason to be abundantly thankful for recovery from a fever which I caught of the sick, in this prison, at my last visit; and would make my grateful acknowledgment to that kind hand, by which I have been hitherto preserved.

At the city prison there were fourteen prisoners: their allowance consists of bread, butter, and small beer. The dungeons were empty.

The unhealthy countenances of the prisoners at the citadel show the pernicious effects of lying in caserns, or damp rooms under the fortifications. 26 May, 1783, here were three hundred and forty prisoners, most of them deserters. In the sick-rooms, which were very close and dirty, there were eighty-six; some of whom, though dying, were in irons. The scurvy has lately made great havoc here. Particular attention should be paid to air and cleanliness, where prisoners have no employment. Humanity to them, and also to their keepers and visitors, demands this. The observation of a sensible magistrate at Hanover, here occurs to my mind: 'We have found', says he, 'that the convicts or slaves who are committed for life, ruin the morals of those who are condemned only for a year or two; therefore, by a late regulation in the electorate, they are now kept apart.' Such a regulation here would be beneficial in every view.

PARIS. In or near Paris the principal prisons were the Conciergerie, Grand and Petit Châtelet, For-l'Evêque, L'Abbaye, and the Bicêtre. But at my visit in 1783 I found two of the worst of them, Petit Châtelet and For-l'Evêque, with their horrid dungeons, entirely demolished. The debtors now are sent to a new prison, the Hôtel de la Force; and criminals are sent to the Conciergerie, or the Grand Châtelet. The king's declaration for this alteration, dated the 30th of August, 1780, contains some of the most humane and enlightened sentiments respecting the conduct of prisons. It mentions the construction of airy and spacious infirmaries for the sick; separate places of confinement, and courts, for men and women, and for prisoners of different classes; and a total abolition of underground dungeons, upon this principle, that it is unjust, that those who may possibly be innocent, should beforehand suffer a rigorous punishment.

Most prisons in the city have three or four doors, from four feet to four and half high, separated from each other by a little area or court. Within the inner door is, in some prisons, a turnstile. The number and lowness of the doors (at each of which you must stoop) and the turnstiles, effectually prevent the prisoners rushing out.

In most of the prisons there are five or six turnkeys, viz., two or three at the doors: one walking in the court, to prevent conferring and plotting (a circumstance to which French gaolers are very attentive): one at the women's ward: and every day one of them is abroad, or otherwise at leisure. This liberty they have in rotation. They are strictly prohibited, under severe penalties, from receiving anything of the prisoners, directly or indirectly, on any pretence whatever. The gaoler is obliged to board them; and to pay each of them at least one hundred livres a year.

I was surprised at seeing that none of the prisoners in the courts were in irons. No gaoler (I was informed) may put them on a prisoner, without an express order from the judge. And yet in some of the prisons, there were more criminals than in any of our London gaols. When I was first there, the number had been recently increased by an insurrection on account of the scarcity of corn. My reader will perhaps presently see reason to conclude, that the manner in which prisons are conducted makes the confinement more tolerable, and chains less needful. Indeed it was evident, from the very appearance of the prisoners in some of the gaols, that humane attention was paid to them.

Most of the courts are paved; and they are washed in summer once or twice a day. One would hardly believe how this freshens the air in the upper rooms. I felt this very sensibly once and again when I was in the chambers: and an Englishman, who had the misfortune to be a prisoner, made the same remark. I seldom or never found in any French prison that offensive smell which I had often perceived in English gaols. I sometimes thought these courts were the cleanest places in Paris. One circumstance that contributed to it, besides the number of turnkeys, was that most of them were near the river.

As prisoners are not properly separated, it is difficult to keep such as become the king's evidence apart from the rest: the gaoler of Le Petit Châtelet was obliged to fit up a separate room for that purpose.

Prisoners, especially criminals, attend mass almost every day, and the gaoler or a turnkey with them: but such of them as are Protestants are excused. No person is admitted into any prison during the time of divine service.

As condemned criminals generally throw off all reserve, and by relating their various adventures and success, prove pernicious tutors to young and less practised offenders; care is taken to prevent this mischief, by sending those who are sentenced to the galleys, to a separate prison, La Tournelle, near the Port de St. Bernard; where they are kept till the time for their being carried off. Before they are sent hither they are branded.

To prevent the frequent consequences of desperation, no one condemned to death by the inferior court is without hopes of life, till the Parliament confirms or reverses the sentence: and they never make known their decision, till the morning of the day on which a prisoner is to suffer. Then they publish a confirmation of the former sentence; and it is sold in the streets. Executions are often in the afternoon: the last that I saw was by torch-light: but the criminal was almost dead by the torture before his execution.

Taking garnish, or footing, is strictly prohibited. If prisoners demand of a new-comer anything of that sort, on whatever pretence; if, in order to obtain it, they distress him by hiding his clothes, etc., they are shut up for a fortnight in a dark dungeon, and suffer other punishment. They are obnoxious to the same chastisement for hiding one another's clothes, or being otherwise injurious.

The daily allowance to criminals is a pound and a half of good bread, and some soup. The soup is not made, nor is any other provision dressed, in the prisons. They have clean linen once a week, from a society, which was instituted about the year 1753. The occasion of it was the prevalence of a contagious disease which in France they call *le scorbut*, the scurvy. This distemper was found to proceed from the prisons; and to spread in the Hôtel-Dieu, whither prisoners that had it were removed. The cause of it was generally thought to be want of cleanliness in prisons; where several of those confined had worn their linen for many months, and infected the most healthy new-comers that were put in the room with them. Eight hundred were ill of it at once in the hospital of St. Louis, to which all that were sick of it in the Hôtel-Dieu had been carried. By the Abbé Breton's exerting himself on this occasion, a fund was raised to support prisoners in the Grand Châtelet with clean linen every week. This put an effectual stop to the malady in that prison. Numbers afterwards joined the society; the king and queen honoured it with their contributions; and the charity extended to three other prisons: so that at last, seven hundred prisoners were provided for in the same manner, and a stock of linen requisite for that purpose, viz., five thousand shirts, was completed. The elder prisoners have charge of the linen that is in the prison; they receive it (every Saturday) and return it, and are gratified by the society; which continues to the present time. Besides this, there is scarce a prison in the city that has not a patroness; a lady of character, who voluntarily takes care that those in the infirmaries be properly attended; supplies them with fuel, and linen; does many kind offices to the prisoners in general; and by soliciting the charity of others, procures not only the relief and comforts mentioned already, but soup twice a week, and meat once a fortnight.

There is also annually at each prison somewhat like our charity sermons; public service in the chapel, and a collection. On these occasions the patroness attends; as I saw at Christmas 1778, and soon after found the prisoners supplied with clothes.

Those who sleep on straw, pay the gaoler no fee at entrance, or discharge; but they pay one sou or halfpenny a day; and have clean straw once a month: those in the dungeons, once a fortnight. These latter are seldom let out; never in the court.

All the regulations are ordered to be read in the chapel to prisoners, the first Sunday of every month, by the chaplain; and they are hung up in the prison for common inspection. If any prisoner tears, or otherwise damages them, he suffers corporal punishment: if a register or gaoler does so, he is fined twenty livres: if a turnkey, he is discharged.

The discipline observed is so exact, that at the fire in the Conciergerie, the numerous prisoners (as I was informed) were removed without any confusion, or a single escape. There are good rules for preserving peace; for suppressing profaneness; for prohibiting gaolers or turnkeys abusing prisoners by beating them or otherwise; forbidding their furnishing them with wine or spirituous liquors, so as to cause excess, drunkenness, etc. Keepers are punished for this, when known to the magistrates, by a fine for the first offence; and for the second by stripes.

They are allowed to sell some things to their prisoners; but the quality, quantity and price must be such as the ordinances of policy define and require.

The turnkeys visit the dungeons four times a day; in the morning when the prisons are opened, at noon, at six in the evening, and at ten at night. I was sorry to find the humanity which is so conspicuous in the forementioned, and other excellent rules, so deficient as to continue the use of those subterraneous abodes; which are totally dark, and beyond imagination horrid and dreadful. Poor creatures are confined in them night and day for weeks, for months together. If the turnkeys find any prisoners sick, they must acquaint the physician and surgeon, who visit them; and if needful, order them to more wholesome rooms till they recover.

A prisoner of rank, a very sensible man, to whom I was speaking concerning gaolers in 1778, said, 'They pay nothing to the crown, and their revenue is not small; at the Conciergerie, it is about fifteen thousand livres; at the Grand-Châtelet, twenty thousand; at For-l'Evêque, twenty thousand; at the Petit-Châtelet, twelve thousand; at L'Abbaye, ten thousand. And all things considered,' he added, 'prisoners have no just reason to complain of this class of men in France.'

The nomination of a gaoler belongs to the magistrates. When he has been nominated, he is proposed to the procureur-general; and if, after a careful inquiry into his character, it appears that he has the reputation of a man of probity, he is fixed in the office, and takes an oath of fidelity. The office is freely given him without any expense whatever; so that keepers are not tempted, by paying for their places, to oppress their prisoners: to remove all pretext for so doing, rents which they formerly paid to the crown are remitted, and the leases given up.

As for debtors, their number is small. Of the two-hundred and two prisoners in the Conciergerie, in 1778, but six were debtors. In the other prisons there were a few more. This perhaps is owing to the following good *arrêts*. Every bailiff who arrests and imprisons a debtor, must pay to the gaoler in advance, a month's aliment or subsistence, i.e. ten livres ten sous, equal to nine shillings English (provisions are at Paris cheaper in general than at London): and if the like sum be not paid within fourteen days after the end of every month, the prisoner is set at liberty. Besides this, the debtor pays no costs of arrests, etc. The whole of them falls on the creditor: and so do all expenses occasioned by his sickness or death.

As the best regulations are liable to be abused, prisoners are not thought sufficiently provided for by enacting good laws: the execution of them is carefully attended to. The substitutes of the attorney-general (should) visit the prisons once a week, to inquire if the rules be observed; to hear complaints of prisoners; to see if the sick be properly attended; and the like. Besides this, the Parliament of Paris sends to all the prisons five times a year two or three counsellers with a substitute of the attorney-general, and two clerks. They go at Christmas, Easter, Whitsuntide, one day before 15 August, St Simon and Jude.

[. . .]

The Bastille may occur to some of my readers, as an object concerning which some information would be acceptable. I am happy to be able to give this, by means of a pamphlet published in 1774, written by a person who was long confined in this prison. It is reckoned the best account of this celebrated structure ever published; and the sale of it being prohibited in France under very severe penalties, it is become extremely scarce. I have extracted the most material circumstances of the description.

> This castle is a State prison, consisting of eight very strong towers, surrounded with a *fossé* about one hundred and twenty feet wide, and a wall sixty feet high. The entrance is at the end of the street of St. Antoine, by a drawbridge, and great gates into the court of l'Hôtel du Gouvernement; and from thence over another drawbridge to the *corps*

de garde, which is separated by a strong barrier constructed with beams plated with iron, from the great court. This court is about one hundred and twenty feet by eighty. In it is a fountain; and six of the towers surround it, which are united by walls of freestone ten feet thick up to the top. At the bottom of this court is a large modern *corps de logis*, which separates it from the court *du Puits*. This court is fifty feet by twenty-five. Contiguous to it, are the other two towers. On the top of the towers is a platform continued in terraces, on which the prisoners are sometimes permitted to walk, attended by a guard. On this platform are thirteen cannons mounted, which are discharged on days of rejoicing. In the *corps de logis* is the council-chamber, and the kitchen, offices, etc., above these are rooms for prisoners of distinction, and over the council-chamber the king's lieutenant resides. In the court *du Puits* is a large well for the use of the kitchen.

The dungeons of the tower *de la Liberté* extend under the kitchen, etc. Near that tower is a small chapel on the ground-floor. In the wall of it are five niches or closets, in which prisoners are put one by one to hear mass, where they can neither see nor be seen.

The dungeons at the bottom of the towers exhale the most offensive scents, and are the receptacles of toads, rats, and other kinds of vermin. In the corner of each is a camp-bed, made of planks laid on iron bars that are fixed to the walls, and the prisoners are allowed some straw to lay on the beds. These dens are dark having no windows, but openings into the ditch: they have double doors, and inner ones plated with iron, with large bolts and locks.

Of the five classes of chambers, the most horrid next to the dungeons are those in which are cages of iron. There are three of them. They are formed of beams with strong plates of iron, and are each eight feet by six.

The *calottes*, or chambers at the top of the towers, are somewhat more tolerable. They are formed of eight arcades of freestone. Here one cannot walk but in the middle of the room. There is hardly sufficient space for a bed from one arcade to another. The windows, being in walls ten feet thick, and having iron grates within and without, admit but little light. In these rooms the heat is excessive in summer, and the cold in winter. They have stoves.

Almost all the other rooms (of the towers) are octagons, about twenty feet in diameter, and from fourteen to fifteen high. They are very cold and damp. Each is furnished with a bed of green serge, etc. All the chambers are numbered. The prisoners are called by the name of their tower joined to the number of their room.

A surgeon and three chaplains reside in the castle. If prisoners of note are dangerously ill, they are generally removed, that they may not die in this prison. The prisoners who die there are buried in the parish of St. Paul, under the name of domestics.

A library was founded by a prisoner who was a foreigner, and died in the Bastille at the beginning of the present century. Some prisoners obtain permission to have the use of it.

One of the sentinels on the inside of the castle rings a bell every hour, day and night, to give notice that they are awake: and on the rounds on the outside of the castle they ring every quarter of an hour.

I have inserted so particular an account of this prison, chiefly with the design of inculcating a reverence for the principles of a free constitution like our own, which will not permit in any degree the exercise of that despotism, which has rendered the name of Bastille so formidable. I was desirous of examining it myself; and for that purpose knocked hard at the outer gate, and immediately went forward through the guard to the drawbridge before the entrance of the castle. But while I was contemplating this gloomy mansion, an officer came out much surprised; and I was forced to retreat through the mute guard, and thus regained that freedom, which for one locked up within those walls it is next to impossible to obtain.

[. . .]

Austrian Flanders

In the Austrian Netherlands I found the prisons in general clean; and no sickness prevailing in any one of them: and yet few of the prisons have a court: in most of them every prisoner is confined to his room. In some places, as at Antwerp, etc., the allowance to criminals is scanty; a pound and a half of bread a day, and a pound of butter a week: but the deficiency is fully made up by supplies from the monasteries, etc. Debtors are very few: they are alimented by their creditors.

[. . .]

There is at Ghent a new prison building by the States of Austrian Flanders. It is a house of correction for those provinces (as that at Vilvorde for Austrian Brabant) and is called La Maison de Force. It is situated near a canal. The plan is an octagon; only four sides finished: in one of them were, in 1775, one hundred and fifty-nine men criminals: in 1776, one hundred and ninety-one. Another of the sides is for women, of whom there were fifty-nine. In the middle of this court is a basin of water, for washing the linen of the house.

On each of the four floors there is a corridor, or arcade, six feet nine inches wide, quite open to the air of the court; which, however, is not attended with any inconvenience, even in winter. In the recess of every corridor, except the lowest, is a range of bedrooms, six feet ten inches by five feet four, and seven feet eight inches high: the doorway two feet. These are uniformly furnished with a bedstead (six feet and a half by two and half), a straw bed, a mattress, a pillow, a pair of sheets, two blankets in winter, and one in summer. Each room has a little bench, and a shutter to the lattice window (nineteen inches by fifteen, in the door) which, when opened and turned down, serves for a table. In the wall is a little cupboard, two feet by one, and ten inches deep. All the rooms are vaulted, to prevent fire from running from story to story. No person is on any pretence admitted into the bedroom of another. They have a clean shirt once a week, and clean sheets once a month. The women have not separate rooms. Some of theirs are ten feet and a half by nine and a half.

In order to (effect) the admission of a prisoner, previous notice must be given by the city or province that sends him. When he comes, he is shaved and washed: a surgeon examines him; and if healthy, he is clothed with the uniform of the house, viz., a linen coat and breeches, and cloth waistcoat, which are marked with the number of his room; to it he is conducted by one of the most orderly of the prisoners; who is appointed to that service, and who also acquaints him with the rules of the house. Commitment (is) from one year to twenty or more, according to their crimes.

A bell is rung in the morning to summon the prisoners into the dining-room; in the summer at five; in winter the hour varies with the length of the days. Half an hour after the bell rings, their names are called over; and they go to prayers in a chapel. They are then allowed half an hour to breakfast. At noon they have two hours for dinner, making their beds (which in fair weather they bring out to air) and for recreation. I was present during the whole time the men criminals were at dinner, and much admired the regularity, decency, and order, with which the whole was conducted. Everything was done at a word given by a director; no noise or confusion appeared; and this company of near one hundred and ninety stout criminals was governed with as much apparent ease, as the most sober and well-disposed assembly in civil society. At night they have an hour for supper, etc. The bell gives notice of all these successive hours: it is rung at a window over the gateway by a sentinel, who there overlooks the whole court; and, should there be any disturbance, is to give the alarm to a company who keep guard. There are eight small rooms (*cachots*) without beds, for the punishment of the refractory; but I always found them empty.

On the ground-floors of the building are workrooms. Those for the men are too small for the looms, etc. The women's workroom is one hundred and seventy feet long, twenty-six wide, and nine to the springing of the arch. In this, many were spinning and combing wool, mending linen, etc. Others were washing the linen in places proper for that purpose.

[. . .]

I revisited this prison in 1778 with one of the magistrates, and found that they were still carrying on a well-regulated manufactory. There were two hundred and eighty men prisoners and one hundred and seventeen women. These latter had on the house clothes, and were at work. Most of them were spinning or knitting, ranged in proper order, attentive and quiet. I was informed that all the prisoners were allowed one-fifth of their earnings for themselves. I brought home specimens of the cloth, as I did of the paper from Brussels; which I mention, because I know an idea has prevailed, that no manufacture can be carried on by convicts to any valuable purpose.

I have been very particular in my accounts of foreign houses of correction, especially those of the freest States, to counteract a notion prevailing among us, that compelling prisoners to work, especially in public, was inconsistent with the principle of English liberty; at the same time that taking away the lives of such numbers, either by executions, or the diseases of our prisons, seems to make little impression upon us. Of such force is custom and prejudice, in silencing the voice of good sense and humanity!

[. . .]

Notes

1. This is also the case in many workhouses and farm-houses, where the poor and the labourer are lodged in rooms that have no light, nor fresh air; which may be the cause of our peasants not having the healthy ruddy complexions one used to see so common twenty or thirty years ago. The difference has often struck me in my various journeys.

2

Elizabethan houses of correction

Austin van der Slice

In 1589 the bench of aldermen of Amsterdam objected to pro-
nouncing the usual death sentence for theft on a sixteen year old
boy. They urged the burgomaster to find a better way to deal
with juvenile offenders. They suggested that they be compelled to
labor, to give up their evil habits and amend their lives. Finally it
was ordered that a house should be established for the confinement of vagabonds and criminals. Here they should be imprisoned
and put to work for as long a time as the magistrates ordered. An
old convent was set aside for the purpose and the Amsterdam
house of correction was opened, in 1596, with twelve inmates.[1]

We have the regulations for this establishment.[2] Their probable
date is between 1599 and 1602. From the regulations we find that
a board of regents consisting of four burghers met regularly each
week to supervise the government of the institution. There were
to be likewise two towns-women who were responsible for the diet
and household economy. There was a resident warden whose wife
assisted by two servants performed the housework. There were
two spinning-masters, a rasping-master, a school teacher, and a
medical man. These regulations laid down by the founders and
regents outline a detailed routine of work, education, and wor-

Source: *Journal of Criminal Law and Crimonology*, vol. XXVII, 1937, pp. 45–57
and pp. 63–67

ship. The inmates were to do a required amount of work for their maintenance and if they did more than that they were to receive additional remuneration. Punishment for lack of discipline might be extra work, fetters, or a lengthened sentence. If the inmate obstinately continued in his defiance, branding and finally the death penalty were prescribed. The inmates were of two classes: those imprisoned on the order of a magistrate, and those admitted at the request of their parents or relatives.[3] In the first class able-bodied beggars, vagabonds, idlers, and in addition among the women, prostitutes, predominated and gave its characteristic stamp to the Amsterdam house of correction. However other criminals, especially thieves, were received from the beginning.[4] The penal reforms introduced by this Amsterdam house of correction had a widespread effect. A more humane treatment of petty offenders, the indeterminate sentence, the corrective influence of work, the industrial rehabilitation of the prisoner, even the idea of reformative treatment and of imprisonment were not established practices at the time.[5] Other European institutions were established as a result of Amsterdam's influence. The Hanse towns of Germany led the way. Houses of correction were set up at Lubeck and Bremen in 1613, at Hamburg in 1620, at Wachsenburg in 1660, at Breslau and Vienna in 1670, in 1671 at Leipzig, at Luneburg in 1676, at Brunswick in 1678, at Frankfurt a.M. in 1679, at Munich in 1682, in 1687 at Spandau and Magdeburg, and in 1691 at Konigsberg in Prussia.[6]

This information was first brought to the attention of students of penology by the notable research of Prof. R. von Hippel in 1898.[7] In 1910 Dr. van der Aa, in a paper before the Eighth International Prison Congress claimed for Holland the distinction of beginning prison reform and of introducing the new penalty of labor.[8] His claim was almost entirely based on the previous work of von Hippel. But the Dutch in substantiating this position are met with the obstinate fact that forty years before the establishment of the Amsterdam house of correction the English had set up a similar institution. And for the next generation first by local action and then by national legislation they had established this type of penal institution in the frame-work of their system of criminal justice and national economy. Prof. von Hippel was aware of the earlier English institutions but said that with the information available at that time the influence of the English houses of correction on the Amsterdam reformatory could not be established definitely although there was a possibility.[9] Dr. van der Aa dismisses the English influence somewhat lightly.[10] However, Dr. Franz D. von Dolsperg, a student under von Hippel, in 1928 undertook a more thorough discussion of this question. He devotes the last one-third of an essay on the early history of imprisonment in England to a comparison of the Amsterdam house of correction and two English ones, Bridewell and the establishment at Bury.[11] Dr. von Dolsperg while still unable to find definite proof of English influence in the founding of the Dutch institution nevertheless points out the strong probability of such an influence. He demonstrates the similarity of the administration of the houses of correction in each country, the fact that they had similar regulations concerning commitment, that the types of inmates were the same, and that the institutions in both countries gave a predominant place to the corrective influence of labor. He finds identical disciplinary measures were used – corporal punishment, fettering, and restricting the diet. Both nations were facing problems of poverty and vagrancy of a similar nature and early English legislation against vagabonds in 1530 had found ready acceptance in Holland in 1531.

This brings us to a realization of the importance of the English houses of correction as pioneer institutions in the field of criminal treatment. Yet there is almost no literature on these early English establishments. This paper after a careful survey of available printed sources attempts to fill this gap in our knowledge of the historical development of modern penal institutions.

Elizabethan England was caught in the throes of a changing world economy. A new capitalistic organization of trade on a world basis was being born out of a local agricultural economy still encumbered by feudal usages. The changes in land tenure and the enclosures, the dismissal by the lords of their bands of retainers, the dissolution of the monasteries, the return of soldiers from foreign campaigns, the inflationary movement brought about by the increase in the supply of precious metal and by the debasement of coins, all these were contributory factors in the economic distress of this transitional era. Naturally the brunt of these forces fell upon the weakest groups in society and thousands of agricultural laborers found themselves on the English highways, with no home and no employment. These vagrants remained a constant threat to internal order and inevitably acted as a breeding ground for crime.[12]

Nor was the situation entirely novel. Ever since the passage of the Statutes of Laborers as a result of the disrupted labor market in the fourteenth century, vagabondage had become an increasingly harassing problem which must be met by the criminal law of the land. Statute after statute was passed from the reign of Richard II on, referring to the number of persons who wandered about the country, leaving their masters, associating in bands, and overawing the authorities.[13]

The first of these statutes with which we are concerned is the one passed in 1530–31 during the reign of Henry VIII. It was this law which was in force at the time Queen Elizabeth took the throne. Under the act impotent beggars were to be licensed by the Justices of Peace to beg within certain limits. All vagabonds and beggars without such license were to be stripped to the waist and whipped until bloody, or set in the stocks for three days and three nights on a diet of bread and water. They were then to be sent to the place of their birth or last three years residence and set to work. Similarly begging scholars without license, shipmen, proctors, pardoners, fortune tellers, fencers, minstrels, and the like without proper license were to be whipped two days in succession. For the second offense this punishment was repeated and in addition they were to stand in the stocks and have one ear cut off. For the third offense they were to undergo the same punishment and lose the other ear.[14]

In this way the able bodied vagrant and beggar were to be suppressed by the machinery of the criminal law.[15] It would be hard to exaggerate the feeling of alarm with which contemporaries, private individuals and public officers, faced this problem.[16] Yet despite the concern and despite the severity of the laws pauperism and vagrancy remained and even increased.[17] It was out of this necessity that the idea and actuality of the English houses of correction were born.

The first experimental attempt to reform the vagrant instead of merely to punish him and send him on his way was made in London. Here under the leadership of Richard Dobbes, Sir George Barnes, Richard Grafton, Bishop Ridley, and others a comprehensive scheme of municipal relief had been established between 1551 and 1557.[18] The poor had been divided into three categories and a hospital had been assigned for the care of each group. Christ's Hospital housed and educated the pauper children; St. Thomas and St. Bartholomew hospitals provided for the sick and maimed; and in Bridewell palace 'the Vagabond and ydle strumpet' were 'chastised and compelled to labour, to the overthrow of the vicious life of ydleness.'[19]

These four royal London hospitals were in 1557 under joint governorship. There were to be sixty-six governors, fourteen of whom were to be aldermen, and fifty-two grave commoners, citizens and freemen of the city. Two of the six 'Graye Cloke' aldermen were to be appointed governor generals of all the hospitals. The senior of the two was comptroller, the other was surveyor. The remaining twelve aldermen and fifty-two commoners were divided equally between the four hospitals. One of the aldermen was to be president and one of the commoners to be treasurer of each.[20]

Our interest of course lies with Bridewell which had been granted to the city of London by Edward VI in 1553 and was established as a house of correction by 1557.[21] Each day the beadles were to make the round of their respective wards and bring the vagrant and idle people to Bridewell where any two of its governors had the right to take in 'lewd and idle' persons. The governors held meetings, once a fortnight, and discussed the various cases that came before them. Nearly all concerned petty offenders, thieves or vagrants. There were a few instances however of persons admitted simply because they had become a charge on the city.[22] The chief hope for the reformation of these vagrants and misdemeanants lay in the discipline of work. Work also would make the institution more nearly self-supporting. There was a spinning room, a nail house, a cornmill, and a bakery, each under the supervision of several of the sixteen governors. The dissolute women were set to work in the spinning room, the more skilled persons were employed in the nail house, and the bake house and the mill were reserved for the worst vagrants. Two inmates made the beds and swept the rooms. The prisoners were paid for their labor and in turn the stewards were to charge those employed for their meals. Gradually the range of occupations increased. Women mended, men dredged sand and burned lime to make mortar.[23] In 1563 a system of apprenticeship was instituted at Bridewell where the children of poor freemen as well as young rogues could learn a trade. By 1579 twenty-five occupations were practised in Bridewell including such as the making of pins, silk, lace, gloves, felts, and tennis balls. Besides this discipline of work other punishments were used such as whipping, restriction of diet, and torture.[24]

We look back upon Bridewell as a unique experiment in the reformative treatment of the vagabond and the strumpet. Yet it is difficult to determine just how clear a purpose its founders had. There is little contemporary evidence that they considered themselves pioneers in penal reform. There is some evidence however that the corrective or reformatory character of Bridewell was understood. The playwright Thomas Dekkar in the second part of 'The Honest Whore,' published in 1608 gives us an interesting description of Bridewell. After narrating its origin he continues:

All here are but one swarm of bees, and strive
To bring with wearied thighs honey to the hive.
The sturdy beggar, and the lazy lown,
Gets here hard hands or laced correction.
The vagabond grows stayd, and learns to 'bey,
The drone is beaten well, and sent away;
As other prisons are (some for the thief,
Some by which undone credit gets relief
From bridled debtors; others for the poor),
So this is for the bawd, the rogue, and whore.
　　　　.　.　.
Nor is it seen
That the whip draws blood here, to cool the spleen
Of any rugged bencher: nor does offence
Feel smart or spiteful, on rash evidence;
But pregnant testimony forth must stand
Ere justice leave them in the beadle's hand;
As iron, on the anvil they are laid
Not to take blows alone, but to be made
And fashioned to some charitable use.[25]

Bridewell was not long established before other English communities founded similar institutions. Thus Oxford in 1562,[26] Salisbury in 1564, Norwich as early as 1565, Gloucester before 1569, Ipswich in that year, Acle by 1574, and Chester in 1575 founded or ordered the establishment of houses of correction modelled upon the London one. A campaign against vagrants had gotten under way in the meantime due to the initiative of the Privy Council. They had ordered general searches for vagrants to be made throughout all the counties of England between 1569 and 1572.[26] In 1569 13,000 idle masterless men were apprehended, and it was estimated that 10,000 more had escaped.[27] In 1571 a bill was introduced into Parliament for the suppression of rogues and vagabonds and in the course of a most interesting debate the Lord Treasurer urged that 'he would have a Bridewell in every Town, and every Tipler in the county to yield twelve pence yearly to the maintenance thereof.'[28] This particular bill did not pass but in 1572 the famous 'Acte for the Punishment of Vacabondes, and for Relief of the Poore and Impotent' became law.[29]

It provided that vagabonds were to be taken into custody and held in the common gaol or some other place designated by three or more Justices of Peace in their General Sessions, until the next session of peace or general gaol delivery. At which time the accused, if duly convicted of his or her 'Rogishe or Vacabonds Trade of Lyef' either by inquest of office or by the sworn testimony of two honest and credible witnesses, was to receive punishment as a vagabond. For the first offense they were to be grievously whipped and their right ear was to be bored by a hot iron one inch in circumference. This penalty might be averted if a substantial person would bond himself for the rogue's safe keeping and take him into service for one year. If after sixty days a vagabond eighteen years old or more should again fall into his old way of life he should be deemed a felon unless taken into service for two years under a £10 bond. For the third offense the statute read: 'suche Roge or Vacabound shalbe adjudged and deemed for a Felon and suffer paynes of Death and loss of Land and Goodes as a Felon without Allowance or Benefyte of clergye or Sanctuary.'

To make it perfectly clear who should be considered as rogues, vagabonds, and sturdy beggars and thus be liable to the penalties fixed by this act the legislators included the well known definition of a vagabond. Within its terms came: all who are or claim to be Procters and Procurators, without sufficient license from the Queen; all other idle wandering persons using subtle crafty and unlawful games or plays, 'and some of them feigning themselves to have knowledge in Phisnomye Palmestrye, or other abused Scyences, whereby they beare the people in the Hand they can tell their Destinies, Deaths and Fortunes, and such other lyke fantasticall Imaginacons', all able bodied persons, having neither land nor master, employing no craft and unable to explain how they lawfully obtain their living; all fencers, bearwards, common players in interludes, minstrels, jugglers, peddlers, tinkers, and petty chapmen who do not have a license from two Justices of Peace of the district where they wander; all able bodied common laborers who loiter and refuse to work for the wages fixed and commonly given in their community; all counterfeiters of licenses and passports, and all wilful users of the same; all scholars of Oxford or Cambridge who beg without a license from the University; all shipmen pretending losses at sea, except for those hereinafter exempted; all persons delivered out of gaols who beg for their fees unless they have a license; and finally all the poor who left settlements established by the second part of this act.[30]

The Justices of Peace were to register all aged and impotent poor, born or three years resident in their district, settle them in convenient habitations and assess the district for their maintenance. If any of these aged and impotent poor were able to work but refused to carry out the task allotted by the Overseer of the Poor they might be whipped and stocked for their first offense and treated as vagabonds in the 'said firste degree of Punyshement' for their second offense. Any three Justices of Peace, if some of the money collected to care for the impotent poor remained, might set to work the rogues and vagabonds who were so disposed. These persons must be residents of the district and should be held to work by the supervision of the Overseers of the Poor. They were to be sustained only upon their own labor. This last provision of the act is perhaps the faint beginning of a nationwide system of bridewells.

At any rate in the next session of Parliament the act of 1576 does provide for the establishment of houses of correction. The act of 1572 is continued in force and the following noteworthy additions are made. Stores of wool, hemp, flax, iron, and the like were to be provided in cities and towns and put under the care of collectors or Governors of the Poor. The poor were to be set to work on these stores and the finished products were to be sold so that the scheme was self-maintaining. Those poor persons who refused to work or who spoiled the materials were committed to the houses of correction provided by this act. These houses of correction were to be established by the Justices of Peace in their General Sessions. Material and equipment was to be provided 'for setting on worcke and punishinge not onlye of those wch by the Collectours and Governours of the Poore for causes aforesaid to the said Houses of Correction shalbe brought, but also of suche as bee or shalbe taken as Roges, or once punished as Roges, and by reason of the uncerteynetye of their Birthe or of their Dwelling by the space of Three yeres, or for any other Cause ought to bee abidinge and kepte within the same Countye.' These houses of correction were to be erected in every county. Although the act sets one year as the desired time limit for the establishment of these institutions in the last analysis it leaves the matter of the time to the discretion of the Justices of the several counties. The Justices of Peace at their General Sessions were to appoint 'Censors or Wardens of the Howses of Correction' who should have the 'Rule Government and Order of suche Howses of Correction, according to suche Orders as by the said Justices of Peace, or the more parte of them, in their Generall Sessions in everye Countye shalbe prescribed.'[31]

This legislation, while not immediately compulsory, undoubtedly stimulated the development of houses of correction throughout England. A house of correction was established at Bodmin in Cornwall shortly after the passage of the act, and at Bristol in 1577. In that year orders were given for the establishment of houses of correction at Worcester and at Exeter. In 1578 at Winchester and at Devizes, and by 1581 at Plymouth, houses of correction were built. A second one was established at Norwich in 1583. By 1584 Leicester had such an institution and York followed in 1586. In this year the Justices ordered the erection of the famous Bury house of correction. In 1590 a bridewell was established at Reading and in 1595 at Coventry.

At this juncture let it be noted that in 1595 the Amsterdam house of correction had not yet been founded. In England however at least twenty-one such institutions were existent and for two decades their establishment had been stimulated by national legislation.

[. . .]

Perhaps the best known of all these Elizabethan houses of correction was that ordered in 1586 at Bury, St. Edmonds.[32] The

Justices of Peace in their General Sessions on 22 April 1589 worked out an elaborate set of regulations to govern the 'punishinge and suppressinge of Roags, Vacabondes, idle, loyteringe, and lewd persons' who wander in eight designated hundreds of Suffolk county.[33] The Justices of these hundreds were to appoint 'one able and honest man' to be Keeper of the house of correction. He was to take charge of the administration, under the supervision of four wardens appointed each year by the Justices. Likewise under the supervision of the Wardens were the four 'Forren Officers' of the house of correction who together with the Constables seized suspects and bringing them before a Justice of Peace had them committed to the bridewell. The Keeper besides his lodging was to receive thirty pounds yearly. He was furnished with all the necessary equipment (a sum of 200 pounds being given him for that purpose) for correcting and setting to work the inmates. In carrying out the provisions of these regulations he was required to keep a careful inventory, keep a record of the inmates, and was under obligation to care for the children of persons kept in the house of correction. The Forren Officers were to receive yearly stipends ranging from 4 li. to 6 li. 13 s. 4d. The Wardens served without salary. Taxation was provided for the maintenance of this house. The range of prisoners received was large, including all the types listed as vagabonds by the law of 1572.[34] The Justice of Peace before whom these persons were brought was to decide whether they should be sent to the gaol or the house of correction. When a Justice of Peace committed a person to the latter he must indicate on his warrant what kind of rogue, either sturdy or otherwise, and the length of the sentence. At the end of this time the Keeper must obtain from a Justice a license or testimonial for the rogue's passport to his place of birth or his last place of residence for the space of three years. Upon entrance every strong and sturdy rogue was to receive twelve stripes of the whip on his bare back and 'have putt uppon hym, her, or them, some cloggs, chaine, collers of irons, ringle, or manacle.' Whatever money the individual may have on his person was removed and held in safe-keeping until his release. Besides this corporal punishment there was a corrective routine of prayer, work, and good behavior which must be lived up to on pain of more whippings, heavier shackles, and finally, for the most obstinate, commitment by a Justice to the nearest gaol, there to be punished as a rogue according to the provisions of the statute. The men and women were to have separate living and working quarters. In the summer the inmates must be ready for work at four and continue in their work, with time off for meals, until seven. In winter the morning hour was advanced to five o'clock. Each morning on rising and each evening on ceasing work they must meet in common prayer. The order of worship included the Confession of Faith, the Lord's Prayer, the Articles of Belief, the Ten Commandments, a short prayer of thanksgiving, and the 'praier that is instituted for the whole estate of Christ's Church militant here on Yearth.' The diet of the inmates is fixed and is reduced to bread and beer alone if an individual refuses to work. Whipping could be administered to any who persisted in swearing, making lewd speeches, and the like. The Keeper was required to 'kepe a booke by itselfe, wherin shal be wrytten the names of every person shal be sente to the said hous of correction, the daie and yeare he shall receyve him or them; and the lyke of their delyverie owte of the said howse, together with theire age, stature, color of hare and face, there mannor of apparell, there place of abode for the three last years, and by whose warrante they be sent in and delyvered; with such other marks as whereby every person maie be knowne yf they shall come ageyne to the said house.'

We have briefly surveyed the administrative set up, the types of individuals committed as well as the manner of their commitment, and the corrective discipline characteristic of the Elizabethan house of correction. It has long been assumed that these institutions were merely part of the machinery of the Elizabethan Poor Law.[35] And indeed they were intimately connected with it, but it must be clear to the reader by this time that these bridewells were penal institutions as well. The Webbs classify the houses of correction with the local gaols as prisons, but they do not emphasize the importance of this role.[36] They point out the administrative superiority which the houses of correction introduced, since they were put directly under the authority of the Justice of Peace rather than being left as in the case of the gaol to the greed of the individual gaoler seeking profits.[37] But they fail to mention the fact that in these houses of correction punishment by imprisonment was given a new importance and that labor was introduced as a corrective discipline. Misdemeanants formerly punished under the criminal law by other methods. were now committed by warrant to the houses of correction, there to be held prisoner under a severe discipline and compelled to work. Gradually the variety and number of offenses which made one liable to commitment to a bridewell increased and the house of correction had merged with the gaol in all except the name.[38] This did not happen however until after the houses of correction had made their special contribution to English and European penal procedure.

It is easily understood that as long as these English houses of correction were considered merely as adjuncts of the poor law their influence on the founding of the Amsterdam houses of correction should have been minimized. Now, however, with the penal character of the English institutions reestablished it is difficult to come to any other conclusion than that they did form the model for the later Dutch houses of correction. Some day evidence will be turned up which will definitely and unmistakably establish this influence.

In conclusion let us turn to an appraisal by contemporaries of the effectiveness of these English houses of correction. At Bodmin and at Exeter the results seem to have been disappointing, but in the main they were accepted as necessary and useful institutions. Edward Hext, a Justice of Peace in Somerset, in writing to the Lord Treasurer in 1596 gives us this picture of their usefulness:

> Your lordship may behold 183 most wicked and desperate persons to be enlarged: and of these very few came to any good; for none will receive them into service. And, in truth, work they will not; neither can they, without extreme pains, by reason their senews are so benumbed and stiff through idleness, as their limbs being put to any hard labour, will grieve them above measure: so as they will rather hazard their lives than work. And this I know to be true: for at such time as our houses of correction were up (which are put down in most parts of England, the more pity,) I sent divers wandering suspicious persons to the house of correction; and all in general would beseech me with bitter tears to send them rather to the gaol. And denying it them, some confessed felony unto me, by which they hazarded their lives, to the end that they should not be sent to the house of correction where they should be forced to work.[39]

James I in one of his speeches to Parliament says: 'look to the

houses of correction, remember that in the time of Ch. J. Popham
there was not a wandering beggar to be found in all Somersetshire,
being his native county.'[40] In the preamble of the statute passed
in 1609 we find England's faith in the effectiveness of houses of
correction expressed in this way:

> Whereas heretofore divers good and necessarie lawes and statutes have
> been made and punishings of rogues, vagabonds, and other idle
> vagrant, and disorderly persons, which lawes have not wrought so good
> effect as was expected, as well for that the said houses of correction
> have not been built according as was intended, and also for that the
> said statutes have not been duely and severely put in execution, as by
> the said statutes were appointed.[41]

Edward Coke, eminent jurist of the time, commenting on the
first of these reasons says:

> For seeing education of youth, and setting of work of idle and
> disorderly persons are such essential parts of the well being of the
> commonwealth; and the only means to compell them to worke (as the
> law now standeth) is by houses of correction, seeing there hath been
> a default in the justices of peace heretofore, and the mischiefe so daily
> increasing, we hope that the justices of peace having yet power, will
> erect more houses of correction (which are also called work-houses)
> so as we shall have neither beggar (as the law of God commandeth)
> nor idle person in the commonwealth.[42]

Coke believes if the statute against vagabonds were enforced
conditions would be better. He goes on: 'And this excellent work
is without question feasible; for upon the making of the statute of
39 Elis. and a good space after, whilest justices of peace and other
officers were diligent and industrious, there was not a rogue to be
seen in any part of England, but when justices and other officers
became tepidi or trepidi, rogues &c. swarmed againe.'[43]

And finally that these houses of correction had a reformative
function which they successfully carried out is attested to also by
this famous jurist, our most valuable contemporary witness. Coke
continues: 'Thus much have we written for the better and more
speedy execution of these excellent statutes and the rather, for
that few or none are committed to the common gaole amongst so
many malefactors, but they come out worse than they went in.
And few were committed to the houses of correction, or working
house, but they come out better.'[44]

Notes

1. This account was taken from an abstract of an article by Dr. Simon van der Aa, University of Groningen, found in the *Report of the Proceedings of the Eighth International Prison Congress*, p. 52 ff. Also see R. von Hippel. 'Beiträge zur Geschichte der Freiheitstrafe' in the *Zeitschrift für die gesamte Strafrechtswissenschaften*, (1898) 18: 419–94, 609–66.
2. These regulations were found by von Hippel in the Danziger Stadtarchiv, quite by chance. He believed them to be the oldest regulations for a house of correction and set their probable date between 1599 and 1602. See R. von Hippel, *loc. cit.*, 472 ff.
3. R. von Hippel, *loc. cit.*, 446.
4. *Ibid.*
5. See the article by Simon van der Aa, *loc. cit.*
6. R. von Hippel, *loc. cit.*, 420 ff.
7. *Ibid.*, entire article.
8. Simon van der Aa, *loc. cit.*
9. R. von Hippel, *loc. cit.*, 419 ff., 472.
10. Simon van der Aa, *loc. cit.*
11. Franz Doleisch v. Dolsperg. *Die Entstehung der Freiheitsstrafe* in the *Strafrechtliche Abhandlungen*, Heft 244 (Breslau, 1928).
12. The preambles of the statutes on vagrancy and the poor are among the most interesting contemporary witnesses concerning these conditions.
13. Sir J. F. Stephens, *A History of the Criminal Law of England*, III, 267 ff.
14. *The Statutes of the Realm*, 22 Henry VIII, c. 12.
15. See W. S. Holdsworth, *A History of English Law* (1924), vol IV, 392 ff.
16. Publicists warned of the danger to the nation and exposed the artifices of the vagabond and the thief, magistrates and statesmen were aware of the grave threat to internal security. In the preambles of the various acts passed to cope with the situation we find crystallized the contemporary concern. 'Where all parts of this Realme of England and Wales be presentlye with Roges, Vagabonds and Sturdy Beggers exceedinglye pestered, by meanes whereof daylye happeneth in the same Realme horryble Murders Thefts and other great outrages, to the highe displeasure of Almightye God, and to the great annoy of the Comon Weale . . .' read the opening words of the act for the punishment of vagabonds which was passed in 1572. [. . .]
17. The penalty for vagabondage had been increased in severity by Edward VI, c. 3 passed in 1547. All able bodied persons not working were to be judged vagabonds. They might be seized by their former masters, branded with a V on the breast, and made a slave for two years. If they ran away and were caught they were branded with a

letter S on the chest and made slaves for life. [. . .] There were at different times a number of estimates made as to the extent of vagrancy. Thus we learn from Strype (Annals 1824, I. ii, 346) that in 1569 13,000 masterless men were apprehended in England and 10,000 more escaped. In 1594 the Lord Mayor of London estimated that there were 12,000 rogues in London alone (Aydelotte, Elizabethan Rogues, app. 4) [. . .]

18.   Richard Dobbes as Lord Mayor had taken active measures to meet the problem of pauperism and further service was rendered by the succeeding Lord Mayor. Sir George Barnes. Bishop Ridley who was in close contact with the King and Richard Grafton, alderman, were also largely instrumental. It was Grafton who was probably the one who pointed out to Ridley the need for Bridewell and thus influenced the latter to intercede with the king (O'Donoghue, *Bridewell*, 137). In Richard Grafton, who often made business trips to the Netherlands, we have a direct link with the Continent whose influence on English ideas concerning relief was a potent one. In 1522 Martin Luther had written two pamphlets on new methods of poor relief which became the basis for numerous experiments in Swiss and German cities. A more direct influence was that of Juan Luis Vives (1492–1540), the humanist and educator, who attached to the court of Henry VIII resided in London from 1522–28. He made frequent trips back and forth to the Netherlands and in 1526, upon the request of a magistrate of Bruges, he wrote an essay on poor relief. The scheme outlined was the one which had been put into effect at Ypres in 1525, and was essentially the same as the one adopted in London twenty-seven years later. A census was to be made of all the poor, in hospitals, almshouses, and in their own homes. Begging should be prohibited and all applicants should be made to labor if fit to work. The children of the poor should be educated and the sick and maimed hospitalized. Vives must have seen this system in action as well as Grafton and other London aldermen on trips to the Netherlands. [. . .]

19.   R. Grafton, *A Chronicle at Large* (1809), vol. II, 531.

20.   *The Order of the Hospitals of K. Henry the Eighth and K. Edward Sixth*, 1557. The Ridgway branch of the Library Company of Philadelphia has a copy.

21.   The story of Bishop Ridley's part in obtaining Bridewell for the city of London has been told many times. Grafton in his *Chronicle at Large* claims to have the story of Ridley's interview with the king from the Bishop himself (vol. II, 529). Glocester Ridley in his *Life of Dr. Nicholas Ridley* gives us a similar account (396–400). Other accounts of Bridewell are found in: Leonard, *Early History of the English Poor Relief*; O'Donoghue, *Bridewell Hospital* (1923); and the chronicles of Holinshed, Stow, and Strype. A. J. Copeland, *Bridewell Royal Hospital Past and Present* (1888) is much quoted but was not available in New York, Philadelphia, or Washington, D. C., libraries. Original records can be found in J. F. Firth, *Memoranda*

Relating to Royal Hospitals (1863); and T. Bowen, *Extracts from the Records and Court Books of Bridewell.*

22. Leonard, *op. cit.*, 38.
23. O'Donoghue, *op. cit.*, 197–8.
24. Leonard, *op. cit.*, 100; O'Donoghue, *op. cit.*, *passim.*
25. Thomas Dekkar, *The Honest Whore.* The play is contained in Dodsley, *A Select Collection of Old Plays*, Volume III, 407–9.
26. See *Victoria History of the Counties of England, Huntingdonshire*, vol. II, 86; *Calendar of State Papers, Domestic. Addenda* for 1566–79. Cf. 1569–72.
27. Strype, *Annals* (1824), I, ii, 346.
28. D'Ewes, *Journals* (1682), 165.
29. *Statutes of the Realm*, 14 Eliz. c. 5.
30. *Ibid.*
31. *Statutes of the Realm*, 18 Eliz. c. 3.
32. Crofton, '*Early annals of gypsies in England*' in the *Journal of the Gypsy Lore Society*, vol. I, 20 (1889).
33. Eden, *op. cit.*, vol. III, Appendix VII (cxxxvi–cxlvi).
34. Those who commit any of the following offenses: '(viz.) by breaking or carrienge awaie of any man's hedge, or cuttinge downe any wood which he cannot justifie to doe, or by takinge geese, ducks, turkies, capons, hennes, pigges, fruite, or such like, not amounting to the some or valewe of xij d.' were to be apprehended and upon warrant of a Justice of Peace sent to the gaol or house of correction to be whipped and then dismissed. (Eden, *loc. cit.*, cxli.)
35. See Leonard, *op. cit.*, 65–6; also Holdsworth, *op. cit.*, vol. IV, 392.
36. Sidney and Beatrice Webb, *English Prisons under Local Government*, 1.
37. *Ibid.*, 12. [. . .]
38. Webb, *op. cit.*, 17. By the Prison Act of 1865 the house of correction and the gaol were made identical and called local prisons.
39. Strype, *Annals of the Reformation* (1824), vol. V, 405. Quoted in Ribton-Turner. *A History of Vagrants and Vagrancy and Beggars and Begging*, 125.
40. Quoted in Barrington, *Observations on the More Ancient Statutes* (1796) form King James' Works, p. 567.
41. *Statutes of the Realm*, 7 Jac, c. 4.
42. Coke, *The Second Part of the Institutes of the Laws of England* (1809), vol. II, 728.
43. *Ibid.*, 728.
44. *Ibid.*, 734.

3

Punishment and social structure

Georg Rusche and Otto Kirchheimer

The evolution of the prison system

Carcer enim ad continendos homines non ad puniendos haberi debet (Prisons exist only in order to keep men, not to punish them.) This was the dominant principle all through the Middle Ages and in the early modern period. Until the eighteenth century, jails were primarily places of detention before trial, where the defendants often spent several months or years until the case came to an end. The conditions defy description. The authorities usually made no provision for the inmate's upkeep, and the office of warden was a business proposition until the end of the eighteenth century. The wealthier prisoners were able to purchase more or less tolerable conditions at a high price. Most of the poor prisoners supported themselves by begging and by alms supplied by church fraternities founded for the purpose.

Sentences to imprisonment did occur, but only exceptionally. The largest group of prisoners not awaiting trial probably consisted of members of the lowest classes who were jailed for their inability to pay a fine. That led to a vicious circle. Men were imprisoned bcause they could not pay fines, and they could not leave the prison because they were unable to repay the jailer for maintenance. The first task of a liberated prisoner was frequently

---

Source: extracts from pp. 62–9 and pp. 84–113 of *Punishment and Social Structure*, 1939, Columbia University Press

the repayment of his debt to the jailer, which explains why the conception of the sturdy beggar in the English Vagrancy Act of 1597 includes ex-convicts who begged for their fees. What created this appalling state of affairs was not so much intentional cruelty as the universally accepted administrative method of operating prisons on a commercial basis.

The idea of exploiting the labor power of prisoners, as against the jailer's way of deriving income from them, already existed in the *opus publicum* of antiquity, a punishment for the lower classes which persisted through medieval times. The smaller states and towns saw in this institution a method comparable to the galleys for disposing of prisoners. They transferred their convicts as cheaply as possible to other public bodies who employed them in forced labor or military service. But the modern prison system as a method of exploiting labor and, equally important in the mercantilist period, as a way of training new labor reserves was really the outgrowth of the houses of correction.

A theoretical distinction can be drawn between a house of correction (*Zuchthaus*), a prison for duly sentenced thieves, pickpockets, and other serious offenders, and a workhouse (*Arbeitshaus*), an institution for the detention of beggars and similar people who had run foul of the police, until they mended their ways. In practice, however, the recognition of this distinction took a slow and uneven course.

The minutes of the Amsterdam town council of July 15, 1589, read:

> Whereas numerous wrongdoers, for the most part young persons, are arrested in the streets of this town daily, and whereas the attitude of the citizens is such that the juries hesitate to condemn such young persons to corporal punishment or life imprisonment, the mayors have asked whether it would not be advisable to set up a house and decree where vagabonds, wrongdoers, rogues, and the like, may be shut up and made to work for their correction.[1]

No differentiation is proposed for the various categories of offenders. An administrative order sent to the managers of the *Tuchthuis* on March 27, 1598, ruled that persons not handed over by court sentence could be accepted only upon approval of the mayors. This was a mere matter of form, however, for the same order proceeded to instruct the regents to arrest all able-bodied persons found begging without the permission of the authorities. Real differentiation was hardly to be expected, for a respectable Amsterdam merchant would find little distinction between an idler arrested by the regents' officers and a thief duly tried and sentenced. Both were guilty of violating the principles of Calvinist ethics. When the council decided on November 12, 1600, to enlarge the establishment and to subdivide it according to new principles, the division was not made between condemned criminals and persons arrested for administrative reasons. The new establishment erected in 1603 housed the children whom their parents, respectable citizens, interned for correction. Elsewhere we find the same failure to divide condemned persons from other inmates.

The regulations of the Lübeck house drew no distinction, but it is worth noting that the administrators constantly refused to accept prisoners who had been condemned by the courts. Was this due to pedagogical considerations and practical objections or simply to a bureaucratic conflict between the administration of the houses and the council, as the correspondence of the council leads one to suspect? In opposition to the latter's policy of sending more and more criminals to the house, the administration wished to uphold its honorable character. The same situation developed in Hamburg, where the necessity of wider application of prison sentences led to the establishment of a spinning house for dishonorable persons in 1669. In Danzig, beggars, idlers, and persons interned by their relatives were separated from convicts as early as 1636 when the house of correction was instituted. In 1690, the courts proposed the erection of a special house for the incarceration and employment of serious offenders against whom the death sentence could hardly be applied and who could not be reformed by other punishments. These instances did occasionally lead to a separation. Since the exploitation of labor power was the decisive consideration, however, local conditions, and particularly population problems, usually determined whether the separation indicated for pedagogical reasons would be carried out in practice.

As late as the end of the eighteenth century it was common to combine the most widely different purposes in the same institution. The Pforzheim house, supported with such affection and care by the princes of Baden, was an orphanage, an institution for the blind, deaf, and dumb, a lunatic asylum, an infant welfare center, and a penal colony, all in one. The Leipzig house bore the following inscription: *Et improbis coercendis et quos deseruit sanae mentis usura custodiendis* (In order to correct the dishonest and to guard the lunatic). In 1780, only 148 of the 283 inmates of the Ludwigsburg institution were convicts; the rest were orphans, paupers, or lunatics. The same variety was to be found in the *Hôpitaux généraux*, although only minor criminals were included at first, because of the harsh sentences under the *ancien régime*. They, too, gradually took on the character of prisons, but without abandoning the practice of admitting the aged, the insane, and children.

The early form of the modern prison was thus bound up with the manufacturing houses of correction. Since the principal objective was not the reformation of the inmates but the rational exploitation of labor power, the manner of recruiting the inmates was not a central problem for the administration. Nor was it an important consideration in the matter of liberation. We have already seen how the period of detention in the case of young or newly trained inmates was determined solely by reference to the needs of the institution or its lessees. Valuable workers whose maintenance and training involved considerable expense must be retained as long as possible. The length of confinement was, therefore, arbitrarily fixed by the administrators in all cases except those voluntarily committed by their relatives. We hear of houses in Brandenburg where, in the absence of determinate sentences laid down in the judgement, some inmates were set free after a fortnight while other minor offenders were retained for years.

The gradual rise of imprisonment was implemented by the necessity for special treatment of women and for differentiation in the treatment of the various social strata. The majority of the women in the *Hôpitaux généraux*, for example, were guilty of crimes punished by galley slavery in the case of male offenders. Incarceration in a *Hôpital* or house of correction was often employed in order to spare members of the privileged classes the humiliation of corporal punishment or galley slavery. Thus, a son of a wealthy citizen of Bremen was tried for housebreaking in 1693 and sentenced to the house of correction for life at the request of his father. He was released on August 20, 1694, on condition that he go to India and not return. The *poena extraordinaria*, which allowed the judge arbitrarily to increase or decrease punishments, everywhere paved the way for a broad extension of the practice of incarceration in the houses of correction.

An especially interesting privilege is found in the decisions of the Tübingen faculty of law and in Württemberg decrees of the seventeenth and eighteenth centuries. The practice had developed of replacing capital or corporal punishment and banishment in the case of craftsmen by public works or confinement in houses of correction. Confirmed by several ducal decrees, this practice had two grounds. One grew out of considerations of social policy, as shown by an edict of 1620 – a dishonorable judgement would have condemned the craftsman and his family to ruin by depriving him of the right to exercise his trade. The second motive was the desire to use trained craftsmen in the service of the state, and one decision explicitly justifies a sentence to public works by reference to the shortage of labor power. The same motive was responsible for the replacement of banishment by the houses of correction. The legislator who exiles evil-doers is not a good householder, people argued, for every subject is a treasure and no sane man would throw a treasure away. Furthermore, it was becoming clear that banishment was the least effective method of suppressing crime. It merely led criminals to shift their fields of activity and had no more utility than present-day expulsion of aliens.

The tendency became rather general to replace even physical punishment by forced labor, and to retain only those forms which 'gave old Adam as much pain as possible without doing the slightest damage to a single limb of his body.' The necessity of keeping the state supplied with labor power was complicated by the desire not to withdraw labor power from the employers. As a result, economic considerations occasionally led to the opposite of the prevailing tendency, that is, to the retention of corporal punishment, especially in agricultural regions. An additional argument in the case of farm servants arose from the fact that imprisonment was no deterrent when their conditions were so bad. Knapp relates that in Upper Silesia as late as the end of the eighteenth century many punishments administered to farm laborers and gardeners failed to stop their stealing. When the master threatened them with hard labor, they would tell him to his face that they preferred ten years of that to one year on his lordship's estate.[2] The landowners drew the conclusion that some form of punishment should be chosen for serfs which did not entail a loss to the landowners themselves. It must be emphasized that these were exceptional cases created by the social and political situation of the eastern farm laborer, which temporarily increased the value of corporal pubishment.

The increasing proportion of sentences to houses of correction was brought about by judicial practice and by the sovereign's prerogative of confirmation and mercy, not by general rules.

Seventeenth-century writers favored this development because of the useless character of the prevailing system of punishment and because of the anticipated value of the new establishments. Henelius called for the restriction of the death penalty to criminals guilty of the most heinous offenses.[3] The good record of the Amsterdam house of correction was widely broadcast as a concrete example of the efficiency of the new system and the uselessness of the old. Henelius's principle, *Mittantur igitur fures ad Sanctum Raspinum, non ad Carnificem*,[4] was accepted by everyone. Complete abolition of capital punishment was, of course, inconceivable at this time, but the number of executions diminished considerably. In the seventeenth and eighteenth centuries, the mere existence of certain forms of punishment, like galley slavery, transportation, and incarceration in houses of correction, limited the use of the capital sentence.

Of all the forces which were responsible for the new emphasis upon imprisonment as a punishment, the most important was the profit motive, both in the narrower sense of making the establishment pay and in the wider sense of making the whole penal system a part of the state's mercantilist program. The secondary interest that the state took in criminal justice was largely due to the fact that the state did not expect to profit by the penal system and sought to deal with the prisoners in the most inexpensive way possible. The state was not expected to make any important outlays apart from salaries, which often amounted to interest payments on the purchase price of a job, as in France. The salary bill of the Paris *Parlement* under Henry III, for example, amounted to 100,000 livres, whereas the payments which, according to an ordonnance of March, 1498, covered general items, such as transportation and maintenance of prisoners and expenses and wages of several lower officials, came to a total of 1,000 livres. The evolution of this unprofitable judicial business into a system which was partially self-supporting from the standpoint of the treasury and a successful part of nation industry from the stand-point of mercantilist policy paved the way for the introduction of imprisonment as a regular form of punishment.

[. . .]

Social and penal consequences of the Industrial Revolution

The movement for the reform of criminal law gained real momentum during the second half of the eighteenth century. The first edition of Beccaria's work: *An essay on Crimes and Punishments*, was published in 1763, the *Allgemeine preussische Landrecht* in 1794. But the basis for the new system of punishment, the need for man power, was disappearing during the same period. We have already indicated that the reform found fertile ground only because its humanitarian principles coincided with the economic necessities of the time. Now, when attempts were being made to give practical expression to these new ideas, part of the base from which they arose had already ceased to exist. That situation was reflected in the conditions of prison life, as we can see from the descriptions in the fourth edition of Howard's *State of the Prisons in England and Wales*. Visiting the Osnabrück prison, he completely disregarded the warden's information – we are vividly reminded of similar cases today – after he saw the misery expressed in the faces of the prisoners. In Ghent, his inquiries led him to the same conclusions. We have similar evidence from Thuringia in the second half of the eighteenth century, where there were not enough instructors nor adequate markets for the commodities produced in the prisons. Lack of space made it necessary to herd people together. The report of the Weimar *Zuchthaus*, for example, said that conditions were 'thoroughly bad'.

Historians agree that the houses of correction had passed their heyday, when they were clean and tidy and well managed, and that, after spreading throughout Europe, the system gradually decayed 'until finally the deplorable state of affairs characteristic of the eighteenth century was reached.' They have tried to account for this development in different ways, but, operating from the idea that progress is a necessary element in evolution, they have generally restricted themselves to moral judgments. Thus, Hippel has nothing but extravagant praise for the Amsterdam methods, but subsequent developments dissatisfy him. In this connection, he writes that the prison system might have developed and prospered if the authorities had followed the Dutch example, built the necessary houses of correction in every town, and really used them as places of punishment. But the development in that direction was only partial. It is true, he continues, that we find houses of correction established in growing numbers from the middle of the seventeenth to the end of the eighteenth century. We find further that imprisonment continued to take the place of physical forms of punishment and the death penalty until, by the end of the eighteenth century, it predominated. At the same time, we find the deplorable tendency to make houses of correction perform the functions of charitable institutions and poorhouses, and to deprive them of their real aim by combining them with orphanages and asylums in which the most heterogeneous elements were herded together. In these institutions, we look in vain for the spirit of the earlier houses of correction with their organization of prison life on a definitely educational basis. Neglect, intimidation, and torment of the inmates became the rule of the day, and they were given work only for their discomfort or for the profit to be gained.[5]

The house of correction grew out of a social situation in which the conditions of the labor market were favorable to the lower classes. But this situation changed. The demand for workers was satisfied and a surplus eventually developed. The population of England increased by one million in the first half of the eighteenth century, and by three million in the second half. It was 5.1 million in 1720, 6 million in 1750, and 9.18 million in 1801. Between 1781 and 1800 the rate of increase was 9 to 11 percent, and between 1801 and 1820, 14 to 18 percent. The population of France was 19 million in 1707, 24 in 1770, and 26 million in 1789. What the ruling classes had been seeking for over a century was now an accomplished fact – relative overpopulation. Factory owners need no longer hunt for men. On the contrary, workers had to search out places of employment. The rapidly growing population could not support itself on the land, especially after certain changes had taken place in agricultural production, resulting in enclosures and large estates. From the beginning of the eighteenth century agricultural workers began to stream into the towns, a movement which reached its climax in the first decades of the nineteenth century. [. . .]

The end of the mercantilist social policy

The organization of industry was revolutionized by the new condition of the labor market. Formerly only those enterprises which received government assistance could hold their own, but now anyone with a little capital could establish some sort of business. The middle classes were coming into their own, and they felt themselves seriously hampered by those privileged groups who used their monopolies and other advantages to keep them out of business. The bourgeoisie demanded freedom of manufacture and freedom of trade. They spread the ideals of liberal optimism; free competition was to be the guarantee of harmony among conflicting interests. Strongly influenced by Adam Smith, this agitation against the old system of state regulation also affected the relationship between employer and employee. At first the generally accepted view was that the interest of the worker himself required that freedom of employment should replace the former rule and regulations limiting the terms of the contract. *Laisser faire, laisser passer, le monde va de lui-même* was the new motto, and both employers and employees saw the key to the millennium in this principle of pure individualism. The effect of this freedom on the condition of the workers, however, was quite different from what its proponents had expected. If there had still been a shortage of labor, the worker would certainly have benefited from the new freedom, for he would have been able to raise the price of his labor. But since the labor market was oversupplied, the workers were more downtrodden than ever and wages lower. Marshall remarked that this period saw the working class fall into the greatest misery it had ever suffered, at least since the beginning of trustworthy records in English social history.[6]

The process was neither continuous nor parallel in all countries, but the course of development was generally the same on the Continent as in England, though delayed. There, too, the change brought about the impoverishment of the lower classes. We do not have the same reliable records on the condition of the German workers, but, as Neumann has pointed out, there can be no question about the sharp widening of the gap between rich and poor in Prussia. While the number of people of moderate means was rapidly decreasing, the number of the extremely rich and the extremely poor was increasing.[7]

The ruling classes had no further need for the coercive measures employed in the mercantilist period to make up for the absence of economic pressure on the working class. The exhaustive system of laws and regulations designed to check rising wages became obsolete. The English laws restricting freedom of movement from one job or trade to another had begun to go out of use in the eighteenth century and they finally disappeared altogether. The justices of the peace refrained from fixing wages. In fact, the machinery for the assessment of fair wages virtually disappeared toward the end of the seventeenth century. It was originally created to fix maximum wages, and that was no longer necessary.

[. . .]

The question of the criminal character of beggary also underwent a significant transformation. Logically one should reach the conclusion that begging is a crime only when it is voluntary, that is to say, when there is no industrial reserve army. Nearly every reply to the circular of the Academy of Chalons, requesting suggestions for the best means of destroying begging in France while making the mendicants useful to the state without rendering them unhappy, insisted that begging is not a crime. The Archbishop of Aix used the common argument, that where there is no crime there is no proportional basis for inflicting punishment. The same opposition to the punishment of beggars developed in England.

Humanitarian reasoning cannot hide the fact that it was the new economic system and the pressure of increasing population which revolutionized the poor-relief problem. Absolutism and its successor, democratic national sovereignty, reacted in the same way by declaring it to be the duty of the state to assist the poor; then the state had the right to proceed against beggary by punitive measures.

England requires special consideration. According to Colquhoun, poverty in London was so great that more than 20,000 miserable individuals rose every morning without knowing how they were to be supported through the day or where they were to lodge on the succeeding night, and cases of death from starvation appeared in the coroner's lists daily.[8] It was in this atmosphere that Malthus came forward with his doctrine that the living standard of paupers can be raised only at the expense of the remaining members of the working class, and that the benevolent intentions of the poor-law reformers must lead to an increase in population and hence to the creation of more misery.[9] He is thus a significant example of the impact of the newly created industrial reserve army upon theoretical considerations. But even Malthus never drew the conclusion that people in distress should be allowed to go hungry, and such a policy was inconceivable to English statesmen merely in the interest of social peace. Clapham goes so far as to say that the poor laws were the only means of preventing discontent and despair from giving rise to revolution.[10] Because of the industrial reserve army, it was no longer necessary 'by savage punishments to discipline the whole propertyless class to the continuous and regular service in agriculture and manufactures,' so that increasing pauperization of the masses was accompanied by more lenient treatment of the poor.

The outcome was a tremendous increase in the poor rates. In 1775, the cost of public assistance was more than a million and a half pounds, and the sum rose rapidly until it reached nearly eight million in 1817, an amount which remained fairly constant to 1834. The propertied classes began to rebel against this expense, and a royal commission appointed in 1832 formulated the principle that all outdoor relief to the able-bodied should be abolished in favor of workhouse relief so that the situation of relief recipients should not be 'so eligible as the situation of the independent labourer of the lowest class.' This principle, incorporated in the Poor Law of 1834, is the leitmotiv of all prison administration down to the present time.

[. . .]

The factory replaced the house of correction, for the latter required large outlays for administration and discipline. Free labor could produce much more and it avoided the drain on capital involved in the houses of correction. In other words, the house of correction fell into decay because other and better sources of profit had been found, and because with the disappearance of the house of correction as a means of profitable exploitation the possible reformatory influence of steady work also disappeared.

[. . .]

New aims and methods of prison administration

Contemporary reformers attributed the shortcomings of the prison system at the beginning of the nineteenth century to incompetent and often ineffective administration, the operation of prisons as private enterprises of the jailer, the internment of convicts together with men awaiting trial, and the internment of men with women. All these abuses gradually disappeared in one country after another, but the crucial question remained: according to what principles and by what methods should prisoners be treated? Writers emphasized the fact that the great majority of prisoners came from the lower ranks of society. The question, then, was to devise treatment which would even have a deterrent effect on those strata. This seems to have been a very difficult task, for we find complaints everywhere that the slight difference between prison conditions and normal existence was a major reason for the rapid increase of the prison population.

As early as 1802, the anonymous author of a pamphlet entitled *Warum werden so wenig Sträflinge in Zuchthaus gebessert? (Why Are So Few Prisoners Improved in the House of Correction?)* commented that conditions in the Leipzig house of correction were too good, and that the inmates themselves were aware of that fact and expressed the desire to remain instead of returning to their customary life outside. This, he asserted, was a very bad state of affairs, for what could be more opposed to the true purpose of imprisonment than for a convict to feel that the comforts of prison life made up for the loss of freedom. And one need not wonder that they feel that way, the pamphlet concludes, when one compares their freedom from care, their light and pleasant work, the pocket money which they could save or spend as they wished, their daily meals, and their good clothing with the life to which they were accustomed, dressed in rags, condemned to work hard, feeling the eternal torment of trying to buy enough food with their inadequate earnings, unable to save a penny for a rainy day or for amusement, often unable to protect themselves against frost and disease. The result was that many people who had committed a crime were not afraid of the house of correction, and some actually offended in order to be sent there and then begged to be allowed to remain permanently. Impoverished citizens and journeymen were saying quite correctly: 'Convicts are better off than we are; they throw more bread away than we can earn; they live a carefree life, feasting and drinking while we live in misery and cannot improve our lot.'

In like manner, the 1825 report on the prison of the canton Waad, one of the most valuable documents of the whole prison literature of the period, insisted first of all that mere deprivation of liberty is no effective punishment for the lower classes. The conclusion was reached that the necessary condition for the prisoner's reentry into society is unconditional submission to authority, a conclusion which has remained unshaken by reform programs and tendencies up to the present. If the prisoners resign themselves to a quiet, regular, and industrious life, punishment will become more tolerable for them. Once this routine becomes a habit, the first step toward improvement has been taken. As far as possible there must be a guaranty that the improvement will continue after the prisoner has been released. Obedience is demanded not so much for the smooth functioning of the prison but for the sake of the convict himself, who shall learn to submit willingly to the fate of the lower classes. That is a difficult task. Obedience to the law is simple and self-evident for the upper classes, but it is almost hopeless to lift the ragged and starved prison inmates to such a level.

All agreed that nothing beyond the barest minimum should be supplied to the prisoners. In discussing the reproduction costs of labor power as the determining factor in wages, Marx remarked that political economy deals with the worker only in his capacity as worker:

> Political economy therefore does not take account of the idler, the member of the working class, insofar as he finds himself excluded from the process of production. The scoundrel, the rogue, the beggar, the unemployed, the miserable, the starving, and the criminal, occupied in forced labor, are types which do not exist for it, existing only for the eyes of the physician, the judge, the grave digger, and the prison commissioner – ghosts outside of its realm.[11]

In the period when houses of correction were centers of production, the necessity of providing for the reproduction of labor power was extended to prisoners too. Now, however, this need no longer exists, or, as Marx put it 'political economy does not take account' of them.

The upper margin for the maintenance of the prisoners was thus determined by the necessity of keeping the prisoners' living standard below the living standard of the lowest classes of the free population. The lower margin, accepted everywhere and explicitly prescribed by a Royal English Commission in 1850, was set by the minimum requirements of health. But the possibilities of variation between these two were merely theoretical. Wages in the first half of the nineteenth century were frequently lower than the minimum necessary to reproduce the labor power of the workers. In other words, the lower margin prescribed by prison regulations was often not attained by free men. That means that the miserable conditions of the working class reduced the standard of prison life far below the officially recognized minimum level.

The old and once satisfactory arrangement whereby the feeding and care of the prisoners was entrusted to entrepreneurs who were financially interested in their physical well-being and capacity for work now had very distressing consequences. As rations were cut down to the very minimum, we hear a great deal about starvation in prisons, about the eating of candles and even of refuse. Voit reports that it was considered sufficient to buy the cheapest foodstuffs available and to cook them in the simplest way, at least in most European countries, so that prisoners were virtually limited to a vegetable diet of mashed potatoes and bad bread in large quantities, clearly one of the chief causes of the poor health and the high death rate in the jails.[12] There was no medical attention even where special sick rooms were set aside for the prisoners, since the superintendent often had to pay doctor's bills and the cost of medicines out of his own small salary. It is not surprising that sixty to eighty percent of the prison deaths were the result of tuberculosis, even according to official figures.

The new attitude toward prison labor

Bad as prison conditions were because of the deliberate policy of starving the prisoners and because of the steadily increasing number of convicts without a corresponding increase in the funds available, they were made still more intolerable by the change in the system of convict labor. It was not necessary for a cruel tyrant to appear and turn the houses of correction into places of torment. The simple fact that they were no longer paying propositions was sufficient. The profit which had accrued to prison managers when men were scarce and wages high disappeared, driving them into bankruptcy or forcing them to abandon the enterprise; and, further, the revenues were no longer sufficient for the upkeep of either prisoners or warders.

The Webbs correctly emphasize the fact that the industrial revolution was making it more and more difficult to obtain any real profit from the demoralized and indiscriminately assembled prisoners.[13] The development of machinery had so destroyed the value of work by hand that it was entirely out of the question to support a remunerative system of nonmachine labor in the jails.

On the basis of French experience, Lucas drew the general conclusion that the European prison system everywhere was operating under the hypothesis that the state could not meet the costs by the products of convict labor.[14]

With the new economic conditions, the competition on the open market between the products of prison labor and free labor became a serious problem. There had never been a time when people did not complain about it. In the mercantilist period the corporations placed difficulties in the way of convict labor, especially by refusing to accept apprentices from the prisons. This opposition could not accomplish its purpose, however, because there was a shortage of labor and because prison-made goods were often superior. Now matters had changed, and convict work was vehemently attacked by the working class and employers alike. Beaumont and Tocqueville emphasized the difficulties in determining the precise moment when manufactories, or any system of productive labor, might be established in the jails without detriment to free citizens.[15] They maintained that the system prevailing in American prisons, which was to make the labor of the convicts as productive as possible, was quite correct in that country where the price of labor was high and where there was no danger that the establishment of prison manufactories would injure the free workers. In countries where the expansion of production has already reduced the price of commodities to its lowest level, however, production cannot be further increased without harm to the working class.

We have seen that the houses of correction used to spur the inmates to greater industry by paying them according to their work or by giving them a share of the profits. They were punished only if they failed to perform their task, whether from lack of skill or from laziness. Now that it no longer paid to employ prisoners, however, they were frequently left with nothing to do. This raised the whole problem of the purpose of imprisonment, and brought its repressive, deterrent side to the fore. The way was open for the realization of the programs of reformers like Pearson and Mittelstädt, who sought to make the prisons rational and efficient means of deterring the lower classes from crime, means which would not allow the convict to perish, but which would impress him once and for all by fear and terror. England, with its large industrial reserve army, led the way. Work was introduced as a form of punishment, not as a source of profit, and moral arguments were brought forward as a justification. One experienced administrator explained in 1821 that work which was to produce profit would interfere with discipline and moral improvement, because, for purposes of manufacture, the taskmaster would seek to assemble prisoners who would otherwise not be permitted to associate with each other.

Prison labor became a method of torture, and the authorities were expert enough in inventing new forms; occupations of a purely punitive character were made as fatiguing as possible and were dragged out for unbearable lengths of time. Prisoners carried huge stones from one place to another and then back again, they worked pumps from which the water flowed back to its source, or trod mills which did no useful work. A simple form of treadwheel, easily applicable to all prisons, was devised by William Cubitt about 1818 for use in the Suffolk County Gaol at Bury, and it was from this example that the practice spread. The cheapness and simplicity of the 'stepping-mill' or 'everlasting staircase,' as it was called, the severe physical exertion required, and the hatred engendered by 'wheel-stepping' commended the new device to Quarter Sessions, and models were set up in every reformed prison, grinding corn or grinding nothing, raising water, supplying power for hemp-beating, cork-cutting, or other machines. Not only was the treadwheel regarded as a success because it afforded a cheap and easy method of forcing prisoners to work, but also because it deterred persons who might use the gaol as a place of ultimate refuge.

The prisoners tried desperately to avoid such punishments. A strong outside opposition also developed on the ground that the treadwheel was so exhausting as to destroy the prisoners' health and that it often amounted to actual torture. Furthermore, it was argued, such punishment counteracted every effort to reform the prisoner's character. But official English opinion continued to favor strictly punitive labor, and it spread from prison to prison despite the attacks of the humanitarians. It was even to be found in the colonial penitentiaries of Hobart Town and Sidney.

These developments also attracted attention outside of England. A German writer insisted on the infliction of penalties having a humiliating effect; if corporal punishment is abolished, he argued, there must be a substitute like the treadmill, which would soon come to be regarded as humiliating. Mittelstädt welcomed the changes because they indicated a realization that the principles of justice demanded that imprisonment should be something more than mere deprivation of liberty and hence should entail a certain amount of positive pain and hardship.[16] German penal practice adhered to this conception until the middle of the nineteenth century. Judges did not trouble to distinguish between different degrees of imprisonment or to fix the term according to definite principles. Legislators and judges were indifferent to prison conditions. They were content to assume that hunger, flogging, and hard labor would do their work, and that there could be no one so poor and miserable but that fear and shame would ultimately force him to do everything in his power to stay outside the prison walls. The possibility that imprisonment could lose its intimidating effects lay beyond the realm of rational thought.

Notes

1.   The quotation is found in R. von Hippel, 'Beiträge zur Geschichte der Freiheitsstrafe,' *Zeitschrift für die gesamte Strafrechtswissenschaft*, XVIII (1898), p. 440.
2.   F. G. Knapp, *Die Bauernbefreiung und der Ursprung der Landarbeiter in den älteren Theilen Preussens* (Leipzig, 1887), I, 68.
3.   Christian Henelius, *Tractatus politicus de Aerario* (Berlin, 1670), p. 323–4.
4.   *Ibid.*, p. 326.
5.   Hippel, 'Beiträge,' pp. 656–7.

6. A. Marshall, *Principles of Economics* (8th edn.; London, 1930), p. 177.
7. F. J. Neumann, 'Zur Lehre von den Lohngesetzen,' *Jahrbücher für Nationalökonomie und Statistik*, LIX (1892), pp. 366–97.
8. P. Colquhoun, *A Treatise on the Police of the Metropolis* (6th edn.; London, 1800), p. 313.
9. Malthus, *Parallel Chapters from the First and Second Edition of an Essay on the Principle of Population* (New York and London, 1895), pp. 34–8.
10. J. H. Clapham, An Economic History of Modern Britain (2nd edn.; Cambridge, 1930), *I*, 580.
11. Marx, 'Ökonomisch-philosophische Manuskripte aus dem Jahre 1844,' *Marx-Engels Gesamtausgabe*, ed. by V. Adoratskij, Abt. I, Vol. III (Berlin, 1932), pp. 97–8.
12. C. von Voit, 'Die Ernährung der Gefangenen,' in *Handbuch des Gefängniswesens*, ed. by F. von Holtzendorff and E. von Jagemann, II. (Hamburg, 1988), pp. 165–6.
13. S. Webb and B. Webb, *English Prisons under Local Government* (London, 1922), p. 89.
14. C. Lucas, *De la Réforme des Prisons on de la Théorie de L'emprisonnement* (Paris, 1838), III, p. 304.
15. G. de Beaumont and A. de Tocqueville, *On the Penitentiary System in the United States and Its Application in France*, tr. by Francis Lieber (Philadelphia, 1833), p. 157.
16. O. Mittelstädt, *Gegen die Freiheitsstrafe* (Leipzig, 1879), p. 36–7.

4

The establishment of modern prison practice in continental Europe

Dario Melossi

Department of Sociology, University of California

John Howard, appointed Sheriff of Bedford in 1773, took an active interest in prison conditions throughout his county. Indeed he was to dedicate the remainder of his life to the question of prison reform, for which purpose between 1770 and 1780 he travelled extensively throughout Britain and Europe. His account provides us with the fullest survey we have of the way prisons were developing in the latter part of the eighteenth century.[1]

If as we have seen, the English prisons were in serious decay, things were different in the German-speaking areas of Europe which had become the natural breeding-ground of houses of correction. Throughout the seventeenth and eighteenth centuries, houses of correction and workhouses had also flourished in countries not mentioned here but, above all, in Germany. In particular this widespread growth took place at the same time as a decline in the usage of old punitive forms consistent with capital or corporal punishment and frequently coincided with the general economic, political and cultural awakening of the Enlightenment (some of the institutions Howard visited were in fact of recent construction). Thus Rusche and Kirchheimer's thesis, according to which there was an overall decay in prisons during this period, should be treated with a certain

---

Source: *The Prison and the Factory*, D. Melossi and M. Pavarini, pp. 47–62, 1981, Macmillan

amount of caution.[2] To be precise, by 'decay' these authors do not mean that there was a reduction in the use of *detentive* punishment or, therefore, in the growth of institutions designed for this purpose, that is, houses of correction (as opposed to the old custodial gaols which Howard frequently found to be semi-deserted). What they are referring to is the deterioration in their internal regimes in which economic functions – and indirectly rehabilitation – were increasingly abandoned in favour of punitive and repressive aims. They attribute this new course to the social consequences of the industrial revolution which through the creation of an enormous reserve army of unemployed throughout Europe, made prison labour (underpaid labour) redundant and the need for open intimidation and socio-political control, if anything, more urgent than ever. If, as Rusche and Kirchheimer contend, the process of decline is linked with the industrial revolution, then we should hardly be surprised to find that most of the evidence supporting their view comes from England. In the same way, it is no surprise that Howard could only discover sporadic signs of deterioration in a more backward country such as Germany, or that the process did not become really general until the influence of the French Revolution and of the English industrial progress was felt in the first years of the nineteenth century and, above all, after the 1815 Restoration.

Howard reserved his highest praise for the Dutch prisons,[3] most of which were still *Rasp-* or *Spin-huis* with a distinctly higher criminal population than had been the case in the seventeenth century. The internal organisation of these institutions was still quite similar to their earlier form. Most of the practical work consisted of rasping wood for dyes; however, as Sellin points out,[4] the daily workload had been reduced by a third and the prisoners fashioned small objects in their spare time to sell to visitors.

About sixty workhouses existed throughout Germany[5] at the end of the eighteenth century. Howard visited many of them:[6] Osnabrück, Bremen, Hanover, Brunswick and Hamburg. The actual gaols housing debtors and those awaiting trial or execution were usually in a horrendous condition: old, unhygienic, often with secret underground floors packed with instruments of torture. However, their population was sparse and many were actually empty. On the other hand, the houses of correction and work-houses were more highly populated; here the men worked on wood (following the Dutch model) whilst the old, the young and women did spinning. There was a great confusion of petty criminals locked up with beggars, vagabonds and those merely suffering from poverty. Often, the only distinction between them was the fact that they were prohibited from mixing or trading with each other. Workhouses thrived in Hamburg in particular, which was a highly-developed city rich in trade: when Howard made his later visits, the Hamburg authorities were preparing a scheme based on workhouses to employ the city's numerous poor.[7] The introduction of the scheme had a remarkable effect and Hamburg proudly proclaimed that begging had disappeared from its streets. But then ten years later, in 1801, the administration fell into heavy debt. The appearance of spinning machines had reduced the competitiveness of the old methods of production. In these circumstances the rapid propagation, primarily of the technological results of the English industrial revolution, effectively made itself felt even when it came to forced labour in Germany. The importation of English machinery and French revolutionary ideas prompted a return to methods of prison control based on terror, which was to characterise the major part of the nineteenth century, long before it produced any great changes in the labour market (though the introduction of machines, among other things, did swell the ranks of the unemployed).

Howard visited other workhouses: in Copenhagen, Stockholm (founded in 1750), Petrograd (still under construction at the time of his visit), in Poland (where, however, there was no work). Berlin (founded in 1758), Spandau, Vienna, in Switzerland, Monaco and Nuremberg (the German and Swiss ones were generally much older). There were numerous houses of correction in Austrian Flanders (Belgium), the most famous of which was the *Maison de Force* at Ghent. This was completely rebuilt in 1775, under Maria Theresa, on the foundations of an old house of 1627.[8]

The *Maison de Force* in particular must have had a great impact. It was one of the first great prison establishments built in the form of an eight-pointed star. The building was divided into sections, each corresponding to a different classification. Whilst criminals had separate cells and were subject to nightly separation, the women and vagabonds slept in dormitories. Textile manufacturing was carried out in large communal areas. However, Howard's enthusiasm for its order, moderation and hygiene waned during his last visit in 1783: 'I found here a great alteration for the worse;

the flourishing and useful manufactory destroyed; and the looms and utensils all sold, in consequence of the Emperor's too hasty attention to a petition from a few interested persons – that which ought to be the leading view in all such houses is now lost in this house.'[9] Even the food had deteriorated and the small wage earned by each inmate had been reduced to little or nothing. The 'few interested persons' were probably producers competing with the institution; they were in fact the source of most attacks on prison labour. For as long as the development of industry depended on the mercantilist system of privilege and monopoly, the authorities could easily get the better of opposition from competing producers, as we have seen in seventeenth-century Holland. But as capitalism grew and imposed the new doctrine of *laissez-faire*, forms of enterprise outside the laws of the free market, such as those making use of forced labour, began to meet with successful opposition. As a result, prison work either tended to disappear or to become totally unproductive with purely disciplinary and deterrent aims. Opponents could now embroider their attack on convict labour with the very convenient excuse that in a situation of extensive unemployment from which *they* prospered, this kind of work endangered the livelihood of the free unemployed labourer. As a matter of fact, the first working-class organisations increasingly adopted a similarly hostile stance towards convict labour.

There were hardly any examples of this sort of institution in Portugal[10] or Spain.[11] In France, the system was seen right from the start much more as a means of suppressing mendicity rather than as a way of providing work.[12] The late economic development of the *ancien régime* weighed heavily upon France. But the abysmal functioning of the *hôpitaux* was primarily attributed to the idleness of the residents, despite all the efforts of the Constituent Assembly's Committee on Mendicity.[13] Howard found thousands of inmates of every kind in the various *hôpitaux généraux*: debtors, criminals (awaiting sentence), the poor, prostitutes, the insane and those suffering from venereal diseases. Continual revolts broke out and torture was widely used. Many died of frostbite during the bitter winters. There was hardly any work.[14] Howard concluded his analysis of Parisian prisons with a description of the Bastille. He was obliged to rely on second-hand information here since he was rudely refused permission to make a personal inspection of the building.[15]

Looking at Howard's account, it is important to realise that the relationship between prison labour and the standard of living of inmates is more than casual. It would be wrong to establish a strict correlation between work and a rehabilitation attitude on the one hand, or between the non-existence of work and a deterrent attitude on the other. These attitudes have been in constant interaction since the institution's earliest days, a fact that is readily apparent from the conception of the *punitive* character of prison labour (though it should be remembered that capitalist ethics also apply this concept to 'free' labour). Nevertheless, it is true that the very conditions of prison life (the level of hygiene, the possibilities of communication and solidarity between inmates, the standard of food, the possibility of earning small personal allowances, etc.) vary according to how far the internal organisation is part of a framework based on productive or unproductive work. Obviously, in the former case, whoever is in charge is presented with the twofold task of exploiting the labour force as rationally as possible while ensuring their daily reproduction (which is more than simply a question of physical subsistence). This produces a situation in which the standard of living of inmates must be inferior to that of employed workers in the outside world (in accordance with the *less eligibility* principle), although it may well be superior to that of someone who is unemployed outside and may, paradoxically, imply a 'material improvement' for the *lumpenproletariat*. This explains why tough methods are revived and the internal conditions of institutions become most harsh when unemployment rises – as tended to happen in the whole of Europe during the first half of the last century. In general, at least in the period examined up to this point, one can see that the inmates' strength and their living and working conditions tended to keep one step behind that of the proletariat as a whole. As a matter of fact, if this did not happen, prisons would lose all their deterrent power as far as the ruling classes are concerned. At times of great poverty and social change, it is not unusual for the most dispossessed sections of society to rise up in protest in a context in which even prison living standards are superior to those they must endure outside. In his description of conditions in poorhouses resulting from new legislation, Marx observes that prison rations were better than those received by the poor.[16] This is because prisons (which had less social impact in any case on account of their sparse population) were part of the reform movement of the previous century – which from the Restoration onwards was to be derisively termed as Enlightenment philanthropy – while the new English workhouse of 1834 conformed to the objectives laid down by the bourgeoisie. A few years later, the English institutions, like those in Europe, took a sharp turn away from the principle of productive work towards a drastic tightening up of its deterrent role.

In the climate of heated ideological debate during the second half of the eighteenth century, a discussion on pauperism, crime and its remedies developed in France. In 1777 the *Gazette de Berne* held a competition to find 'a complete and detailed plan for criminal legislation'. The future revolutionary leader, Dr Jean-Paul Marat, took part with his *Plan de législation criminelle*, published at Neuchatel in 1780.[17] Having dealt with social order and laws in the first part, entitled *fundamental principles for good legislation*, Marat dealt with *the obligation to submit to the law*.[18] Let us take a close look at Marat's argument in order to appreciate fully the consciousness and sensitivity shown by this epoch towards the whole problem.

Marat based his whole argument on an analysis of the concrete situation to which law related. Having noted how 'wealth quickly accumulates in the bosoms of a restricted number of families', producing as a result, 'a multitude of needy persons who will leave their offspring in poverty',[19] he continues:

> Here is why they must die of hunger: the earth has become other people's property and they have no chance of getting anything for themselves. Now, since this disadvantage excludes them from society, are they obliged to respect its laws? Definitely not. If society abandons them they return to a state of nature. So when they forcefully vindicate the rights they have lost with the sole aim of improving their lot, any authority which stands in their way is tyrannical and the judge who condemns them to death is nothing but a vile murderer. If it is true that society must oblige them to respect the established order for the sake of its own self-preservation, it is also true that society must before all else, shelter them from temptation born of need. Society must therefore assure them of adequate means of subsistence and of the chance of suitable clothing, guaranteeing moreover to give them the best possible protection, to look after them in time of illness and old-age: they cannot renounce their natural rights until society has made available to them a way of life that is preferable to the state of nature. Society has no right therefore to punish those who violate its laws

without having made shift in this way to fulfil its obligations towards all its members.[20]

Marat then goes on to examine these principles in relation to a particular crime: theft. But 'any theft presupposes property rights'.[21] and, having challenged the various contemporary theories on the origins of such rights, Marat hands over to 'someone unfortunate enough to find himself before the judges':

> Am I guilty? That's not the point. The real point is that I've done nothing I shouldn't have done. The first right of man is to keep body and soul together and you know yourselves that there's no more important right than that; he who has no way of keeping himself alive other than by stealing is only exercising his rights. You accuse me of disturbing law and order. But how do you expect me to care about your precious law and order when it only reduces me to such misery? It doesn't surprise me at all that you go around preaching that everyone should obey the law – it's the law that allows you to rule over so many unfortunate people. You tell us we've got to work. Easier said than done. What sort of chance did I have? Reduced to poverty through the injustice of a powerful neighbour, in vain I sought the refuge of a peasant's cottage: I was torn away from the plough by a cruel illness which consumes me and made me a burden to my master. There was nothing left for me to do but beg for my bread: but even this pathetic expedient failed me . . . your turning me away made me desperate, having nothing and driven by hunger I took advantage of the darkness of the night to snatch the alms your hard hearts had denied me from a passerby. It's because I've used my natural rights that you've condemned me.[22]

So what is the answer? The authorisation of theft and anarchy? Certainly not!

> Evil doing is warned against; but what is done to remedy it? Beggars are classed as vagabonds and put in prison. This is not good politics: I will not discuss whether the government has the right to deprive them of their liberty in this way but I will merely observe that the houses of detention in which they are locked up can only be maintained at public expense, and that the spirit of idleness which they nourish rather than remedying the poverty of the individual, can only raise the general level of poverty. Very well then, what is the remedy? Here it is. Don't keep the poor in idleness, give them work, make it possible for them to satisfy their wants through labour. They must be given a trade, they must be treated as free men. This means that numerous public workshops must be opened for the use of the poor.[23]

During the deep-seated economic crisis which preceded the great revolution, this problem imposed itself on everyone who lived in France. In town and country alike, the endless 'reserve army' of unemployed were forced to beg, thieve and turn to vagrancy or in the last resort to banditry, if they were to avoid starvation.[24] The revolt of the poor against the process Marx describes as 'primitive accumulation' worked its way through the countryside without pause. By the second half of the eighteenth century, the collective rights, which had always greatly assisted the poor peasants, had been severely eroded by the great property owners and government-supported tenants.[25]

> At the end of the *ancien regime*, people everywhere were searching for land; the poor took over the common land, overran forest, open country and the borders of marshland; they complained about the privileged classes who used bailiffs and foremen to farm their land; they demanded the sale or even the free distribution of the King's estates and sometimes of the clergy's property too; there was a very strong movement against the existence of the great estates, for their division into small lots would have provided work for many families.[26]

As a result, 'at least one tenth of the rural population did nothing but beg from one year to another'.[27] The local communities were not always hostile to vagabonds; in certain 'pamphlets of complaint', protests were made against the confinement of vagabonds in houses of detention. The arguments were probably similar to those of Marat. Bands of unemployed beggars and vagabonds roamed town and country; the greater their numbers, the greater the poverty and as their numbers grew so did their sense of desperation: beggars gravitated towards brigandage. Even if those not paying the requested alms did not take the lead from an Arquebus, they still ran the risk of finding their crops dug over, their cattle mutilated or their houses burned down.[28] It was quite clear from the fact that 'when the almshouses were full, the doors were opened'[29] that they were quite inadequate. In fact, objections were raised because of the contamination that resulted from allowing the poor to mix with real criminals. Lefebvre states that this was not the least cause of the 'great fear' pervading France when revolution was imminent in 1789.

The revolutionary penal code of 25 September 1791 crowned the intense agitation for reform of the preceding half-century with the introduction of the principle of legality both in relation to crime and punishment and with the declaration that detention should reign supreme over any other punitive form. At the same time it was emphasised that *hôpitaux* and prisons must be made into places where society would be truly defended on the basis of labour.[30] The idea that punishment should no longer be arbitrary but should be proportional to the gravity of the crime, as laid down in an explicit legal code, played an important role in the struggle of a now confident and developed bourgeoisie against the old state forms (though this approach to penal practice had been formulated as much as two centuries earlier). As the Russian, E. B. Pashukanis, very acutely observed in 1924:

> Deprivation of freedom, for a period stipulated in the court sentence, is the specific form in which modern, that is to say bourgeois–capitalist, criminal law embodies the principle of recompense. This form is unconciously yet deeply linked with the conception of man in the abstract, and abstract human labour measureable in time . . . For it to be possible for the idea to emerge that one could make recompense for an offence with a piece of abstract freedom determined in advance, it was necessary for all concrete forms of social wealth to be reduced to the most abstract and simple form, to human labour measured in time . . . Industrial capitalism, the declaration of human rights, the political economy of Ricardo, the system of imprisonment for a stipulated term are phenomena peculiar to one and the same historical epoch.[31]

The notion of proportionality in relation to punishment had already assumed this significance for a writer representing the summit of bourgeois consciousness in its 'classic' period – Hegel.[32] The refusal to use corporal and capital punishment, the notion that a specific crime must correspond to a *quantum* of punishment and that internal prison conditions must be 'humane' therefore began with the practice established in workhouses under the direction of public authorities and merchants. To this the revolutionary impulse of the eighteenth-century bourgeoisie added its struggle for the establishment of a legal code. The origin of this struggle lay not in the confrontation between the bourgeoisie and the proletariat but in the confrontation between the bourgeoisie and the absolute state. Nevertheless, it is important to understand that it was no accident that such principles were to become an increasingly strong weapon in the hands of the proletariat. Enlightenment thought of the second half of the eighteenth century explains and summarises this development. The spread of houses of correction throughout Europe was by no means the only reason why such thought was not simply confined to a declaration of principles. Nor is it at all the case that reformers and politicians were the only ones who saw the connection between penal reform and workhouses; in those works dedicated to law, discussion was not limited merely to principles of natural law but, for example, it was made very clear that there were connections between poverty, unemployment and the widely varying forms of delinquency.

On the other hand, Hegel and Pashukanis were to express in the most theoretically rigorous terms the formalisation of criminal law according to revolutionary principles: the concept of *labour* represents the necessary welding of the institution's content to its legal form. To calculate, to *measure* a punishment in terms of labour-value by units of time is possible only when the punishment is filled with this significance, when one labours or one is trained to labour (to wage labour, capitalistic labour). This is also true if one does not work in prison: time (measured, broken up and regulated time) is one of the great discoveries of this period in relation to other ancillary institutions such as the school.[33] Even if the time spent in prison does not reproduce the value of the injury (the basis of retaliatory punishment as Hegel observes), the propaedeutic, ancillary nature of the institution is precisely such as to exact retribution through the very fact of having to serve time, calculable time, measured time, that 'empty form' which is never a mere ideology but which gnaws away at the body and mind of the individual to be reformed, and which shapes him according to *utilisable* parameters for the process of exploitation.

The content of the punishment (the 'execution') is thus linked to its juridical form in the same way as authority in the factory ensures that exploitation can assume the character of a contract. After all, is it not *value* which determines, in Hegel's view, as much the equality between the two sides of the bargain in contractual exchange as that between the two sides of retribution, crime and punishment?[34] Again, it is not a question of analogy, but an expression of the two mutually essential moments in the capitalist structure: circulation and production. Once more, the realm of law (the circulation of goods), the great pride of the revolutionary bourgeoisie in the sphere of law, is intrinsically linked to the relationship of exploitation, that is, the authority and violence which reigns in production (in the factory, in the prison). Such bourgeois conquests, therefore, have much more to do with the consolidation of class hegemony over the social structure as a whole and therefore objectively against the proletariat *as such*, than with bourgeois defence against the absolute state. In any case, in so far as the latter adopts such principles itself, it is increasingly in bourgeois hands.

These are therefore genuine bourgeois-revolutionary conquests in the sense that they revolutionise old methods of handling punitive problems by the application of the new criteria of capitalist relations of production (as workers destined to find themselves behind bars – 'dangerous classes' – will very quickly come to appreciate). And, in fact, whilst the revolutionary bourgeoisie found that a sentence served by working was a concretisation of its conception of life based on labour-value measured in terms of time, the lower classes, in their turn protagonists of the Great Revolution that shook Europe, viewed prisons in a totally different light. The destruction of the Bastille was no isolated fact; although it is true that it was a specific type of prison, that is a fortress for political prisoners, it is not without some irony that the English workhouses of 1834 were, as we have seen, immediately renamed 'poor-law bastilles'. From then on, attacks on prisons and the liberation of prisoners were a constant feature of every uprising and popular insurrection. Although assaults on prisons usually had the aim of releasing 'political' prisoners or at least popular leaders and brigands, etc., to whom the masses felt some kind of affinity, things did not stop there; guided by an acute class instinct, they also unlocked the cells of ordinary thieves, vagabonds and so on without any moralism.

After some delay, the more backward regions of Europe were also affected by the growth of an immeasurably large industrial reserve army, with a concomitant growth in pauperism and criminality. Indeed after the revolution and Jacobism, whilst working-class organisation was still in its infancy, class war was largely fought out on the terrain of criminality, the violent individual solution. This period was fraught with massive unemployment, extreme poverty and disorganisation of the masses; real wages plummeted to what was possibly an all-time low in the history of capitalism; the masses were driven into begging, stealing and, in some circumstances, violence, banditry and primitive forms of class struggle, for example, incendiarism and machine-breaking. In the face of this phenomenon, the creation of capital itself, its bourgeois political agents no longer had to rely on forced labour in order to drive down free labourers' wages, nor did they have to worry about training and returning the forced labourers to factory work. Prison remained the definitive and increasingly dominant acquisition of bourgeois punitive practice, but its function throughout Europe – at least while the circumstances described above prevailed (until just after the middle of the century) – increasingly acquired a bias towards terror and direct social control; the principle of discipline *tout court* prevailed over that of *productive* factory discipline.

In the more advanced countries the reactionary turn of the 1815 Restoration brought about an alliance between the victorious bourgeoisie and what remained of the old absolutist order together with its theoretical and practical remnants. This turn was an expression of anti-liberal resistance on the one hand, and a growing anti-working-class stance on the other. From the Restoration onwards, the emergence of an incipient political potential among the lower classes made it impossible to divorce the question of crime and prison in particular from the more general class struggle. What had been an unconscious relationship between the new classes of capitalism during its formative period now emerged as a conscious relationship of *political* hostility. During the first decades of the last century, various European governments demonstrated a mounting concern over the question of prison reform as a result of the 'terrible rise in recidivity'.[35] Foreign observers were sent out to other countries, particularly the United States.[36]

It is no accident that statistical research into criminality began in this period and revealed a particularly rapid rise in crimes against property in England and France.[37] A slow but continuous movement in favour of greater severity in penal doctrines and practices began with the Napoleonic Code of 1810 and joined in the attack on revolutionary *philanthropy*.[38] The French code essentially envisaged three types of sanction: capital punishment; forced labour; and the house of correction. The death penalty, however, was not the exceptional measure it had tended to be in earlier revolutionary legislation but was applied to practically all crimes threatening state security, counterfeiting, larceny and arson; in this way, it struck at every kind of subversion which had immediate political–military repercussions and at the two crimes common to the urban and country masses. For the less serious crimes of these classes – vagrancy, mendicancy, rebellion not constituting a serious threat to state security, the offences of striking and of association, etc. – the use of the house of correction was envisaged, of a short, sharp punishment, and above all, one that centred on compulsory labour; in this way, the practice we have seen being used from the foundation of the very first workhouses or houses of correction was formalised. The refinement of legal technique; the ever more complete incorporation in penal law of fundamental civil rights; both went hand in hand with the strengthening and stiffening of repression in other codes as well, such as the Bavarian Code of 1813, which was the work of Anselm Feuerbach.[39]

As we have already seen, one of the main aims to be achieved by coerced labour since prisons first began was the levelling down of wages outside. This could only partially be achieved, however, by means of an economic mechanism pure and simple, that is, by placing unfree labour at the disposal of certain branches of production (if for no other reason than the scarcity of those kinds of labour). It was due, more than anything, to the terror struck in those refusing to work, either at all or in particularly bad conditions, by the idea of prison as their unavoidable fate. Then according to the less eligibility principle, freedom and outside work must always be preferable to confinement. In the period of mounting unemployment and pauperism now being examined, the only possible way of intimidating people who had no chance of finding work anyway was politically, in the sense of deterring the unemployed, the vagabond, etc., from turning to crime, begging and so on, in the attempt to keep alive. But the risks at stake for the poor and the unemployed in these first decades of the nineteenth century were precisely those of survival or of starving to death with their families, and not just of haggling over the *conditions* of exploitation. It was extremely difficult for prison to intimidate them in the light of this, as it only had to provide the bare minimum necessary for subsistence to be preferable to freedom.

Thus, in this period, protests against the work of reform carried out in the late eighteenth century multiplied. Whilst it was conceded that reforms contained some merit, objections were raised as to the excessive improvement of prison conditions. It was said that too much attention had been paid to the *material* aspect and too little to the *spiritual* aspect of detention.[40] That prisoners should enjoy a standard of living similar to that of any free 'artisan', whose own standard was in any case frequently below the minimum level of subsistence, was held to be an impossible state of affairs.[41] As a result, prisoners became ill and died of starvation; Malthusianism was being taken towards its logical conclusion – genocide of the proletariat.[42]

It was in this climate that the reformers now turned their attention towards the American scene. By the end of its first century, the Quaker state of Pennsylvania had already established a prison regime based on solitary confinement: this typically Calvinist system was entirely founded upon the *spiritual* work ethic (just what they were looking for in Europe!) and had no place for productive work. Production, by contrast, was at the basis of the Auburn *silent* system which envisaged solitary confinement at night and silent collective labour during the day.[43] In the new and rapidly growing states of North America, this system soon gained ground as a result of the great shortage of labour that had arisen, in contrast to Europe.[44]

At this point in the history of the Old World, the debate on prison reform fused with a discussion on the merits of these two systems, cross-fertilising each system into a number of possibilities which generated new solutions.

Though some taking part in the debate propounded what was by now a different ideology, they carried on in their activity the tradition of Enlightenment *philosophes*: as scholars representing the widest range of human sciences, they frequently wrote essays, articles and travelogues. Though these projects for reform dealt with different matters, they all had in common the overall organ-isation, in its multifaceted complexity, of nascent bourgeois civil-isation and especially of its state. They were often personally involved in legislative or administrative activity and their interest in the prison question, as it came to be known, was never casual but was always with an eye to the possibilities of practical application. Carlo Ilarione Petitti di Roreto from Piedmont was typical of this breed. In his work of 1840, *Della condizione attuale delle carceri e dei mezzi di migliorarla* ('The present condition of prison and ways of improving it'),[45] he provides an extensive survey on the state of reform in the nations of Europe at the time and the accompanying theoretical discussion.[46]

Both positions presupposed that it was necessary to avoid the corruption of contact between the various categories of prisoners. Such corruption was said to form the basis of what was considered to be the most worrying phenomenon in the prison question, the rise in recidivism. The supporters of the Auburn system, who were however, in the minority,[47] denounced the remarkable rise in cases of insanity and suicide found in prisons conducted on the Philadelphian model of solitary confinement. At the same time, the supporters of the Philadelphian system made use of the Quaker theory of the great moral effectiveness of meditation and of the comfort offered by sound and reliable visitors, who were allowed for despite the system's rigidity.[48] They further accused the silent system of being very difficult to put into practice and of giving the warders too much scope for the excessive use of violence in the attempt to ensure adherence to the rules. The marked lack of interest shown by European culture on the question of convict labour showed itself in the fact that the fundamental difference between the two systems – the one facilitating the installation of real productive work, the other not – was usually missed or at least was not seen for what it was. For the treasuries of various states, however, the consideration that the Philadelphian system with its costly requirement of cellular buildings would involve great expenditure was much more important. This was later the reason why a number of states which had declared themselves in favour of this solution in principle did not put it in practice.

The system of solitary confinement was the final outcome of a series of international prison conferences, the first one of which took place in Frankfurt. The reasons for this were precisely those stated at the start: the lack of interest in forced labour (provided for under the Auburn-system) when labour was abundant; a preference for the use of terror, never openly admitted but embodied in the choice of the 'Philadelphian System': an awareness of the horror inspired in the potential offender by the prospect of spending a five, ten or twenty-year sentence in solitary confinement – often relieved only by some form of 'work' so pointless and repetitive that it would really amount to physical torture. Again, for the complex reasons we have tried to explain, the serious decline in prison conditions was thus accompanied by an ever more limited use of work. Moreover, the use of work was also impeded by technical considerations: in an age which gave birth to the real modern factory, with its expensive and cumbersome machinery, with the first development of a more structured organisation of labour, only a very single-minded policy bent on transforming prison into factory through capital investment, etc., could have sustained efficient use of convict labour.

On the other hand, it was not only the reservations of reactionaries that discouraged this kind of prison regime. The popular masses themselves were very conscious of the menace convict labour represented in competition with free labour, especially in a situation of widespread unemployment. For many years, the working-class movement thus became one of the principle obstacles to prison labour. In the United States, for example, perhaps the only country which had had significant experience of convict labour, its continual decline from the end of the last century up to 1940 was above all due to the hostility of a strong and organised workers' movement. Even in a situation closer to that under examination – the 1848 Revolution in Paris – one of the first victories of the popular masses was the abolition of work in prisons, promptly restored after their defeat.[49] However, it is interesting that the fundamental social struggle of the 1848 Revolution was around the demand for 'the right to work'. This led to the opening of the *Ateliers Nationales* along the lines proposed by Considérant and Fourier. Even if the consciousness of the time probably did not make a link between the two problems, it seems to me that there is a direct connection from the workers' point of view between the fight for the right of everyone to work and the fight against convict labour. Free labour must be available to all without the economic and political blackmail of the house of correction! The views of the Parisian Proletariat were to be echoed by Marx many years later in his comments on a demand relating to convict labour in the German Social Democratic Party's Gotha Programme.[50] Marx wrote that prisoners should neither be deprived of 'productive labour' nor be treated 'like animals' from fear of their competition. However, the organised working class's attitude *vis-à-vis* prison work belongs to a history which begins where we finish. Towards the middle of the last century, prison came of age and was able to take its place in line with the other bourgeois social institutions of capitalism. Its further history is above all the history of a *crisis* which, like the history of the organised working class, already belong to a different sort of capitalist society.

Notes

1. The complete title of Howard's first volume cited here is: *The State of the Prisons in England and Wales, with Preliminary Observations, and an Account of some Foreign Prisons and Hospitals.*
2. Cf. Rusche and Kirchheimer, *Punishment and Social Structure*, ch. VI, pp. 84 ff.
3. See Howard, *The State of the Prisons*, pp. 44 ff.
4. See T., Sellin, *Pioneering in Penology* (Philadelphia, 1944), p. 59.
5. See M., Grünhut, *Penal Reform* (Oxford, 1948), pp. 19 ff.
6. See Howard, *The State of the Prisons*, pp. 66 ff.
7. See Rusche and Kirchheimer, *Punishment and Social Structure*, p. 91.
8. See Howard, *The State of the Prisons*, pp. 145 ff. which includes a reproduction of the plan of the *Maison de Force*; Grünhut, *Penal Reform*, p. 22; L. Stroobant, 'Le Rasphuis de Gand, Recherches sur la repression du vagabondage et sur le système pénitentiaire établi en Flandre au XVIIe et au XVIIIe siècle', *Annales de la Soc. d'Histoire et d'Archéologie de Gand*, vol. III (1990) pp. 191–307. The prison at Ghent was generally considered to be the fundamental starting point for the development of the modern prison; it is cited in practically all historic studies on this subject.
9. Howard, *The State of the Prisons*, p. 148.
10. *Ibid.*, p. 150.
11. *Ibid.*, p. 153. For Italy cf. pp. 63 ff.
12. See M., Foucault, *Storia della follia* (Milan, 1963), pp. 109 ff.
13. *Ibid.*, p. 110; Rusche and Kirchheimer, *Punishment and Social Structure*, p. 91.
14. See Howard, *The State of the Prisons*, pp. 165 ff. For an analysis of the various human types locked up in the Parisian hospitals, see Foucault, *Storia della follia*, pp. 126, 127.
15. See Howard, *The State of the Prisons*, p. 174.
16. See K., Marx, Capital (London, 1977), vol. I.
17. See J. P. Marat, *Disegno di legislazione criminale* (Milano, 1971). Refer to the preface by M. A. Cattaneo and the scholarly introduction by M. A. Aimo for further material on this work.
18. *Ibid.*, pp. 71 ff.
19. *Ibid.*, p. 72.
20. *Ibid.*, pp. 72–3.
21. *Ibid.*, p. 73.

22. *Ibid.*, pp. 74–5.
23. *Ibid.*, p. 78.
24. Cf. G. Lefebvre, *The Great Fear of 1789, Rural Panic in Revolutionary France* (London, 1973). There is extensive material in French on this subject. I will limit myself to citing the following: C. Paultre, *De La répression de la mendicité et du vagabondage en France sous l'Ancien Régime* (Paris: 1906); L. Lallemand, *Histoire de la Charité, t. IV, Les temps modernes* (Paris: 1910 and 1912); 'Crimes et criminalité en France sous l'Ancien Régime, XVIIe–XVIIIe siècles', *Cahier des Annales*, vol. 33 (Paris, 1971); A. Vexliard, *Introduction à la sociologie du vagabondage* (Paris, 1956).
25. See Lefebvre, *The Great Fear*, pp. 10, 11.
26. *Ibid.*, p. 14.
27. *Ibid.*, p. 14.
28. *Ibid.*, p. 17.
29. G. Lefebvre, *The Great Fear*, p. 21.
30. Cf. Rusche and Kirchheimer, *Punishment and Social Structure*, pp. 81–2, 91–2; Foucault, *Storia della folia*, p. 110.
31. E. B. Pashukanis, *Law and Marxism: A General Theory*, ed. C. Arthur (London, 1978).
32. In para. 101 of his *Philosophy of Right*, trans. S. W. Dyde (London 1896), Hegel states in relation to the *lex taliones*: 'This identity, involved in the very nature of the case, is not literal equality, but equality in the inherent nature of the injury, namely, its value.'
33. Cf. Foucault's brilliant discussion in *Surveiller et punir* (London, 1977), pp. 158 ff. on the new mode of controlling time *'par découpe segmentaire, par sériation, par synthése et totalisation.*
34. See above, note 32.
35. These words are from Petitti di Roreto, *Della condizione attuale delle carceri* (1840) (Opere Scelte Turino 1969), p. 372.
36. Probably the best known reports came from G. de Beaumont and A. de Tocqueville, *On the Penitentiary System in the United States and its Application in France* (Southern Illinois University Press, 1964).
37. See Rusche and Kirchheimer, *Punishment and Social Structure*, pp. 96–7.
38. *Ibid.*, pp. 98, 99. In the nineteenth century this came to be a common point from which eighteenth-century social policy was attacked.
39. *Ibid.*, pp. 99–100.
40. See Petitti, *Della condizione attuale delle carceri*, pp. 374–5 and 469.
41. See Rusche and Kirchheimer, *Punishment and Social Structure*, pp. 106–7.
42. See information recorded in Rusche and Kirchheimer, p. 109.
43. See *ibid.*, ch. VIII, p. 127.
44. See Rusche and Kirchheimer, p. 130.
45. See the work of Sellin, note 4, and Grünhut, note 5, above.
46. See Petitti, *Della Condizione*, p. 374 ff.

47. Petitti lists the following as being amongst the supporters of this system: 'Messrs Lucas, Mittermaier, Madam Fry, Aubanel, Leone Faucher and Grellet Wammy and himself', p. 450.
48. The following supported solitary confinement: 'Moreau-Cristophe, Aylies, Demetz, Blouet, Jurlius, Crawford, Russel and Ducpetiaux' (p. 452). The people cited here and in note 47 above are amongst the main artificers, both in practical and theoretical terms, of European social policy during the first half of the last century.
49. See Rusche and Kirchheimer, pp. 94–5.
50. On the position of the French workers' movement on this subject at the beginning of the last century, see Foucault, *Surveiller et punir*, pp. 291 ff.

PART 2

Contemporary penal policies and practices

Introduction

In the past decade, renewed interest in comparative criminology and penology has been evident in the growing number of international surveys of crime rates, victimisation rates and sentencing practices as well as prison population sizes. It is now well known that the size of the prison population varies markedly from one country to another. In Europe this information is regularly provided by the Council of Europe's biannual *Prison Information Bulletin*. It shows, for example, that on 1 September 1988, while the average rate of detention was 78.2 per 100,000 population in Europe, this ranged from 35.6 in Iceland to 114.2 in Northern Ireland. These basic comparisons which have revealed such wide discrepancies in what are presumed to be otherwise comparable jurisdictions have been the foci for a growing number of comparative European research studies. To date these have largely been restricted to northern European countries. Thus, it is far more common to find comparative analyses of, say, England and Wales and Holland, or Scandinavia and West Germany, than, say, Cyprus or Portugal, even though the latter also produce a wide variation in rates of detention.

The selection of readings in this section mirrors this current partiality in the development of a pan-European penology. Each chapter takes England and Wales as its major point of reference and uses comparative material to try and uncover divergent practices and policies, usually with the underlying aim of trying to establish the exact parameters of 'good practice'. England and Wales is a common starting point in such European studies (not just for British researchers), largely because its high rate of detention usually places it towards, or at the head of, the European imprisonment league table. It stands as a somewhat 'extreme' example against which the policies and practices of other countries can most readily be measured.

The section opens with Muncie and Sparks' overview of prison populations in Europe. Drawing on the statistical data provided by the Council of Europe, they identify a central paradox in all European penal systems, that while each may be concerned (in different ways and to different degrees) to reduce its prison population and to tackle the degrading aspects of prison life, the overall prison population of Europe is consistently expanding. Prison building programmes, revisions to sentencing practices and the development of non-custodial measures, have all been advocated as a means of breaking out of this impasse. However, the problems of comparing one country's policies with those of another are complex and daunting. At the very least the heterogeneity of penal practices and the gathering of quantitative data make it difficult to arrive at any indisputable comparative judgements. For example, basic data on prison population size needs to take account of types of detention, length of sentence and different categories of prisoner (e.g. long-term, remand, women, juveniles) before any meaningful conclusion can be arrived at regarding what can be considered progressive practice. Equally, any wholesale transference of the seemingly progressive from one jurisdiction to another would fail to take into account the differing socio-political contexts and rationales for imprisonment.

Notwithstanding such difficulties in making sense of the available comparative data, the cases of Holland in the 1960s and 1970s and West Germany in the 1980s are commonly cited as examples where prison populations have been reduced without any measureable increase in risk to the nation's internal security or safety. The chapters by Downes and Feest both provide insights into the efficacy of reductionist policies and practices. For Downes, the Dutch were able to reduce their prison population through a combination of policies: limiting penal capacity, emphasising the rehabilitative aspects of incarceration, and supporting a culture of tolerance. In West Germany, Feest contends that the prison population was dramatically reduced through the changing *practices* of criminal justice personnel. In particular the public prosecution service made more sparing use of prosecution and of requests for remands in custody, and the legal profession consistently spoke out against the excessive use of imprisonment before trial. Above all, a growing practitioner-led disillusionment with imprisonment appears to underlie West Germany's reductionist developments.

The evidence presented in these two chapters stands as a testimony to the fact that levels of imprisonment are not solely determined by crime rates, levels of unemployment or, as Rusche and Kirchheimer contended, labour market conditions. Rather, the adoption of official policies and discretionary practices can have a direct impact on rates of detention. Imprisonment is also a matter of political choice. Whether such reductionist strategies can be expected to have more than a minimal and shortlived success is, however, open to question. It is worth recalling that England and Wales was able to achieve significant reductions in the inter-war period largely through decision-maker scepticism of the benefits of imprisonment and a practitioner-based movement, but this was easily overturned in the post-war political climate. Reductionist policy and practice may then be more successful in providing short-term relief from prison population pressures than promoting a viable alternative to expanding penal systems.

The following two chapters shift attention away from the relationship between penal systems and external questions of sentencing practices, and towards the possibilities of the 'internal' reform of penal regimes and prison administrations. The key issues here concern the treatment, rights and responsibilities of those who do find themselves subjected to incarceration. For example, Vagg's descriptive comparison of prison grievance and inspection procedures in the penal administrations of four northern European countries, finds a wide variation in both the form and outcome of prisoners' complaints. For example, England and Wales and West Germany have low success rates in prison litigation compared to the Netherlands. This is due in part to the related issue of prison conditions, but also reflects the greater recognition of a wide range of inmate rights and possibilities for mediation that are present in the Dutch penal system. Paradoxically, while England and Wales accords inmates the fewest rights, it also has the most sophisticated and independent arrangements for prison inspection. However, despite often being heavily critical of regimes and conditions, the effectiveness of the inspectorate appears to be circumspect: being, in the main, hostage to the broader policy concerns of government. In contrast Holland offers the strongest of inmate rights – albeit in prison regulations and not prison law – but has the smallest and least elaborate inspection office. There appears, then, to be something of an inverse relationship between 'internal' grievance and 'external' inspectorate procedures: with the greater possibility for establishing penal reform lying in the expansion of prisoners' legal rights, than with advisory inspectorate reviews.

As well as providing a timely reminder (at least to an English audience) that the United Kingdom contains the three separate and distinct jurisdictions of England and Wales, Northern Ireland and Scotland, Adler and Longhurst catalogue the gathering strength of penal policy reform in Scotland within a new philosophy of 'opportunity and responsibility'. Rejecting the view of the 1979 May Committee that treatment and training has had its day, Adler and Longhurst note how the Scottish Prison Service has developed a new philosophy in which prisoners should be treated as responsible people and offered a full range of opportunities for personal development. In particular they advocate that what are regarded as prisoner privileges should be incorporated into penal regimes as prisoner rights. Home leave, conjugal visits, single-cell occupancy and preparation for release schemes are all promoted as avenues by which prison life can be 'normalised'. The problem remains, though, as Vagg's contribution suggested, that the granting of opportunity, without providing legally enforceable prisoners' rights, may be self-defeating.

The final contribution to this section moves us back to broader questions of penal policy in terms not of *how* we should treat the incarcerated but *whether* we should incarcerate at all. Mathiesen, a leading proponent of the abolitionist movement which has its roots in the 1960s in Scandinavia and in England, argues that while abolition may be currently politically unacceptable, a more modest, but no less urgent, requirement is to impose a permanent international ban on the expansion of penal capacity. By listing the failures of prison to reduce crime rates, to prevent recidivism, to promote rehabilitation, to prevent violence and to be financially cost-effective, Mathiesen reminds us that reformist efforts to reduce prison populations or to enhance the quality of prison life lose sight of that most fundamental of questions: why do we have prisons at all?

5

Expansion and contraction in European penal systems

John Muncie and Richard Sparks

Lecturer in Social Policy, The Open University
Lecturer in Criminology, The Open University

Concern about the size of the United Kingdom prison population appears to rise constantly. Prison riots and occupations are now regular events in England and Scotland. The Chief Inspector of Prisons, Stephen Tumim, has consistently argued that conditions are deteriorating, with prisoners incarcerated in regimes which 'offend against any reasonable standards of decency'. To make matters worse, at the end of the 1980s the United Kingdom imprisoned more people per 100,000 population than any of the other member states of the Council of Europe, including Turkey. In an attempt to reverse this trend in England and Wales, the Home Office in England has responded with a package of measures: the expansion of penal capacity, longer sentences for serious offenders and an array of devices to encourage the judiciary to use non-custodial sentences for the less serious offender. In short, the government proposes that the twin levers of expansion *and* contraction will begin to ease the burdens of an overstretched prison service.

Such concerns are perhaps particularly acute in the United Kingdom given the scale and intensity of its penal problems. However, they are by no means unique. Most European jurisdictions (with some salient exceptions) have experienced some

Source: Commissioned for this volume

combination of similar problems and have often sought similar solutions. Perhaps the most widespread of these developments has been the tendency towards polarisation between the milder and the more severe ends of the penal range (what in the context of the English debate is now generally called 'bifurcation').

In this chapter we will begin to assess the viability of these tactics by providing a brief review of recent literature on prison populations in Europe. In so doing we will seek to clarify

(a) what in particular we are able to learn from a comparative approach to prison populations;

(b) which recent trends are local phenomena and which are common across jurisdictions; and

(c) what this tells us about the viability of different strategies for reducing prison populations.

Comparing rates of prison use

The Council of Europe's biannual *Prison Information Bulletin* provides a regular resumé of statistics on prison populations in its member states. At 1 September 1988 it was found that the average overall rate of detention was 78.2 per 100,000 population, a grand total 321,700 people (a city larger than Sheffield). This represented a rise of 2.6 per cent from 1987 and 7.6 per cent from 1983 (when figures were first available). Between 1983 and 1988 substantial increases were recorded in a majority of countries including the Netherlands, France and the United Kingdom, while Austria, Germany and Turkey saw a downward trend in their rate of detention. The largest prison populations were to be found in the United Kingdom, West Germany and Turkey, with the United Kingdom also leading the list for the highest rate of detention per head of population. Of the three UK countries, Northern Ireland attained the dubious honour of incarcerating 114.2 people for every 100,000 in the population compared to Scotland's 99.3, England's 96.7, Turkey's 95.6 and West Germany's 84.9. Those achieving the lowest incarceration rates were Iceland at 35.6, Cyprus at 39.3, Holland at 40.0 and Greece at 44.0 (Table 5.1).

These statistics reflect the bare bones of existing knowledge of the use of imprisonment across Europe. But as Fitzmaurice and

Table 5.1 Number of prisoners at 1 September 1988

	Number of prisoners	Population Total (thousands) (*)	Population % aged 15–64 (*)	Rate of detention per 100 000 inhabitants Total	Rate of detention per 100 000 inhabitants 15–64
Total	321 700	411 588		78.2	
Austria	5 862	7 613	68	77.0	113.3
Belgium	6 450	9 862	67	65.4	97.6
Cyprus	219	577	65	39.3	60.4
Denmark	3 469	5 101	67	68.0	101.5
Finland	3 598	4 929	68	73.0	107.4
France*	46 423	57 242	66	81.1	122.9
Fed. Rep. of Germany	52 076	61 338	70	84.9	121.3
Greece	4 288	9 745	66	44.0	66.7
Iceland	89	250	65	35.6	54.8
Ireland	1 953	3 551	60	55.0	91.7
Italy	34 675	57 409	68	60.4	88.8
Luxembourg	322	372	70	86.5	123.6
Malta	221	330	66	67.0	101.5
Netherlands	5 827	14 567	69	40.0	58.0
Norway	2 041	4 217	65	48.4	74.4
Portugal	8 181	9 857	65	83.0	127.7
Spain	29 244	38 712	66	75.8	114.8
Sweden	4 716	8 421	65	56 0	86 1
Switzerland*	4 679	6 401	68	73.1	107.5
Turkey	51 810	54 195	59	95.6	162.0
UK	55 457	56 919	66	97.4	147.6
England and Wales*	48 595	50 243		96.7	
Scotland	5 076	5 112		99.3	
N. Ireland	1 786	1 564		114.2	

Notes:
(*) Total population has been recalculated on the basis of the number of prisoners and the rate of detention provided by administrations.

Proportion in the 15–64 age group: INED, 'Tous les Pays du Monde', *Population et Sociétés*, No. 237, 1989.

FRANCE: The data represent all persons imprisoned in metropolitan France and the Overseas Départements (metropolitan = 44 912, overseas = 1511). For metropolitan France, the rate of detention is 80.3 per 1 000 000.

SWITZERLAND: The number of prisoners and the rate of detention are estimates, since no figures were available for persons detained on remand at 1.9.1989. Latest figure for persons detained on remand: 1521 (17.3.1988). Number of persons serving sentences at 1.9.1988 = 3158.

ENGLAND AND WALES: In addition to the 48 595 prisoners, 1511 persons are being held by the police (most of whom have not been sentenced).

Source: Council of Europe, 1990, p. 6.

Pease (1982, p. 575) remind us they are 'statistics which represent the end of a decision making process which has involved the offenders concerned, their victims, the police, the courts and various welfare oriented organisations'. Rates of imprisonment then reflect a variety of factors which are overlooked simply by examining prison populations. Fitzmaurice and Pease also rightly warn us of the dangers of making simplistic comparisons between countries which use different categories for the incarcerated, different means of recording imprisonment and different ways of classifying adulthood for penal purposes (see also Collier and Tarling, 1987). For example, in Holland, until recently, criminals thought to be insane were sentenced to a mental hospital for a fixed period after having received a term of imprisonment. Similarly, do all the statistics include prisoners, mainly unsentenced, who are held in police custody? Or equally complex, the Belgians have the power to hold vagrants in state care or custody after the expiry of their sentences simply because they were vagrants at the time of the offence (Fitzmaurice and Pease, 1982, p. 575). The age of eligibility to enter an adult prison also varies from sixteen years in France, seventeen years in England and eighteen years in Switzerland. Whatever comparisons can be made between different jurisdictions is thus likely to be wrought with complexities. As De Haan (1990, p. 65) argues: 'The scarcity of detailed data often results in extremely global comparisons between countries. Theories explaining differences lack a solid empirical foundation, seriously risking the distortion of reality. Consequently, these comparisons are rarely more than wild guesses.'

It is not simply a matter of how populations are classified and counted. Rather, apparently similar rates of imprisonment can conceal radically divergent practices, often in surprising ways.

The rate of detention per 100,000 population (the commonest way of summarising and comparing national practices) is in fact a partial and sometimes misleading measure. Recent commentaries on prison populations (e.g. Heinz, 1989; Collier and Tarling, 1987; Fitzmaurice and Pease, 1982; Council of Europe, 1990) have begun to introduce some important conceptual and practical distinctions.

The classic 'rate of detention' (conventionally expressed in numbers per 100,000 inhabitants) is a measure of the 'stock' of the prison population. It is a snap-shot. Most prison administrations make such a head-count on one particular day each year, for the purpose of facilitating comparison of yearly trends. (Some, as in the United Kingdom, also record the average daily population taken over the year as a whole.) Table 5.1 expresses information of this kind. Such data graphically summarise sharp national differences in the use of imprisonment. In much recent discussion they have given particular focus and bite to the assessment of the United Kingdom's record, for instance; such discussions have emphasised, most especially in comparing the English and Dutch situations, that it is perfectly possible for another industrial society, with a recorded crime rate comparable to that of the United Kingdom, to have a much lower proportionate prison population. Comparing England and Wales with Sweden would enforce a similar conclusion (Bondeson, 1989).

However, such comparisons can easily degenerate into a rhetorical game. The 'stock' of imprisonment is in some respects a quite limited index of prison use, and in any case is a figure which stands in need of explanation. The other key dimension of information on imprisonment is provided by measures of 'flow'. The determinants of 'flow' are the number of committals to prison (whether on remand or under sentence) and the length of time spent there. It is only when these more dynamic 'flow' data are used to illuminate the blunt figures on 'stocks' that international comparisons really become interesting or useful (Council of Europe, 1990, p. 5).

'Stocks' and 'flows'

Consider the figures given in Tables 5.2 and 5.3. Let us re-examine the exceptionally high stock of prisoners in the United Kingdom in the light of this information.

We have now supplemented our knowledge of the stock of prisoners with additional information on the flow of persons into custody (re-expressed as a rate of imprisonments per 100,000 inhabitants). Once one knows both the overall rate of detention (the prison population on a given day) *and* the rate of imprisonments (the number of committals per 100,000), one can also work

Table 5.2 Flows of imprisonment in 1987

	Number of imprisonments	Rate of imprisonments per 100 000	Proportion of unconvicted prisoners at entry (%)
Belgium	18 437	185.1	77.2
Cyprus	574	104.1	26.5
Finland	9 467	212.9	27.9
France*	90 697	163.0	71.9
Fed. Rep. of Germany	89 220	145.9	–
Greece	3 966	40.7	26.3
Iceland	326	133.8	32.5
Ireland	7 275	206.3	43.4
Italy	70 479	123.0	93.3
Luxembourg	629	170.2	79.2
Malta	278	84.0	70.1
Norway	21 394	510.2	51.4
Portugal	9 716	98.7	80.7
Turkey	129 613	255.9	65.7
UK	199 068	350.7	43.5
England and Wales*	153 708	307.1	43.8
Scotland	39 297	767.7	43.5
N. Ireland	6 063	388.6	35.3

Notes:

(*) FRANCE: Data refer to metropolitan France.

ENGLAND and WALES: The number of entries has been obtained by summing entries of convicted and unconvicted persons. The English Administration assesses the number of persons imprisoned (without double counting) as 119 681. From that figure we obtain a rate of imprisonment of 239.1 per 100 000. But this index is not directly comparable to those of other countries, calculation of which is based on the concept of imprisonment and not on that of persons imprisoned.

Source: Council of Europe, 1990, p. 11.

out the average duration of imprisonment. Prison populations are fairly simple sums: given any two of the terms (population, numbers committed, time served) you can work out the third.

What all this tells us is that some jurisdictions with overtly similar stocks of imprisoned people are actually behaving very differently, while others which we already thought of as different, in fact also differ in unexpected ways. For instance, compare England and Wales with Portugal in Table 5.2. Portugal has a much, much lower rate of imprisonments than England and Wales (less than one-third). Yet rates of detention in the two countries are much more similar. This is because the average duration of imprisonment in Portugal is unusually long. Alternatively, com-

Table 5.3 Average duration of imprisonment in 1987

	Rate of imprisonments per 100 000	Rate of detention per 100 000 at 1.9.87	Average duration of imprisonment expressed in months
Belgium	185.1	67.4	4.4
Cyprus	104.1	39.0	4.5
Finland	212.9	86.0	4.8
France*	163.0	88.2	6.5
Fed. Rep. of Germany	145.9	84.9	7.0
Greece	40.7	40.9	12.1
Iceland	133.8	27.9	2.5
Ireland	206.3	55.0	3.2
Italy	123.0	60.8	5.9
Luxembourg	170.2	95.5	6.7
Malta	84.0	14.8	2.1
Norway	510.2	46.0	1.1
Portugal	98.7	84.0	10.2
Turkey	255.9	99.4	4.7
UK	350.7	95.8	3.3
England and Wales*	307.1	94.1	3.7
Scotland	767.7	105.9	1.7
N. Ireland	388.6	119.1	3.7

Notes:
(*) FRANCE: Data refer to metropolitan France.

ENGLAND and WALES: Using the figure for the number of persons imprisoned without double counting as a basis for calculation, we obtain an indicator for the average duration of imprisonment of 4.7 months.

Source: Council of Europe, 1990, p. 11.

pare Norway with Greece. In common with other Scandinavian countries, Norway has a moderately low rate of detention. It is somewhat higher than that of Greece (46.0 per cent versus 40.9 per cent respectively). Yet Norway has a rate of imprisonment more than twelve times as great as that of Greece. Their apparently similar rates of detention mask an enormous disparity in the duration of imprisonment (a reversal of the picture: the average duration of imprisonment in Greece is nearly twelve times as long as in Norway).

It is now generally agreed that the exceptionally large stock of prisoners in England and Wales results from the combination of rather (though not exceptionally) high rates of imprisonment with rather (though not exceptionally) long periods of detention. That is, the English flow is both strong and slow (as Table 5.3 indicates). Moreover, this characteristic strongly influences not only the absolute size of the population but also the tendency towards overcrowding. Since (i) each person incarcerated for one year occupies as much space as twelve people detained consecutively for one month each, and (ii) it is the general policy of the English Prison Service to sustain single-cell occupancy as far as possible in the long-term prisons, what results is the concentration of pressure on remand and short-term facilities (i.e. the local prisons and remand centres).

The cases of Norway and the Netherlands present a striking contrast with the English experience. The rate of detention in Norway is less than half that of England and Wales. Yet its rate of imprisonments is unusually high. (Something similar is true of Denmark, according to Heinz, 1989, p. 190.) This is because Norway is among the countries with the lowest mean detention periods. The flow of prisoners is very high but also very fast. The Netherlands ostensibly presents a less extreme case. Blankenburg (1985), comparing penal policy in the Netherlands and in the Federal Republic of Germany, reports that the Netherlands has a higher rate of imprisonments but a lower rate of detention than its neighbouring German state, largely because the vast majority of sentences imposed are of under six months' duration (quoted in Heinz, 1989, p. 191).

What is particularly striking in the case of the Netherlands is that immediate sentences of imprisonment constitute a rather high proportion of all punishments administered by the courts (11.0 per cent as compared with 3.6 per cent in England and Wales (Council of Europe, 1990, p. 30)). This produces a lower rate of detention not simply because of the shorter sentences but also because fewer cases come before the courts as a result of police and prosecutorial discretion. The English system is not *prima facie* more 'punitive' (a far larger proportion of defendants are fined in England and Wales than in comparable jurisdictions (*idem*)), but it is far more *extensive*, and apparently less given to channelling cases out at an early stage (cf. Feest, this volume). It is also more sharply polarised in that more serious offenders go to prison for a very much longer time in England and Wales than in the Netherlands or Norway. The penal range is great, thereby pushing up the average duration of imprisonment.

Such comparisons raise a succession of difficult and absorbing issues when it comes to assessing the following:

(a) the relation between imprisonment and 'alternative' measures in different jurisdictions;
(b) the 'mildness' or 'severity' of the penal climate in different countries (and its relation to macro-economic or social structural factors) and
(c) the viability of different strategies for reducing prison populations.

We will hazard some tentative judgements on each of these matters. First, however, we should consider some instances of contraction or expansion in individual countries.

Contractions and expansions

Notwithstanding the difficulties of making accurate comparisons, certain jurisdictions have been traditionally cited as instances of 'good practice' in keeping prison populations relatively low. The Netherlands, for example, has long been regarded by penal reformers as a model case. Downes (1988) notes that although for most of the century before 1955 the Dutch prison population rate exceeded that in England and Wales, the average daily population of Dutch prisons fell from around 6,000 in 1950 to under 3,500 by 1955. Further decreases occurred in the next two decades despite a rising crime rate. In England and Wales the numbers have more than doubled since 1950. Recent rises in the Dutch population still leave its relative size at only one-third of that of England and Wales. Downes (1988) attributes this mild penal climate to a number of factors. These include a greater emphasis on rehabilitation, the use of prosecutorial guidelines to encourage greater consistency in sentencing and a presumed Dutch 'culture of tolerance' towards its deviant minorities. However, even after a lengthy and rigorous examination of empirical data and his own qualitative research, Downes remains inconclusive in attributing Holland's move to reductionism to any one cause.

The picture is also complicated by De Haan's argument (1990, p. 65) that although the Dutch prison population did fall in the 1960s and 1970s, the *number* of prison sentences increased continuously. The cause of the small prison population, then, appears to lie more in a reduction of sentence length. A practice of frequent, but relatively lenient, prison sentences leaves the question of Dutch 'tolerance' open. But, whatever the reasons, the unquestionably smaller numbers in Dutch prisons has clearly aided the development of prisoners' rights and welfare amenities which appear so lacking in the English system.

The trend to increase prison populations has also been reversed by West Germany. Between 1983 and 1988 the German prison population declined by an average of 3.5 per cent per year. Graham (1990) attributes this not to offenders receiving shorter sentences but to a decline in the number of offenders actually being sent to prison. In turn this is not due to a decrease in crime rates, or indeed to any legislative changes, but to a 'radical change in the practice of public prosecutors and judges, which in turn has been brought about by a shift in their perceptions of the efficacy and legitimacy of incarceration' (Graham, 1990, p. 167). Combined with these changes has been a growth in diversion from custody projects which, unlike in England and Wales, have been established and organised by members of the judiciary.

Attempts to stem the increase in the use of imprisonment have also been in evidence in other countries. For example, Norway introduced a waiting list system in the mid-1970s in an effort to stabilise its prison population. The waiting list has, however, increased by 49 per cent between 1981 and 1985, so that although there were 2,000 prisoners at any one time there were another 6,500 convicted 'queuing up to serve their sentence' (Mathiesen, 1990, p.3). A decline is also noted in Italy which introduced shorter periods of remand in 1985 and a selective amnesty in 1986. In 1983 Sweden was able to stabilise its prison population by introducing half-time parole for a majority of its prisoners. In 1982 Denmark initiated a similar development by reducing maximum sentences for property crimes and liberalising the rules concerning drunken driving.

Despite these cases of limited 'decarceration', the overall trend in Europe has been one of expansion. Between September 1983 and September 1988, the Council of Europe statistics suggest a twelve per cent increase in the rate of detention in its twenty member states. For Mathiesen (1990) this reveals that the conscious efforts to reduce prison populations within the decarcerative ideology of the late 1960s and 1970s have now been overturned by a renewed tendency in which 'a more severe criminal policy, with more relentless use of prison seems to be an underlying pattern in a wide range of Western countries' (p. 10). As evidence, he cites the fact that in many countries, recent growths in prison figures have been followed by major prison building programmes. In the mid-1980s in England and Wales, sixteen new prisons were planned which would add 12,000 new prison places. (By 1990 this had increased to twenty-four new prisons providing over 21,000 additional prison places. By June 1990 eight of these had been built and a further twelve were under construction). In Holland, five new prisons were planned which would add 2,250 new prison places. In smaller European countries, such as Sweden and Norway, similar developments can be seen.

Despite the exception of West Germany, the underlying trend in Europe suggests that there is a generalised shift in penal policy from one concerned with reducing the number of prisoners and emphasising rehabilitation, to one which assumes expansion and is preoccupied mainly with the management or 'batch-processing' of large numbers of people (Peters, 1986). Few people go so far as to advocate higher prison use, yet most administrations seem reconciled (albeit sometimes reluctantly) to growth.

International comparisons: universality vs specificity

On the basis of the available statistical data from the Council of Europe Prison Information Bulletin and from United Nations surveys, there would appear to be the following four distinct trends in European imprisonment:

1. The overall rate of detention is increasing.
2. The use of longer sentences for serious offenders is increasing.
3. Many prisons have experienced modest or severe overcrowding.
4. Attempts to ease overcrowding have burgeoned, ranging from expansionist prison-building programmes to reductionist diversion from custody policies.

While we would be well advised to note Mathiesen's (1990) warning of a shift to a greater use of punitive sanctions, such generalisations fail to catch sight of the more progressive elements within the criminal justice systems of respective countries. For example, although we know that France was successful in reducing its prison population in 1988, and Holland is apparently reversing its liberality of the post-war period, we do not know the precise reasons why these shifts have occurred. Similarly England and Wales, long the foremost exponent of expansionism in Europe, reduced its average daily prison population by nine per cent between 1988 and 1990. In line with West Germany this shift appears to be practitioner-led. It results from changes in both remanding and sentencing, especially those targeted at particular groups, notably, in the English case, young adults. However, such comparisons over a small time scale may be misleading. Are they minor aberrations or evidence of developing long-term trends? To reach a more complete understanding of the process of incarceration we need to balance generalised statements about Europe as a whole, with more specific analyses of the impact of penal policy and practice in specific jurisdictions (cf. Downes, 1988; Feest, this volume).

Given the diversity of practices and local experiences it is difficult to arrive at adequate global judgements: indeed, it may be unwise to seek to identify pan-European trends. Yet such provisos should not obscure a basic truth, namely, that prison populations have risen sharply in most industrial societies during the last two decades. Perhaps, however, we should attempt some sort of answer to our own earlier questions:

(1) What is the relation between imprisonment and its 'alternatives', in the light of the European experience? It is now something of a commonplace, though still a matter of regret and some puzzlement to many, that the provision of a wide range of alternative sanctions does not, in and of itself, lead to a reduction in the prison population. Commentators have developed a now familiar list of reasons why this should be so: that alternatives are used as alternatives to one another rather than to prison; that people wind up in prison for being in breach of other penalties or because an earlier 'alternative' sanction has already brought them to the notice of police and courts; and that the sheer extent and ostensibly benign character of the system's lower reaches both 'widens the net' and 'thins the mesh', thereby drawing more

people into the maw of formal social control. The paradox of the English case (that a declining proportion of custodial sentences can produce a sharply increasing prison population) is thrown into sharper relief by comparison with other countries which impose proportionately more frequent prison sentences without the same effect. In the first instance, this is primarily a matter of the duration of imprisonment. What is also clear, however, is that those countries which have enjoyed less rapid penal expansion, or even, as in the Federal Republic of Germany, contrived a reduction in the prison population, have done so largely by bringing fewer people before the courts in the first place, and only secondarily by altering sentencing practices. Meanwhile, the general experience of expansion need not prevent the hope that one might still effect the virtual abolition of penal custody for specific groups. This being so, it is necessary to stratify one's analysis of prison populations carefully. A rising curve of imprisonment for adult males need not controvert sharp reductions in the cases of juveniles (Rutherford, 1986) or women (Carlen, 1990).

It is an important problem that reductions (and expansions) in prison populations are so often presented as mystifying and mysterious, and hence as lying outside conscious political control. It is true that practices which favour a smaller prison population may be to some extent inadvertent – a change in the distribution of police attention, for example, which brings fewer minor offenders to court. Alternatively, such changes may be intended, but may be informal and unannounced (as is West German discretion to prosecute). These complexities are still investigable, however. Nor is there any necessary reason why an informal practice cannot later be formalised and integrated into an overall policy strategy. It would appear, in comparing the Scandinavian or Dutch experience with the English, for example, that in the former cases stricter limits have historically been imposed on the propriety of imprisonment as a sanction; whereas the sentencing discretion of the English courts permits a more eclectic and extensive set of rationales for custodial measures. For example, Mathiesen cites recent moves in Swedish policy documents to reformulate sentencing strategy in strict, neo-classical 'just deserts' terms (Mathiesen, 1990, p. 105), thereby deliberately disallowing other candidate justifications, such as deterrence. Mathiesen disapproves of this, as of other rationales and alibis for incarceration, and he and others (e.g. De Haan, 1990) have consistently argued that neo-classical logic is easily co-opted by political ideologies with a positive enthusiasm for punishment. However, in comparative terms it would appear that the Scandinavian approach has had some success in restraining the length (if not the number) of prison sentences. The duration of imprisonment remains crucial to the eventual size of prison population (an issue to which we return below in conclusion).

(2) What other political and economic factors favour larger or smaller prison populations? This is a very large question which we can broach here only briefly. Yet it bears centrally upon an issue which we have already raised, namely: how far does the size of the prison population stand within willed political control? As we have already noted there is a strong tendency to regard prison populations as escaping conscious direction, either because the factors which produce them are so very various and complicated or because there is some sort of inherent embargo on acting upon them (viz. judicial independence, the operational autonomy of Chief Constables, etc.). Indeed, there is a clear sense in which this may be so: no one may *intend* to produce a prison population of a given size, even if their practices will reliably do so (just as no one intends to create traffic jams in the same places every day).

Young (1986) suggests that explanations for the size of prison populations tend to be of two kinds, either 'deterministic' or 'policy choice'. 'Deterministic' explanations emphasise factors extrinsic to the criminal justice system as such: crime rates; labour markets and the impacts of economic crises upon public attitudes; 'transcarceration' between prisons and psychiatric hospitals; Durkheimian 'stability of punishment' theses; prison populations as an automatic (unintended) function of prison capacity (Young, 1986, pp. 127–31). Of these, perhaps the most influential and persuasive has been the work of Box and Hale (1982, 1985) on unemployment and imprisonment. Briefly, Box and Hale argue that the relationship between these terms is mediated by the impact of unemployment on the anxieties and sense of incipient social disorder among the powerful, and hence on the sentencing culture. Thus imprisonment is 'not a direct response to any rise in crime, but is an ideologically motivated response to the perceived threat posed by the swelling population of economically marginalised persons' (Box and Hale, 1982, p. 22). De Haan has since criticised these views, partly on the grounds that Box and Hale do not distinguish sufficiently clearly between the *number* and the *duration* of prison sentences, both of which are, as we have seen, necessary to the understanding of rates of detention. Indeed, De Haan argues, prison populations can easily increase (in the Netherlands during the 1980s) while the proportionate imposition of prison sentences remains static or drops, either because of increased waiting time on remand or because of the increased number of long sentences (De Haan, 1990, pp. 52–3). Again, the duration of imprisonment is central. De Haan is thus cautious about global, law-like theories of penal expansion. Clearly, very general theses which attribute the recent growth of prison systems to 'the fiscal crisis of the state', or indeed to a pervasive 'legitimation crisis' need to be treated with circumspection and called upon to give a detailed account of mechanism. On the other hand, there is clearly a general sense in which it is true that political discourse in the 1980s in several countries (especially the United Kingdom and the United States) has indeed been dominated by a neo-conservative retrenchment, in combination with persistently high rates of unemployment, widening inequalities of income and a preference for fairly hard 'law and order' rhetoric (Mathiesen, 1990; Caringella-Macdonald, 1990; Lowman, Menzies and Palys, 1987), and that all of criminal justice policy needs to be reviewed in that light. Even if this only leads to the tougher sentencing of particular categories of crime which have been vested with particular rhetorical importance, it can still contribute to an increased prison population (De Haan, 1990, p. 63).

On the other side of Young's polarity are the 'policy choice' models (though it should follow from our account of Box and Hale's and De Haan's views on the impact of politico-ideological variation on sentencing that we do not altogether accept a sharp distinction between 'social structural' and 'policy choice' explanations). Young cites both the work of Downes (this volume) and Feest (this volume) as instances of 'policy choice' emphases, since both emphasise the importance of particular professional cultures among decision-makers, especially regarding discretion to prosecute. Rutherford's views would also stand on the 'policy choice' side of the argument. Whatever the pressures may have been, Rutherford argues, the prison system must be seen as having chosen to expand (1986, pp. 43–7), even though no one would have knowingly chosen the present destination. By the same token, one can also choose a definite set of reductionist tactics (based on cross-national comparisons) comprising a general acceptance that few benefits derive from incarceration, preparedness to waive prosecutions, shorter sentences and embargoes on overcrowding (1986, pp. 121–49). More radically, abolitionist thought is almost inherently wedded to a 'policy choice' worldview since it requires the belief that societies can eventually take a collective decision to work towards an end to imprisonment. Christie is perhaps the most thoroughgoing voluntarist of these thinkers. He has consistently argued that if we construe punishment as the knowing delivery of pain, and if we assume it to be desirable to seek a reduction of humanly-created pain, it is open to us to decide jointly what level of 'pain delivery' we accept (Christie, 1981, 1989). Christie insists that as soon as one takes the secular view that 'justice does not exist, but is created' then it follows that 'We are free to decide on the pain level we find acceptable. There are no guidelines, except in values' (1989, p. 9).

Clearly this distinction between 'deterministic' and 'policy choice' explanations can be overdrawn, as Young recognizes (1986, p. 134). Christie is making a polemical point, rather than denying the need for a grounded historical account of why punishments vary. Meanwhile, many of the writers who are at pains to show the contingency of punishment on economic and political circumstances do so precisely in order to sustain the view that things could be otherwise, if one acted to alter those circumstances.

(3) Finally, we have asked, what viable strategies exist for reducing prison populations? The lessons from European comparisons for the English case seem fairly clear. The salient difference between the level of imprisonment in England and Wales and in most other European countries lies in the length of sentences. Fitzmaurice and Pease have argued that even if one took only the 'non-exotic comparison with Scotland', then: 'Were we to keep our present reception rate but behave as regards sentence length in the way in which Scotland behaves, we would effect a 50 per cent reduction in our present prison population' (Fitzmaurice and Pease, 1982, p. 576).

Conversely, this view holds a cautionary note against undue

optimism engendered by recent falls in the English prison population. That is, if government policy continues to favour a 'bifurca-
ted' approach of decarceration for some 'soft' categories of
offence, but tough (tougher?) sentencing for serious crime, then
there is a self-imposed 'floor' below which the population will not
fall because the average duration of imprisonment will not
decrease. This being so, we conjecture that the English prison
population will tend to rise again in the near future.

Finally, there are two outstanding and unresolved issues. The
first concerns the length of sentences. On the one hand, one can
advocate shorter sentences as a reductionist stratagem. On the
other, there is also the uncomfortable recognition that many
jurisdictions have explicitly sought to do away with the shortest
sentences either as the easiest means of embarking on a more
parsimonious use of prison or on the grounds of their inherent
inutility (Heinz, 1989; Bondeson, 1989). One could hardly propose
that the United Kingdom adopt anything resembling a 'Scandinavian' option without acknowledging the difficulty involved in
justifying the short prison sentence, certainly on anything other
than purely retributive grounds.

The second problem concerns one possible defect of comparative penological arguments. Certainly, the penal record of certain
jurisdictions (England and Wales, Scotland, Northern Ireland.
Turkey, Austria – not to mention the United States, Canada,
South Africa, the Soviet Union, New Zealand) is rendered more
intelligible and stands out in sharper relief on the basis of cross-
national comparisons. The argumentative trap would lie, however,
in the assumption that if one 'normalised' the rate of detention
compared with neighbouring countries, then 'the problem' would
have been solved. There is no very evident justification for basing
one's penal policy on the pursuit of a Euroaverage, rather than
seeking a level of prison use (or none) which is rationally defens-
ible on its own terms.

Bibliography

Bondeson, U. V. (1989) 'Commentary on Heinz' in Hood, R. (ed.) *Crime
    and Criminal Policy in Europe*, Oxford, Centre for Criminological
    Research.
Blankenburg, E. (1985) 'Indikatorenvergleich der Rechtskulturen in der

Bundesrepublik und den Niederlanden', in *Zeitschrift fur Rechtssozi-ologie*, vol. 6, pp. 255–73.

Box, S. and Hale, C. (1982) 'Economic crisis and the rising prison population', *Crime and Social Justice*, vol. 18, pp. 20–35.

Box, S. and Hale, C. (1985) 'Unemployment, imprisonment and prison overcrowding', *Contemporary Crises*, vol. 9, pp. 209–28.

Caringella-Macdonald, S. (1990) 'State crises and the crackdown on crime under Reagan', *Contemporary Crises*, vol. 14, pp. 91–118.

Carlen, P. (1990) *Alternatives to Women's Imprisonment*, Milton Keynes, Open University Press.

Christie, N. (1981) *Limits to Pain*, Oxford, Martin Robertson.

Christie, N. (1989) 'Prisons as self-expressions', in *The Meaning of Imprisonment*, Bishop of Lincoln.

Collier, P. and Tarling, R. (1987) 'International comparisons of prison populations', *Home Office Research Bulletin*, no. 23.

Council of Europe (1983–1988) *Prison Information Bulletin*, nos. 1–12.

Council of Europe (1990) *Prison Information Bulletin*, no. 15.

Downes, D. (1988) *Contrasts in Tolerance*, Oxford University Press.

Fitzmaurice, C. and Pease, K. (1982) 'Prison sentences and populations: A comparison of some European countries', *Justice of the Peace*, vol. 146.

Graham, J. (1990) 'Decarceration in the Federal Republic of Germany', *British Journal of Criminology*, vol. 30, no. 2.

De Haan, W. (1990) *The Politics of Redress*, Unwin Hyman.

Heinz, W. (1989) 'The problems of imprisonment' in Hood, R. (ed.) *Crime and Criminal Policy in Europe*, Oxford, Centre for Criminologi-cal Research.

HEUNI (1985) *Criminal Justice Systems in Europe*, Helsinki Institute for Crime Prevention and Control.

Lowman, J., Menzies, R. and Palys, T. S. (eds) (1987) *Transcarceration: Essays in the Sociology of Social Control*, Aldershot, Gower.

Mathiesen, T. (1990) *Prison on Trial*, London, Sage.

NACRO (1989) 'Imprisonment in Western Europe: some facts and figures' *Nacro Briefing*, no. 25.

Peters, A. (1986) 'Main currents in criminal law theory' in Van Dijk, J. *et al.* (ed.), *Criminal Law in Action*, Arnhem, Gouda Quint.

Rolston, B. and Tomlinson, M. (eds) (1986) 'The expansion of European prison systems', *Working Papers in European Criminology*, no. 7.

Rutherford, A. (1986) *Prisons and the Process of Justice* (2nd edn), Oxford University Press.

Steenhuis, D., Tigges, L. C. M. and Essers, J. J. A. (1983) 'The Penal Climate in the Netherlands', *British Journal of Criminology*, vol. 23, no. 1.

Young, W. (1986) 'Influences upon the use of imprisonment: A review of the literature', *The Howard Journal*, vol. 25, no. 2.

6

The origins and consequences of Dutch penal policy since 1945

David Downes
Professor of Social Science and Administration, London School of Economics and Finance

Over the past decade or so, more references have been made by interested foreigners to Dutch penal policy than seems likely to have been the case since the *rasphaus* was founded in the mid-sixteenth century. Though the references are largely rhetorical, of the 'They order this matter better in France' variety, they denote a quickening of interest in the Dutch achievement of a more substantial degree of decarceration than has occurred in other European societies in the post-war period. However, the character of that achievement remains only sketchily known in the English-speaking world, and its origins and consequences have not been of major concern to academic criminologists even in the Netherlands. What follows is an attempt to sketch in rather more fully the character, origins and consequences of that decarceration, though it must be admitted at the outset that breadth of interest has ruled out any considerable depth.

My basic aim was to gather as systematically as possible views and information about how and why Dutch penal trends had developed so distinctively in the post-war period. It is easy to exaggerate that distinctiveness, and there are other states, as diverse as Japan, Sweden and Ontario, which have maintained

Source: British Journal of Criminology, vol. 22, no. 4, October 1982, pp. 325–6; 335–50.

relatively low prison populations, or which have experienced similar or even greater reductions in their prison populations within this period (Yanagimoto, 1970; van Hofer, 1975; Daniels, 1981). However, the Netherlands has proved the most striking and durable example of a trend which is markedly different from that in Britain, Germany and most other European societies.

[. . .]

Origins of sentencing trends in the Netherlands

At least seven theories, or broad ways of explaining [sentencing] trends, have presented themselves, either in the criminological literature on penal changes or in interviews with members of the Dutch judiciary and specialists in allied fields. They are by no means mutually exclusive but, in assessing their merits, it seems in order to ask of each in turn not only how well they fit the facts of the case in the Netherlands, but also how well they do so for England and Wales and other comparable societies. A good explanation would also suggest the processes whereby so-called 'causes' are mediated through the human agencies, in this case primarily the judiciary, who accomplish their apparent effects. Having reviewed the strengths and weaknesses of each theory, the somewhat artificial process of separating out the elements of explanatory approaches can be abandoned and the best possible combination sought.

(i) The economics of 'decarceration'

In his book *Decarceration* (1977), Andrew Scull argued that the trends towards the de-institutionalisation of both punishment and treatment (i.e. of responses to the 'bad' and the 'mad') are increasingly marked in capitalist societies, mainly for reasons of gathering economic stringency rather than from any substantial humanitarian concern or profound therapeutic breakthrough. He puts forward the view that 'welfare capitalism' is increasingly beset by fiscal crises, as the costs of manning burgeoning welfare institutions outpace economic growth. His argument is based chiefly upon trends in the United States and Britain, in both of which prison populations have fallen *relative* to the growth of crime rates. His argument seems much stronger in relation to the mentally ill, in particular the psycho-geriatric, than to offenders. His most striking example of the latter is the case of Massachusetts, in which the juvenile reformatories were closed down virtually overnight.

By Scull's definition, the Netherlands is a classic example of decarceration, particularly in the penal sphere. It does not appear, however, to conform to his theory of fiscal crisis. The major reductions in the prison population, both in terms of average daily populations and its relation to the rise in crime rates, came in the late 1950s and 1960s, precisely when the Netherlands was experiencing an unprecedented growth in prosperity and a relative absence of fiscal crisis. Conversely, plans are now being put forward for an increase in penal capacity of 1,300 places (an extra 34 per cent or so) at a time of considerable economic anxiety. (They may, of course, not be provided.) Nor is there any correspondence between decarceration and the economic crisis in the Netherlands over a longer time span. Indeed, van Ruller (1981) has pointed out that, except for a few extraordinary periods of short-term growth, the Dutch penal population has not increased since about 1840, remaining at about the size of 3–4,000 over the entire period, while the population as a whole quintupled.

There is one sense in which, despite these drawbacks of the theory in the main, Scull's approach chimes with that of Foucault on the 'carceral' society. To Foucault (1979), the prison is unlikely to remain the central focus of formal control in advanced capitalist societies. Instead a web of control institutions will permeate civil society in an ever-tightening mesh of state regulations. People in general, not only the 'deviant', will come under systematic surveillance. The state will hold the prison in reserve for the recalcitrant, but its agencies of control will develop more effective techniques of persuasion and coercion. There is an all too apparent sense in which this model fits the Netherlands, as it fits other industrial societies (of both capitalist and State socialist varieties). The growth of private security, the proliferation of quasi-judicial State agencies in the sectors of economic and administrative control, the tendencies to substitute executive for judicial power in a growing number of respects even in the criminal justice system: in these kinds of ways, the 'carceral' society has taken quite substantial hold. Above all, the 'welfare state' is increasingly viewed as legitimating a form of sanction which 'takes as its object not a citizen but a client, activated not by guilt but by abnormality, establishing a relation which is not punitive but normalising' (Garland, 1981, p. 40). There is not, however, any indication that this 'soft machine' has developed, in its regulatory mode, correspondingly further or faster in Holland than in other societies with a far greater investment in more traditional carceral equipment. And there are many respects in which, despite the awesome growth of the machinery of control, it limps behind the growth of phenomena which it can barely chart, let alone constrain: the informal economy, tax evasion, and allied 'fiddling' occupationally. It sometimes seems as if the only people in gaol, apart from the occasional spectacular gangster, are those unemployed or marginal workers who lack routinised access to occupational crime. But it is hardly to the Netherlands' discredit to have acted on that insight more than other comparably developed societies. It is difficult to impute to the Dutch, in other words, a more developed carceral society than that existing in Britain, Germany, France, Russia, Scandinavia, the United States or any other societies with far higher prison populations than Holland.

(ii) The limits of penal capacity

Broadly stated, this theory maintains that it is penal capacity which determines penal population rather than the reverse. Van Ruller (1981) has provided a well-documented basis for the examination of this approach: 'The suggestion implicit in the rates is that the existing penitentiary infrastructure strongly determines the degree to which the prison sentence is used in the Netherlands.' A more general statement of this view has been made by Blumstein and Cohen (1973). Van Ruller shows the astonishing longevity of the trend towards a reduction in the average prison population relative to the size of the population as a whole in the Netherlands: the reduction is traceable back virtually to the 1840s, and is broken only by short-term increases during the crisis periods of the two World Wars and their immediate aftermaths, after which the progressive decrease is resumed. By contrast, the penal capacity (excluding the nineteenth century beggar colonies and their successor, the State labour colonies, which retained separate but diminishing populations till their abolition in the 1950s) remained relatively stable over the entire period at between 4–5,000 places, declining to below that figure only in the early 1970s, a development which precipitated a crisis of sorts over penal capacity that was temporarily resolved by the pardons of 1975. In short, if penal capacity is assumed to be a constant, then the reduction in prison population relative to the population as a whole is inevitable, given the sharp growth of the latter, irrespective of the crime rate.

The main question which this approach begs is just *why* a certain level of penal capacity should come to be adopted by a society over so extensive a period of time. Van Ruller essays an answer to this question but in terms which raise a fresh set of issues that are of a quite different character: 'The opinion that prison does not solve social problems, and that prison is rather such a social problem itself, and that it should be repudiated, is rather widely propagated in the Netherlands.' By implication, there is a simple remedy for limited penal capacity: build more prisons. If the money for such building cannot be found, and yet more people are sent to prison regardless of capacity, the British at least have found a remedy for that: overcrowding. In sum, to propose penal capacity as the major determinant of penal policy is to reify that capacity, to treat it as a phenomenon *sui generis*, which somehow transcends the will to change, expand or transform institutional infrastructure. If, on the other hand, the question is put in van Ruller's second form, i.e. 'What is it that leads the Dutch to treat penal capacity as a constant, that may in turn affect penal policy?', we are moved onto a different terrain.

Even in its own terms, however, there are difficulties in placing such explanatory emphasis on the penal capacity alone. Not only does it fail to address the issue of why some societies, but not others, seem to stabilise that capacity; it also leaves unexamined the mediation of cause and effect. It is, in a sense, the criminological equivalent of monetarism; a fixed resource somehow promotes desired ends. But the question of why those ends are desired, and how they are in practice accomplished, is left unexamined. Do Dutch judges, for example, pay close attention to penal capacity in their sentencing? (In interviews, virtually all denied that they do, and several were strongly opposed to such a view in principle; nevertheless, it may operate as a background factor to which they pay some regard.) If so, there is a far from exact fit between sentences of imprisonment and actual capacity, as the build-up of 'waiting' prisoners in the Netherlands testifies. Also, in the post-war period, a situation of penal overcapacity developed, in which some closures of penal institutions became feasible. A strict theory of penal capacity would entail that available places were filled. Such anomalies point to serious inadequacies in the theory, even for Holland.

If we regard the second of the two approaches to penal capacity as the more fruitful, i.e. 'What is it that leads the Dutch to treat penal capacity as a constant?', then the post-World War Two period presents a particularly interesting context in which to attempt an answer. There are certain differences of note between the post-war and the pre-war periods. Before 1950, for example, no 'Crimes known to the police' statistics were compiled in the Netherlands, and it is notable that the trend towards reducing the prison population persisted even in the context of a rising crime rate. Also, there are some parallels between Britain and the Netherlands in the pre-war period. The prison population in Britain fell from 1870 or so to rise again only in the economic crisis period of the 1920s. It fell again in the early 1950s, before the steep rises thereafter. The main contrast between the two societies takes on its most striking character only in the post-war period from the mid-1950s as a result. It is in that period that proportionate rises in the penal budget came in England and Wales to exceed those in the fields of education and health.

In both societies penal capacity was a constraint, but it was a constraint overcome in Britain by progressive overcrowding and fresh prison building. In Holland, from the Fick Commission of 1947 onwards, far higher standards of conditions and amenities (including a proscription against exceeding the limits of one prisoner to a cell) were enforced. The constraint of penal capacity was hence a far more realistic one in Holland. The sources of that constraint are not, however, at all apparent. Indeed, if the limits of penal capacity are generalised to the criminal justice system as a whole they become even more formidable. This notion of constraint applies not only to penal capacity, but also to the capacity of the judiciary to handle a progressive increase in caseloads. The numbers of public prosecutors and judges in the penal chamber in Holland are relatively small, and have changed but little over the past twenty years despite a large caseload increase. There are considerable pressures to save time and filter out the less serious cases. An increasing crime rate is met by a reduced clear-up rate (though police strength has increased, it has not done so in proportion to the rise in crime); an increasing caseload for the prosecutors is met by an increasing tendency to waive prosecutions (which does not entail the prosecution in court attendances and extensive dossier production); the judges, aware of the lengthening waiting lists, cut their length of sentence rather than avoid imprisonment altogether. The cumulative effect of overall constraint throughout the entire criminal justice system produces a stabilised prison population. Yet the question remains as to why so high a premium continued and continues to be placed on minimising the resort to prison, not only among the judiciary, but also among Goverments, at the Ministry of Justice, and even among opinion-makers in the media.

(iii) The culture of 'tolerance'

A more straightforward theory is that penal and sentencing policy and practice in the Netherlands is a manifestation of Dutch 'tolerance', a term which connotes a long tradition of relative leniency towards, and acceptance of, deviants, minority groups and religious dissent, and which grants a respectable hearing to views which elsewhere would be dismissed as extreme or eccentric. Evidence of the reality of what amounts, in this view, to a culture of tolerance is a matter of impressive historical record. Indicators are, for example, the low rates of execution in the eighteenth and nineteenth centuries in Holland by comparison with other European societies and in the early abolition of both capital and corporal punishment in Holland in 1876 (though the abolition did not extend to Dutch colonies, and was superseded in wartime and for collaborators tried in the immediate post-war period). Most notable as an acid test of tolerance was the very low number of wartime collaborators who were lynched in Holland after the war: a total of six by comparison with other occupied countries such as Belgium (4–500) and France (3–4,000) (Mason, 1952). This culture

114   David Downes

of tolerance can be said to operate on two mutually reinforcing levels to produce a relatively low prison population: first, directly through the judiciary, who make the actual sentencing decisions; second, through the relative absence in Holland of authoritarian 'public opinion' which in other countries, both as articulated through the media and as directly expressed in everyday life, plays upon the judiciary to enforce harsh penal sanctions.

Dutch tolerance is particularly well documented in the sphere of religious and racial 'pluralism'. Bagley's (1973) study of race relations in the Netherlands also provides useful comparative material with British attitudes and practices towards immigrants. The greater tolerance of the Dutch enabled them to turn what was in all respects a more difficult situation to better advantage than has been the case in Britain. 'The proportion of coloured immigrants in the Netherlands is similar to the proportion in Britain. The Netherlands is a much more crowded country than Britain, and in comparison with this country has an acute housing shortage. Immigrants to the Netherlands arrived, moreover, in much heavier concentrations than immigrants to the United Kingdom. Despite these facts it appears that the Dutch express markedly less prejudice than their English counterparts, and practise markedly less racial discrimination. Social policy on behalf of immigrants has been, moreover, markedly more generous and systematic than social policy in Britain. Such policy was carried through in a country with (then) somewhat less national wealth per head than Britain' (p. 246). Events since 1973 serve to reinforce Bagley's thesis, in particular his prescience on the likelihood of violent responses to indigenous racism in Britain, and continuing good race relations in Holland, with the stated exception of the Moluccans.

Dutch tolerance is not a simple blanket acceptance of all manner of behaviour and opinion. It is rooted in a society 'marked by kindly authoritarianism, deference to one's elders and those in positions of authority, with particular respect for the moral dogmas of Christianity' (p. 171). In this sense, 'Dutch emigrants to South Africa have been deviants from Dutch life, the extreme Protestants for whom any kind of compromise with other religious groups, including reformed Calvinists and Roman Catholics, was unacceptable. It is possible that this emigration of extremists from the Netherlands has indirectly contributed to the stability of Dutch society' (p. 173). Moreover, 'tolerance is extended only to the extent that the minorities conform to the Dutch *verzuiling* rules of restrained and deferential inter-personal behaviour' (p. 171). Over the past fifteen years, perhaps the most formidable and sustained challenge to the tolerant cast of Dutch government and administration has come from the squatters in particular, and youthful radicals in general, groups who explicitly repudiate these rules.

In Bagley's view, the sources of this form of tolerance reside in two major characteristics of Dutch social structure and colonial history. First, drawing on Lijphart's analysis (1975), the rules for overcoming *verzuiling* (the 'pillarisation' of Dutch society) stress decorum, negotiation, accommodation and pragmatic tolerance (by no means the same as sympathy) for the interests and values of other groups. Equality of consideration and the proportional distribution of power mean that minority groups avoid the fate of endless subordination that has so disastrously characterised Northern Ireland's Catholic population, the working class in Britain, or our minority groups more generally. (Bagley arguably overdoes his thesis here, for autonomous institutions of socialisation and communication do exist among Catholics in Northern Ireland, though these have not, of course, brought them any share in effective power. Also – as he acknowledges – some minority groups in Britain, the Jews outstandingly so, have been integrated without any particularly pronounced loss of their identity.) Secondly, colonialism in the Dutch case did not rest, for largely religious reasons as well as by the export of *verzuiling*, on the assumption of racial superiority which has so poisoned the post-war experience of coloured immigrants to Britain. In Bagley's view, this absence of prejudice, relatively speaking, can be explained in functional terms. Dutch society does not *need* to cohere around the scapegoating of coloured, or any other, minority groups, since it has evolved its own institutional devices to promote social integration out of diverse social groupings: the inter-elite 'politics of accommodation' of the different religious and secular blocs. By these means, class conflict (horizontal stratification) is diffused by cross-cutting bloc allegiances (vertical stratification). In other societies, e.g. the United States, this pattern of fragmentation has not minimised conflict, since the blocs have not materialised or become articulated politically.

To the extent that Bagley's theories have substance, much the

same analysis could be made in relation to crime. Marxist criminology in Britain has recently focused on the integrative role
played by crime and its 'control' in the context of an otherwise
class-ridden and structurally divided society (*e.g.* Hall *et al.*, 1978).
Lacking the basis for integrative institutions to form on lines of
religious allegiances (to Bagley, Britain is a 'non-Christian' society
by comparison with the Netherlands), crime has operated as a
basis on which the ruling class can impose the legitimacy of its
claims to hegemony. The rhetoric of 'law and order' is the
justification for punitive sentencing. By contrast, the Netherlands
has never engaged at this level in the 'war on crime' around which
all can unite; it has not needed to invoke such grounds for a
solidarity which it already possesses by other means.

This approach has considerable plausibility. It seems to account
for the relative mildness of Dutch reactions to crime, though it
allows for occasional outbursts of hostility to groups which either
reject or have yet to accept the 'rules of the game'. It is chiefly
lacking in a detailed application to the sphere of crime and its
control, that is, in the specification of the mediating processes at
work whereby 'tolerant' outcomes are accomplished and in particular why tolerance as expressed in sentencing has apparently
actually increased at a time of rising crime in the post-war period.
It also leaves unclear the reasons why 'religion has been so
important to the Dutch nation in the first place' (Bagley, p. 248),
though the most obvious explanation seems to lie in the crucial
symbolic role played by religion in the very formation of Dutch
nationalism in the sixteenth and seventeenth centuries.

(iv) The politics of accommodation

Lijphart's (1975) concept of the 'politics of accommodation' has
been explicitly linked with the reduction of the lengths of prison
sentences in the Netherlands by Johnson and Heijder (1983).
The distinctive quality of the 'politics of accommodation' is
that of bargaining and pragmatic compromise between the élites
which stand at the apex of the four 'pillars' of Dutch society. The
processes of inter-élite negotiation turn to advantage a denominational structure which elsewhere, notoriously in Northern Ireland,
would be the basis for endless and unproductive conflict. Catholics,

Calvinists, secular liberals and secular radicals each form their own constituency, to which their élites are responsive, and which therefore possess by proxy a stake in the system. The major price, so to speak, for such an arrangement is that the élites, both in and outside Government and Parliament, are relatively insulated from criticism, unless in exceptional circumstances. As long as they produce results, the negotiations whereby they are reached are not of immediate public interest. Delays in the post-electoral formation of Governments which in Britain would herald a major constitutional crisis are a normal feature of political process in the Netherlands.

Johnson and Heijder's argument is that, in the crucial post-war period, the 'law and order' issue was effectively neutralised politically by the interlocking character of party coalitions. Quoting van Weringh, they assert that 'issue-oriented bargaining among political parties, none of which hold absolute power . . . has been crucial to criminal justice policy . . . because the long-term rejection of prison by the Social Democrats became politically significant in this bargaining among political parties . . . The Christian Democrats are inclined towards a "law and order" policy in dealing with abortion, homosexuality, pornography, drug abuse, and similar issues because of religious conviction. The Liberals share economic conservatism but do not agree with the Christian Democrats on moral issues. So the Liberals make accommodations with the Social Democrats in support of tolerant policies' (pp. 7–8). The Socialists presided over the major changes in penal policy for twelve years after the war, which ushered in such major reforms as the 1951 Act which contained the principle of rehabilitation.

Within this setting, the criminal justice system operates, as it were, its own politics of accommodation. 'The setting of criminal justice policy operates largely detached from public monitoring . . . A small professional élite, with a fringe of complementary groups, dominates practice in the field of criminal justice. Shared training, position, norms, and values provide an effective boundary-maintaining system shielding the operations of criminal justice from public opinion' (p. 7). No neat consensus prevails, but the system affords a diverse array of flexible devices for achieving solutions to problems as they arise. The various pressure groups lock into the politics of penal reform, and even advocates of extreme positions, such as abolitionism, take the business of participation seriously, avoiding the polarisation so evident in Britain. Criminologists such as Bianchi and Hulsman, whose views on criminal justice would tend to exclude them from advisory roles in Britain or the United States, have served on commissions of enquiry; are quoted by quite orthodox members of the judiciary as holding views that deserve to be taken seriously; produce 'green' papers as alternative policy proposals that are published along with official policy statements by the government; in short, operate perhaps to shift the axis of debate to more radical positions of compromise than would otherwise occur. The flexibility of the system is such that precedents can be invoked for extensions of such devices as 'waiting' for places in prison; for the large number of pardons granted (to judicial objections) in 1975; or the increase in the proportions of cases waived by public prosecutors in the 1950s and 1960s. Freedom of the professional judges and prosecutors from the need to work with lay colleagues or juries was quoted to me many times in explanations of the direction sentencing policy had taken since the war. It tends to be assumed as a matter of course that any involvement of the public is bound to introduce a degree of unwarranted emotionalism into the processes of sentencing and prosecution. The Dutch criminal justice system approximates to the Fabian ideal of small, highly trained élites getting on with their jobs without undue public interference (though with a due regard to public opinion and the public interest).

There is considerable evidence for the view that the media have generally exerted a far more restrained stance towards penal policy in Holland than in Britain or the United States. The sensationalism of crime reporting so endemic in the latter societies is, with the generally cited exception of *De Telegraaf*, notably absent in Holland. Comment tends to be more informed and more inclined to present liberal policy sympathetically. The police do not act as a pressure group lobbying for tougher measures along the lines of the Police Federation in Britain (which indeed is showing every sign of taking the Dutch example as a threat to British sentencing policy: two recent issues of *Police* have carried strongly critical articles on Dutch penal policy, e.g. March 1981). Police evaluations emerged as quite close to those of prosecutors concerning the seriousness of offences in a study by Buikhuisen and van Dijk (1975), with the public ranking offences generally, though not too markedly, as more serious than either group. With the media, the police, the politicians and the administrators taking much the same line as the judiciary, a well-entrenched defence of the policy seems guaranteed. Even so, the last few years have seen an upturn in the proportion and numbers of sentences of over a year in length, and there are indications that the period of sentence shortening is finally over. It seems unlikely, however, that any wholesale abandonment of the generally lenient tariff is imminent. The recommendation of the Van Hijlkema Commission that the penal capacity be increased by 1,300 additional places over the next five years has already stimulated prompt and informed criticism. (See, for example, Soetenhorst, 1981)

Whether or not the two trends are at all connected, the last decade has also seen the undermining to some degree of the 'pillarised' structure, and the accompanying 'politics of accommodation', that Heijder and Johnson regard as the essential context for Dutch leniency in sentencing. Lijphart, in the 1975 edition of his book, views the period 1965–76 as that of its disintegration. Bryant (1981) asserts the emergence of social class as a more potent source of allegiance in this period than denominational loyalties. Undoubtedly some realignments of a politically crucial nature have been going on: it seems premature, however, to infer the demise of the 'politics of accommodation' from this realignment.

What remains lacking in the approach outlined above is as yet any clear analysis of precisely what connections in the political sphere led to the changes in sentencing policy with which we are concerned. After all, sporadic attempts in Britain on the part of the Home Office to persuade the judiciary and magistracy to reduce the length of sentences to prison have in general met with signal lack of success. Given the independence of the judiciary in both societies, why should judges and prosecutors in Holland either accede to or even initiate more lenient policies in line with Ministry thinking, when in Britain no such alignment occurred?

(v) Confluence

The view that Dutch sentencing trends are the outcome, not of any systematic policy, but of a confluence of largely unanticipated prior social developments, is put most vigorously by Hulsman:

'The considerable measure of de-escalation in penal matters during the past decade in the Netherlands and the general situation of the criminal justice system are less the result of deliberate policy (demands for which have only become clear or clamorous in recent years) than of a development evolving more or less fortuitously from the interplay of the factors outlined above' (below, in this case: L. H. C. Hulsman *et al.*, 1978, p. 377). After disposing of two previous myths often invoked to explain the relative mildness of Dutch sentencing, i.e. the 'masking' of institutionalisation (see above) and the alleged homogeneity of Dutch society (which is not necessarily a synonym for its degree of integration), Hulsman singles out five 'environmental' factors that have combined to produce the situation: (1) the comprehensive range of social services; (2) the extensive network and character of youth centres; (3) the multiplicity and client-orientation of welfare and social service agencies; (4) the mass media as integrative and destigmatising agencies (could this statement be made of the mass media in any other country?); and (5) the pressure group activities on behalf of penal reform by the social service agencies (including the probation service). Some of these factors extrinsic to the criminal justice system also operate within it (e.g. the probation service) in a 'de-escalating' manner; and some factors alluded to above, (e.g. the limited manpower of the judiciary) also serve to promote an economical use of prison. Other factors not mentioned in this context by Hulsman also seem to be most compatible with this approach, e.g. the often-quoted argument that the experience of internment by hundreds of thousands of Dutch people, including members of the élites, during the War, led to a widespread association of prison with oppression and an intense awareness of the costs of the deprivation of liberty.

There is much to be said for this approach, not least because it takes account of the oldest sociological truism that 'Social facts are the product of human actions, not human designs.' But it is exceptionally difficult to gauge the extent to which any or all of the above developments are in some way responsible for the mildness of Dutch sentencing, or are themselves products of the same causal matrix. War-time internment, for example, was also the experience of hundreds of thousands of Belgians and French: but their penal policies are relatively harsh. A comprehensive range of social services and youth clubs is – perhaps to a less adequate level – available in Britain (or, at least, was until the past few years' mounting toll of cutbacks in social service expenditure): again, without a similar pay-off. Perhaps the most interesting of the above developments is the character of the *reclassering* agencies in Holland. Founded in the early nineteenth century, closely allied from the mid-nineteenth century with the judiciary, and fiercely independent of State or court control (despite total financial dependence on the State), the *reclassering* agencies do seem to have played a more influential role in penal policy-making and its implementation than the probation service in England and Wales. The most obvious means whereby their agents influence actual sentencing is their recommendation to the court on the social background and situation of the defendant. The balance of opinion among members of the judiciary was that it was a factor, no more, in the trend towards greater mildness. Until the links can be established with greater precision, it seems impossible to say that the developments listed by Hulsman were any more than an accompaniment to sentencing trends rather than in any way causative.

(vi) The culture of the judiciary

A pervasive theme in many interviews was that the judiciary in the Netherlands have evolved a distinctive occupational culture, central to which is the strongly negative value placed upon imprisonment, which is viewed as at best a necessary evil, and at least as a process likely to inflict progressive damage on a person's capacity to re-enter the community. It should therefore be minimised as far as possible. The strength of this negative evaluation is a central feature of legal training, in which lawyers are exposed to criminological teaching and research, including that of abolitionists, which expose them to the weight of evidence against prison as a penalty. For example, several members of the judiciary mentioned an interview in Rijksen's book (1961) on the psychological damage wrought by prison, a book based on prisoners' own accounts, which the Ministry of Justice originally sought to suppress. By contrast, a few also mentioned a more statistical study by Steenhuis (1977), in which a controlled comparison was made of the blood alcohol levels of drivers from areas in West and East Netherlands. In the former custodial, in the latter non-custodial sentencing tended to be the norm for offences of drunken driving. No significant differences emerged from these spot-checks of blood alcohol concentrations in the two samples, from which it was inferred that fines should replace imprisonment as the standard sentence. It is difficult to imagine a similar degree of awareness of criminological literature among British members of the judiciary. This core concern is reinforced when judges enter the penal chamber, and especially when they act in more serious cases with two other judges. Their professional activities can also involve them in greater and more complex contacts with non-jurists who share an anti-penal view, and their likelihood of actually visiting prisons is far higher than is the case with their counterparts in Britain. (Almost every prosecutor and judge whom I interviewed had visited prison at least once, and several had made numerous visits in different capacities, to different types of prison and to Terbeschikkiingstelling van der Regering (TBR) clinics.) The strong commitment of the judiciary to this aspect of their role was exemplified by one instance in Amsterdam. Some twenty judges and prosecutors, along with psychiatrists, spent a Saturday morning viewing a film on the theme of TBR. A minor event, perhaps, but on top of the heavy judicial workload and outside the run of formal conferences, it testified to the seriousness with which the judiciary in Holland approach their job. It is difficult to conceive of the same event occurring in London.

Another much-quoted element in the judiciary's make-up in Holland is the reduced social distance between judges and defendants compared with the situation in Britain. In Holland, some judges questioned whether they were members of the 'upper ten'. Though it seems to me they were too modest on this score, there is no doubt but that in England judges belong to the 'upper one'. (Even magistrates in Britain, for whom there is no Dutch counterpart, are drawn from the upper-middle class to a predominant degree.) This reduced social distance enables judges, so it is said, to establish more *rapport* with defendants under the relatively straightforward rules of Dutch court procedure. By contrast, the ritual and ceremonial aspects of the trial are far more pronounced in England and Wales. 'We are judging the person rather than the facts' was a statement made on quite a few occasions in interview. The Dutch trial process is not conducted on the full-blown adversary model of the Anglo-Saxon tradition. It is more a review of evidence gathered *before* the trial takes place, on evidence assembled in dossiers which judges already know. Victims are rarely present, witnesses have already made their depositions. In the report of the *reclassering* officer, the defendant's needs are given full attention. The prosecutor has to recommend a specific sentence, and as it is his function to represent the 'public interest' but not without taking other parties (victim, defendant, their families, etc.) into account, the judges tend to treat his recommendation as an upper limit within which to exercise their own discretion. Data for 1973–6 indicate that the sentence was the same as the requirement in fully one-third of all cases at the district courts, and that the average difference in the remainder amounted to actual sentences of between 12 and 20 per cent less in length than the prosecutors' recommendations in cases of rape, robbery, burglary, manslaughter and extortion (Zoomer, 1979, pp. 45 and 51–4). (Actual sentences were higher in cases of murder and attempted extortion.) But the overall degree of concordance is remarkably close. In short, a shared community of values does seem to underpin the scheme of sentencing and the adoption of a certain tariff. The directives from the senior prosecutors, and the guidelines which they issue, are by no means capable of yielding a precise set of sentences, and though they are adhered to in general, it would seem, variations obviously exist. Current attempts at a greater degree of co-ordination of sentencing would doubtless iron out some of the extremes, but these (to an outsider) do not seem in the case of some offences to be at all remarkable, being in general a matter of months rather than years. For burglary, for example, the range by district is from 5.3 to 8.1 months' imprisonment, though the dispersion is larger for other offences (Zoomer, p. 41).

This shared community of values does not preclude change, and in recent years sentences to prison have been stiffer, though they remain mild by English standards. There does not seem to be any marked generational effect involved in this change. The RAIO system of judicial recruitment and training, introduced in the 1971–2 period to broaden and systematise these processes, has if anything strengthened the exposure of younger recruits to the anti-penal influences mentioned above. The problem of accounting for the anti-penal character of the culture of the judiciary in terms of these features is, however, that they would – in different circumstances – equally well support a pro-penal ideology. For example,

English magistrates are not necessarily less penally minded than English judges, despite being closer socially to their defendants. In a salutary demonstration that greater professionalisation and criminological training does not necessitate milder sentencing, Stanton Wheeler revealed in one American study that the better trained judges doled out *longer* sentences, since their acceptance of a rehabilitative ideology led them to accept the need for more exposure to such influences in reformatories (Wheeler *et al.*, 1968). In that case, the nature of the criminological training was heavily influenced by psychiatric thinking. How has this linkage been avoided in the Netherlands, where perhaps the most influential post-war school of thought was the 'Utrecht School'? The interplay between the theories and institutional outcomes of some of that School's thinkers perhaps supplies a missing element in the explanation of the trends under scrutiny (Moedikdo, 1976; Bianchi, 1975).

(vii) The rise and fall of rehabilitation

For a relatively brief period, from roughly 1950 until the mid-1960s, the rehabilitative ideal was accepted in Holland by the judiciary to an extent unknown in England and Wales, where its sway (despite the strong rehabilitative emphasis of the 1895 Gladstone Committee) was always more muted among judges and magistrates. The inter-war period in the Netherlands had seen a pronounced move towards the acceptance of psychoanalytical models for the treatment of a small minority of offenders, and the introduction of TBR in 1929 went beyond any equivalent tendency in Britain. However, in both countries, treatment of the individual offender by casework methods was regarded as progressive in social work and probation circles. After the War, however, there emerged in the work of the so-called Utrecht School in Holland a small group of distinguished professors – Baan, Kempe and Pompe – whose advocacy of rehabilitative measures, and whose opposition to penal measures, went far beyond that of any comparable group in Britain. The establishment of several clinics of a largely non-custodial kind in the 1950s in Holland was matched in Britain only by the lone establishment of the Henderson Hospital. The fact that by 1955 a third of all 'prisoners' serving over a year, and a third of the average daily population in liberty-depriving institutions, were in TBR, indicates the extent to which the judiciary in Holland were prepared to invest considerable faith in these measures. By contrast, in England and Wales, the proportions sent as compulsory admissions to mental hospitals were a far smaller fraction of the long-term and average daily population. By 1966, the peak of attempted psychiatrisation was reached with the Hustinx Committee recommendation in Holland that all defendants facing sentences of one year or more should be subject to psychiatric reports and that, to undertake this task, clinics were needed in all five High Court areas. These recommendations were never implemented, and shortly afterwards the reaction against TBR set in. From a number of disparate standpoints – prisoners' rights, the indeterminacy issue, the flaws in clinic security – attacks were mounted, not least by the judiciary, against the over-use of TBR. Its use was progressively curtailed from that point, though it remains a fairly standard sentence in combination with prison for aggressive offenders. Its status and procedures are currently under review by the Mulder Committee, though it seems that its role for a much reduced minority of offenders is secure.

How can we account for this contrast? First, the energies and evangelistic zeal of the chief members of the Utrecht School were obviously formidable. As Frank Kuitenbrouwer put it in an interview: 'They spoke all over Holland, they wrote newspaper articles, they hammered at the Establishment to be more humane. Pompe made the link between the reform of prisons and the reform of sentencing. He had immense moral authority and a very strong personality. And he was teaching lawyers.' Secondly, the talents of the group were complementary: Baan provided psychiatric expertise, Pompe the legal and criminological linkages, and Kempe the concept of the 'dialogue' between therapist and client which lent philosophical lustre to the mental health movement and the professional social workers. *Reclassering* gave strong support to the ideals of the School. Thirdly, the anti-penal critique implicit in their approach reinforced the pre-existing antipathy to imprisonment that had already been fostered by war-time experience. It seems likely that, even when in the 1960s the judiciary abandoned the high hopes that treatment would have discernable *positive* effects on offenders, they retained their acceptance of the School's rejection of prison for its *negative* impact on them. This is not to say that the School was the sole source of anti-penal thinking, merely that it reinforced it at a critical period. Nor is it to deny that the School's treatment orientation was strongly opposed from the outset by certain leading criminologists, in particular Nagel, who none the less endorsed the anti-penal strand in their thinking.

By contrast, in Britain, despite the attempted innovations of the 1959 Mental Health Act, the judiciary have never really been swayed from their belief in the need for the fundamentally punitive and deterrent functions of prison, though a minority perhaps placed some faith in the notion of prison as a context *within* which rehabilitation could occur. The designation of so many establishments in Britain as 'treatment and training' prisons testifies to the lack of serious Establishment opposition to the very compromise that the Utrecht School rejected: that punishment and treatment could be rendered compatible.

There was in some cases sharp disagreement in interviews with the view, expressed most forcibly by Bianchi, that the Utrecht School's impact in Holland was 'enormous' (pp. 53–4) and that they 'converted' the authorities to their views. Also, the nature of the commitment of Baan, Kempe and Pompe to the medical model varied considerably (Moedikdo). They did, however, share an anti-penal, anti-reductionist and in some respects existentialist philosophy of treatment that was unique; and they occupied the plurality of roles necessary for them to mediate their views at all levels of the control system from the Ministry and Supreme Court down.

Conclusion

Adequate tests of theories in the social sciences are in far more parsimonious supply than the theories themselves. Use of the comparative method, however, suggests that the first two approaches have considerable shortcomings in their starkest form. Economic constraints are unlikely to account for reductions in the resort to imprisonment at a period of unprecedented economic prosperity in the Netherlands. Countries similarly placed, or even experiencing greater economic stringencies, failed to match the

Dutch example of relative decarceration. For much the same reason, penal capacity does not seem, even allowing for inertia, to account for the trends under scrutiny. What happened pre-war did not prove much of a basis for predicting what occurred post-war in any society except Holland. Progressive declines in penal population occurred from around the 1880s to around the eve of World War Two in Britain, France, Germany and Belgium, a trend attributed by Rusche and Kirchheimer (1939, Ch. 9) to improvements in economic conditions and falls either in the incidence or the rate of increase of crime from the alarming levels of the early and mid-nineteenth century. If, however, the limits of penal capacity are extended to the criminal justice system in general, then a substantial (though by no means the major) part of the phenomenon can be accounted for by the progressive filtering out of potential inputs by (a) the sharp decline in the clear-up rate, (b) an increase in the proportion of offences not brought before the prosecutor even though they have been cleared up, and (c) an increase in the proportion not passed on to the court by the prosecutor.

Some of these trends can be accounted for by 'policy' considerations. The 'principle of opportunity', whereby the public prosecutor may waive prosecution for reasons of public interest, provides the constitutional *imprimatur* for considerable flexibility. The progressive waiving of prosecutions may thus be linked with the shortening of prison terms by judges. Explanations in terms of a generalised 'culture of tolerance' operating within the context of a 'politics of accommodation', help to explain *how* the élites concerned were enabled to carry their policies through without eliciting fierce opposition and public hostility. The context of an unusually generous welfare state which gave high priority to the assimilation of minority groups would also ease the task of justifying such measures. But the main burden of accounting for the trends seems to fall ultimately on variables closely connected with the actual accomplishment of sentencing by the prosecutors and judges themselves; and here the manner of judicial training and socialisation, and the character and timing of the brief ascendancy of rehabilitative policies, seem to be crucial, in ways which have yet to be analysed at all adequately.

[. . .]

128 *David Downes*

Bibliography

Bagley, C. (1973) *The Dutch Plural Society*, Oxford University Press.
Baldock, J. C. (1980) 'Why the prison population has grown larger and younger,' *Howard Journal*, vol. **19**, 142–55.
Bianchi, H. (1975) 'Social control and deviance in the Netherlands,' in his (co-ed.) *Deviance and Control in Europe*, London, Wiley.
Blumstein, A. and Cohen, J. (1973) 'A theory of the stability of punishment,' *Journal of Criminal Law and Criminology*, vol. **64**, 198–207.
Boyle, J. (1977) *A Sense of Freedom*, London, Pan.
Bryant, C. G. A. (1981) 'Depillarisation in the Netherlands,' *British Journal of Sociology*, vol. **22**, 56–74.
Buikhuisen, W. and Dijk, J. J. M. van (1975) *Official Police Reporting of Criminal Offences*, The Hague, Research and Documentation Centre, Ministry of Justice.
Cross, R. (1975) *The English Sentencing System*, 2nd edn (rev.), London, Butterworths.
Daniels, A. (1981) 'Future for alternatives,' *Correctional Options*, vol. **1**, Fall 1981.
Dijk, J. J. M. van (1980) *Some Characteristics of the Sentencing Process*, The Hague, Research and Documentation Centre, Ministry of Justice.
Dijk, J. J. M. van and Steinmetz, C. D. (1980) *The Burden of Crime on Dutch Society*, The Hague, Research and Documentation Centre, Ministry of Justice.
Fiselier, J. P. S. (1978) *Slachtoffers van Delicten*, Utrecht, Ars Aequi Libri.
Foucault, M. (1979) *Discipline and Punish*, Harmondsworth, Penguin.
Garland, D. (1981) 'The birth of the welfare sanction,' *British Journal of Law and Society*, vol. **8**, 29–45.
Hall, S., Critcher, C., Jefferson, T., Clarke, J. and Roberts, B. (1978) *Policing the Crisis*, London, Macmillan.
Hall Williams, J. E. and Leigh, L. H. (1981) *The Management of the Prosecution Process in Denmark, Sweden and the Netherlands*, Leamington Spa, James Hall.
Hofer, H. van (1975) 'Dutch prison population,' *Nordiska Samarbetsradets for Kriminologi*, pp. 99–143.
Hulsman, L. H. C., Beerling, H. W. R. and Dijk, E. van (1978) 'The Dutch criminal justice system from a comparative legal perspective,' in Fokkema, D. C. *et al.* (eds) *Introduction to Dutch Law for Foreign Lawyers*, Netherlands, Kluwer, pp. 289–377.
Johnson, E. H. and Heijder, A. (1983) 'The Dutch deemphasise imprisonment: A sociocultural and structural explanation,' *International Journal of Comparitive and Applied Justice*, 7, pp. 3–19.
Jongman, R. W. (1981) *Klasse Elementen in de Rechtsgang*, Groningen, Institute of Criminology.

Junger-Tas, J. (1979) *Juvenile Court Structures: Problems and Dilemmas*, The Hague, Research and Documentation Centre, Ministry of Justice.

Junger-Tas, J. (1981) *Some Consequences of Changes in the Processing of Juveniles through the Child Protection Systems in the Netherlands*, The Hague, Research and Documentation Centre, Ministry of Justice.

Lijphart, A. (1975) *The Politics of Accommodation* (2nd. rev. edn), Berkeley and Los Angeles, University of California Press.

Mason, H. L. (1952) *The Purge of Dutch Quislings*, The Hague, Nijhoff.

Ministry of Justice (1981) *De capaciteitsproblemen bij het gevangeniswezen* ('The problems of capacity in the prison system'), Report of the working group.

Moedikdo, P. (1976) 'De Utrechtse School van Pompe, Baan en Kempe,' in Kelk, C. *et al.* (eds) *Recht, Macht en Manipulatie*, Utrecht and Antwerp, Uitgeverig het Spectrum.

Police – Monthly Magazine of the Police Federation (1981) Editorial and article by Hulsman, L. H. C. 'Prisons – must Britain "go Dutch" to end the crisis?' 13 March 1981, pp. 3 and 36–9.

Punch, M. (1979a) *Policing the Inner City: A Study of Amsterdam's Warmoestraat*, London, Macmillan.

Punch, M. (1979b) 'A mild case of corruption,' *British Journal of Law and Society*, vol. **6**, 243–53.

Rijksen, R. (1961) *Meningen van Gedetineerden over de Strafrechtspleging*. Assen, van Gorcum.

Rosett, A. (1972) 'Trial and discretion in Dutch criminal justice,' *University of California at Los Angeles Law Review*, vol. **19**.

Ruller, S. van (1981) 'The number of prisoners in the Netherlands since 1837,' *Tijdschrift voor Criminologie*, October.

Rusche, G. and Kirchheimer, O. (1939) *Punishment and Social Structure*, New York, Columbia University Press.

Scull, A. (1977) *Decarceration*, Englewood Cliffs, NJ, Prentice Hall.

Sharples, K. S. (1972) *The Legal Framework of Judicial Sentencing Policy*, Amsterdam University Press.

Shaw, S. (1980) *Paying the Penalty: An Analysis of the Cost of Penal Sanctions*, London, National Association for the Care and Resettlement of Offenders.

Social and Cultural Report (1978) Chapter 9 'Justice and criminal procedure,' Risjwijk, Social and Cultural Planning Office.

Soetenhorst – De Savornin Lohman, J. (1981) 'Kritische kanttekeningen bij het rapport "De capaciteitsproblemen big het gevangeniswezen".' *Delikt en Delinkwent*, vol. **11**, 721–32.

Sparks, R., Genn, H. G. and Dodd, D. J. (1977) *Surveying Victims*, London, Wiley.

Steenhuis, D. (1977) *General Deterrence and Drunken Driving*, The Hague, Research and Documentation Centre, Ministry of Justice.

Steenhuis, D., Tigges, A. C. M. and Essers, J. J. H. (1983) 'The penal climate in the Netherlands: sunny or cloudy?', *British Journal of Criminology*, vol. 23, no. 1, pp. 1–16.

Thomas, D. A. (1970) *Principles of Sentencing*, London, Heinemann.

Tulkens, H. (1979) *Some Developments in Penal Policy and Practice in Holland*, Chichester, Barry Rose (for London: National Association for the Care and Resettlement of Offenders.).

Wheeler, S., Boniach, E., Cramer, M. R. and Zola, I. K. (1968) 'Agents of delinquency control: a comparative analysis,' in Wheeler, S. (ed.) *Controlling Delinquents*, London, Wiley.

Yanagimoto, M. (1970) 'Some features of the Japanese prison system,' *British Journal of Criminology*, vol. **10**, 209–24.

Zoomer, O. (1979) *Sanctioning in Cases of Serious Offence*, The Hague, Research and Documentation Centre, Ministry of Justice.

7

Reducing the prison population: Lessons from the West German experience?

Johannes Feest
Professor of Criminal Law and Criminology, University of Bremen

Introduction

The 'Breakdown of Council of Europe Member States by Rate of Detention per 100,000 inhabitants' (Tournier, 1987, p. 24) looks very much like the results of some European sports competition. It seems that a low rate of detention (relative to the population) is what everyone is striving for. Interestingly enough, Malta and Iceland are the leading nations in this contest, closely pursued by Cyprus and the Netherlands, Greece, Norway, Sweden and the Republic of Ireland. There is a middle group consisting of Italy, Denmark, Belgium and Spain. And then there are the rest, with the United Kingdom bringing up the rear, in the company of Austria, Luxembourg and Turkey. Until very recently, the Federal Republic of Germany was also in this unenviable position. But, the Germans have somehow managed to squeeze past the British, leaving the latter with the wooden spoon, as it were. Unfortunately, it is not at all clear how these developments came about and what they mean in terms of German, let alone UK, politics. This paper will, however, proceed in three steps. First, it

Source: Commissioned for this volume. Revised version of a lecture given at the NACRO General Meeting, 1988 and published by the National Association for the Care and Resettlement of Offenders, 1988, pp. 2–8.

will describe what has happened. Second, it will discuss a number of possible explanations. And third, it will try to give an answer to the question of whether anything can be learned from this.

Reduction

The West German prison population has decreased within the last five years by more than 11,000 inmates, or almost 10 per cent. This process has taken place with minor variations in all eleven states of the Federal Republic. It encompasses both remanded and sentenced prisoners, juveniles as well as adults.

The process started in 1983 with *remand prisoners*. From an all time high in 1982, their numbers began to fall by about 1,000 per year to a record low in 1987, a reduction of 28 per cent. In my own part of the country, the city state of Bremen, the historical remand prison in the centre of the city was abandoned in 1986 because the city fathers felt that it was too costly to run a prison for so few prisoners. The remaining prisoners and personnel were moved to an empty wing of another prison.

Juvenile prisoners followed: their numbers decreased from their highest point in 1983 by more than 2000, i.e. 32 per cent. In some areas the situation is even more extreme: the youth prison in Bremen, built in the 1960s for a capacity of 300, houses at present a little fewer than 100 prisoners. And the prison employees are afraid of losing their jobs, or at least of being moved to other prisons.

Last but not least, *adult sentenced prisoners* followed the trend in 1985. Since that year their number has been decreasing steadily. And today it is down substantially, in absolute as well as relative terms: more than 5,000 or 18 per cent. This accounts for about half of the total decrease. And the process has not yet come to a halt.

This was *not the first reductionist experience in West Germany*. About twenty years ago, a reduction of similar scope was achieved by means of legislation (Feest, 1982, p. 15 ff.). Some aspects of this legislation became effective immediately, others later. Among the latter was the day fine system, which in 1975 became a sentencing option for all but a handful of criminal offences. In addition, the legislature discouraged prison sentences of less than six months, on the basis that true correctional treatment required more time. As a result, short-term imprisonment decreased, and many smaller local prisons were closed. But at the same time the number of longer sentences increased. And the remaining prisons became more full every year. There was considerable overcrowding in the early 1980s. And there were large building programmes under consideration or already in progress.

You may find it difficult to believe, but this *reduction* went on *almost unnoticed* at first. This was partly due to the fact that West German court as well as prison statistics are published after considerable delay, and partly because no one expected anything of the sort to happen. The conservative Kohl government had just come into power. Progressives were fighting conservative criminal policies, long sentences and prison building programmes. And even when the first signs of a declining prison population appeared, they were seen as an interlude only, without much lasting significance. This may explain why there are still no published studies in West Germany on the reductionist phenomenon. The only two publications on the subject are by British scholars, John Graham (1988) and Andrew Rutherford (1988). And it was only late last year that I received an analysis by my German colleague Professor Christian Pfeiffer (1988). While Rutherford focuses on remand, Graham and Pfeiffer concentrate on youth prisons and youth detention.

Changed behaviour of prosecutors and judges

How did the Germans do it? Maybe they did nothing at all and some larger social forces simply changed for the better? Or perhaps the crime rate dropped and brought the imprisonment rate down? Or again, did they use legislation to solve the problem of their overcrowded prisons? I think I can show that none of these approaches can explain the phenomenon.

Larger social forces

There are two large forces that are worth inspecting: the economy and demography.

The most obvious general variable to examine is the *economy* (Council of Europe, 1985). In traditional criminology, unemployment is seen as an important criminogenic condition, a condition inducing people to commit crimes; but it has also been hypothesised that in a situation of high unemployment judges will be less likely to use fines, and imprisonment becomes the only alternative. So when the German prison population increased in the 1970s, one of the reasons usually given was 'the deteriorating economic situation causing chronic unemployment for juveniles and young adults' (Feest, 1982, p. 43). The unemployment rate in the 1970s was never higher than 4.7 per cent; today it is about twice as high. But the prison population is down by 20 per cent. There goes another simplistic theory.

The *demographic argument* sounds even more convincing: the German population is shrinking. Contraceptive devices, the pill in particular, have led to a marked reduction in the birth rate. We may hypothesise that a smaller population will have proportionately fewer criminals. Quite fittingly, the topic of a recent conference of our National Organization of Juvenile Courts and Youth Probation read as follows: '. . . The challenge of the smaller birth cohorts' (DVJJ, 1987) But these smaller birth cohorts can presently explain, at best, only a small proportion of the dwindling prison populations, because the birth cohorts became smaller after the baby boom of the mid-1960s, but it is only since 1967 that the birth rate has dropped substantially, which means that any major effect could only have reached the adult criminal courts in 1988 at the earliest since almost all under-twenty-one-year-olds are handled by juvenile courts. And even among juvenile offenders, the birth rate can explain only about one-quarter of the reduction.

Crime rate

But could not crime or the number of suspected criminals have decreased even faster than the birth rate? It could have, but it did not. The number of offences known to the police surpassed 4 million in 1981 and has stayed above that magic line ever since. Basically, the same is true for the number of suspects known to the police (it has stuck at a record level of 1.3 million for the last four years). Of course, most offences that the police register are very minor and will not usually lead to imprisonment. But even if we look at imprisonable offences only, we find a slight increase and definitely not a major slump for the years in question.

Legislation

Legislation as an explanation is the easiest to disprove, because no major change in criminal law has occurred in the period under review, let alone decriminalising legislation – which is not exactly the line of the Kohl government. Even in 1983, at the height of prison overcrowding, the government was not prepared to intervene with decriminalising legislation. It took it another three years to make a rather half-hearted step in the right direction: in 1986 the scope of the suspended sentence on the one hand, and parole on the other, were slightly expanded. But at that time the reduction was already in full swing. (As a matter of fact, the Kohl government is divided on criminal policy issues: while the Christian Democrats are basically law-and-order-oriented, their coalition partners, the Free Democrats, are less so; and theirs is the Justice Ministry.)

Criminal justice process

If it was not the economy, demography, the crime rate or legislation, the explanation must lie somewhere within the criminal justice process.

While the police produced and processed about the same numbers and kinds of suspects, the number of prosecutions, remands as well as convictions, decreased. This trend started in 1983 with juveniles and has continued since 1984 for both juveniles and adults. Also, since 1983 the number of people remanded into custody, both juveniles and adults, has decreased. And since 1984 there have been signs that the number of long sentences is at least not rising any more, and may in fact be decreasing. *The reduction of the West German prison population is therefore clearly attributable to changes in the behaviour of prosecutors and/or judges.* It is what the Council of Europe like to call *de facto* as opposed to *de jure* decriminalisation (Council of Europe, 1980).

At this point, a few words on the mechanics of the German

Criminal Justice System would be helpful: in every single case of a person remanded into custody a prosecutor must have requested and received a remand order from a judge. And the same is true for people being placed on trial: a prosecutor must have presented what in British terminology would be an indictment, and a judge must have accepted that indictment. So a reduction can only come about by a judge denying a prosecutor's request for a trial; or by a judge refusing a prosecutor's demand to send people to a remand prison; and/or by prosecutors not requesting these.

Reductions in remands, in particular, *seem to have contributed directly to the more sparing use of the prison sanction* in West Germany. Let me try to explain this: in West Germany, the time spent in a remand prison is automatically deducted from a prison sentence. And there is a well-known psychological tendency on the part of judges to make the prison term fit (at least) the time already spent on remand. It is therefore logical that with less or no remand there will be less or no imprisonment. Over and above that, the chance of being handed a suspended prison sentence will be greater in a case where the offender comes to trial as a free person, possibly working, rather than as a remand prisoner.

Prosecutors seem to have played a more important role than judges with respect to the reduction, as evidenced by the fact that prosecutions have decreased more markedly than convictions. And it would explain why the change came so abruptly and at about the same time in different parts of the country. Independent judges can be influenced only very indirectly, while prosecutors are subject to directions from their superiors; and directions they get. It is important to note here that prosecutors in West Germany have acquired over the years rather broad powers to dismiss cases and even to impose sanctions on their own. Petty cases – such as shoplifting – can be dismissed without conditions. Since 1976 prosecutors have been entitled to dismiss (with the judge's consent) more important cases on the condition that the offender pays a fine, performs community work or promises reparation to the victim. In juvenile cases the prosecutor can dismiss the case if the offender is already undergoing an 'educational measure, which makes a judicial disposition unnecessary' (cl. 45, Juvenile Court Code). And then there is always the 'penal order' (Felstiner, 1979), a court order involving a fine, prepared by a prosecutor and signed by a judge; unless the defendant objects to the penal order within one week, it becomes effective and has the same status as a conviction after trial. As can be seen, prosecutors in West Germany have a number of different options to prevent a case from coming to trial. And they are using these options more and more often.

Background factors

Of course, these possibilities of handling cases without trial and of dispensing with offenders in ways other than by imprisonment have been enshrined in law for at least ten or more years. Why then have prosecutors and/or judges changed their ways since 1982–83? Something must have happened to shake their faith in the usefulness of prisons.

I can find in those years three major movements which seem to have contributed to this sense of disillusionment on the part of criminal justice practitioners: a movement dramatising the remand situation; the so-called 'alternatives' movement in juvenile justice; and the movement against prison construction. I will take these movements, one by one:

Academic *critique of remand* has a long tradition in Germany. When in 1981 a colleague of mine called remand 'the bleakest chapter of German criminal justice' (Wolter, 1981), he was simply quoting from another author writing in 1906. But this long-standing critique of remand did not become a major factor in public opinion until groups outside academia picked it up. One such group has been the National Federation for Offenders' Aid, which decided in 1979 to set up a commission to prepare a report on the problems of remand. After long deliberation, hearing experts and visiting a number of prison facilities, the group finished its work at the end of 1982. The published report commences with the observation, 'by far too many people are arrested and are held on remand much too long' (Jung and Müller-Dietz, 1983). And this formula was picked up and amplified by the German Lawyers Association (representing all practising advocates), which turned its attention to the remand problem towards the end of 1982. Since Andrew Rutherford – on the basis of interviews with participants – has so neatly pieced that story together, let me quote from his account:

> In February 1983, the Association's criminal law section organized a special conference at the Beethoven Hall in Bonn on the theme 'Too many People in Germany are Remanded' . . . The conference

attracted over two hundred people, including judges, prosecutors and administrators from the federal and state governments. As befitted its setting, the proceedings were carefully orchestrated. Formal presentations were made by six leading practitioners from across the country . . . The conference attracted wide coverage in the media. (Rutherford, 1988, p. 108)

Further publicity ensued when the Federal government – prompted by the absence of comprehensive data – announced the funding of a large-scale research project. In the following months and years several local and national conferences on the topic were organised. I still remember a local conference in Bremen organised by the prison chaplain, which brought together lawyers, prosecutors and prison personnel. Such conferences have produced formal as well as informal directions to prosecutors to use remand more cautiously. In Lower Saxonia, for instance, prosecutors have since 1985 been obliged to report to the Justice Ministry all cases of remand for juveniles younger than seventeen years of age. Even though this is only a very small part of the remand population, it may have served as a signal to proceed with more caution generally.

In addition, *community projects* have been organised, providing what is called 'remand decision help' or 'remand avoidance help' (Plemper, 1981). These projects try to find housing and/or work for people who would otherwise have been remanded in custody. I understand that a similar approach was taken by a pilot project at Camberwell Green Magistrates Court. In West Germany, this began in Hamburg and has been imitated by a number of other large cities. Judges, prosecutors and social workers interviewed on this subject have asserted that these projects were of 'central importance' in lowering the remand rate (Pfeiffer, 1988, p. 94). But then again, it may not always be necessary to provide alternatives. Many prosecutors seem to have understood that it is simply not just to remand a person into custody if a custodial sentence is unlikely anyway.

Another important factor is what has become known as the *'alternatives movement'*, that is, the growing number of projects providing judges and prosecutors with alternative non-custodial sanctions. In theory, the German juvenile judge has a broad and practically unlimited range of alternative sanctions. These are called 'disciplinary' or 'educational' measures. In the past the main problem was that, in practical terms, a juvenile judge did not have much of a choice: even if he or she would have preferred to do something other than detain the juvenile, there were no community alternatives. This has been changing: all over the country 'projects' have sprung up, offering the judges and prosecutors such options as community work, training courses and supervised activities, victim–offender–reconciliation, and individual supervision. Most of these projects are organised by private, non-profit-making organisations, even though they are usually subsidised by the state. And, not infrequently, the local juvenile prosecutor is among the organisers of the project. These projects command a lot of local publicity. And since 1982 the number of such projects has grown steadily from 50 to more than 400. Let me quote from a comprehensive report:

> Those 410 projects are the result of a 'criminal policy from below'. The initiative for the setting up of such projects . . . has come sometimes from academics, mainly however from practitioners – from juvenile probation officers, juvenile judges, juvenile prosecutors and social workers, unhappy with the fact that in their region there were not enough alternatives to custodial sanctions. (Pfeiffer, 1988, p. 94)

John Graham has recently described in a Home Office publication two such 'diversion from court and custody' projects, asserting that 'there appears to be evidence that the projects themselves are at least partially responsible for the decline in the number of prosecutions and the declining use of custody' (Graham, 1988, p. 49).

It would be wrong, however, to assume that these projects are directly responsible for the reduction. They operate only in the juvenile field and cannot explain the reduction with respect to adults. Furthermore, not even with respect to juveniles is there enough empirical evidence to show that these projects have directly siphoned off all those nearly 3,000 juvenile offenders who were spared imprisonment over the last five years. But they do constitute an important influence on local public opinion. And they seem to have helped to educate and influence judges and prosecutors towards more sparing use of the prison sanction. This is most plausible in those many areas where juvenile judges or prosecutors are directly involved in such projects.

Finally, the *movement against prison construction* may have had some influence. At first this movement was organised mainly by groups of radical abolitionists in the tradition of the Norwegian sociologist Thomas Mathiesen. The movement was small and initially had little publicity. But with the advent of the Green Party the situation changed. Because the Green Party did not at first have much of a criminal policy, abolitionism–reductionism soon became a plank in its platform. And when the Social Democrats were forced to enter into a coalition government with the Green Party in the state of Hesse, the issue received a lot of publicity because the Social Democrats wished to go ahead with comprehensive plans for building more and better 'modern' prisons. The Green Party made it a condition of their participation in that state's government that a two-day parliamentary hearing be held in September 1984. Experts from the academic as well as from the bureaucratic world were invited. In the words of an interested observer: 'Undoubtedly, these two days were a politically fateful hour (Sternstunde) for abolitionism in West Germany. Never before has this movement had a forum as widely noticed' (Spalt, 1988, p. 81). And to everyone's surprise, the large majority of experts, irrespective of which party had suggested their participation, came out against building more prisons and in favour of non-custodial alternatives.

With the decreasing prison population and the decreasing birth rate, a number of states have indeed scrapped most of their expensive prison building programmes. I do not believe that they were really convinced by the abolitionist ideas, but rather that they used the evidence presented at the hearing to legitimise a certain redistribution of their resources.

Lessons from the West German experience

There is a lot to be said in favour of cross-cultural learning in the criminal justice field. As a matter of fact some of the community options I have mentioned can be traced to UK models, even though the United Kingdom may not recognise them any more. But cross-national learning is not easy. Institutional arrangements are often so different that cultural borrowing must be handled with great care. Take for example, the 'structural problem' (Stern, 1987, p. 189) where in the United Kingdom different ministries are responsible for prisons on the one hand and for the judiciary on the other. There is no such structural separation of sentencing and prisons in West Germany: prosecution, the judiciary and the prison administration all fall within the jurisdiction of one and the same ministry, the Ministry of Justice. But, then, there is not just one Ministry of Justice in the Federal Republic of Germany; in addition to the federal one there are eleven State Ministries of Justice. Since I found it difficult enough to trace exactly what happens in West Germany, where I know the institutional arrangements well, it would be foolhardy for me to suggest on this basis any easy recipes for the United Kingdom. Let me close, therefore, with a few general comments on what I think can nevertheless be learned from the West German experience and, conversely, in what respects the Germans should not be taken as a model.

First of all, *West Germany cannot be a model with respect to the length of time that people are kept in prisons*, both remand and otherwise. Indeed, when one looks at the latest EC statistics, West Germany, despite its declining prison population, is still among those countries with the longest mean detention period (Tournier, 1987, p. 29). And the United Kingdom looks relatively good in this respect, if only for the fact that short sentences are so numerous as to statistically outweigh long sentences. If we look at long sentences only, West Germany and the United Kingdom have about equally high per capita rates. So both would have to look for models elsewhere, to Norway or the Netherlands, for instance.

The same is true for the length of remand custody. Whatever upper limits exist in West Germany (six months) are easily overruled by judges feeling that their brethren in the prosecutor's office simply need more time. I suggest that both countries examine recent Italian legislation as a model: if the prosecution, the trial or the appeal proceedings are not completed within certain time-limits, the suspect has to be released from remand prison; and there are no exceptions to this *scadenza del termine* (Conti and Macchia, 1989, pp. 92 ff, 279 ff), that is, expiry of the time-limit. Here is definitely a way to speed up trials and/or shorten the time spent on remand.

Second, if there is any really important lesson to be learned from the recent experience in West Germany, this concerns the fear of crime: developments during the last five years show that a *substantial reduction of the prison population is possible without any negative effects on public order and safety.* The reduction has not led to an increase in major crime, nor has it made the streets any less safe.

With respect to non-trivial juvenile offences, a recent study has even demonstrated that numbers are decreasing for the first time, most clearly so in those areas where imprisonment has been least used (Pfeiffer, personal communication). It is still too early to tell whether this decrease in juvenile crime is happening despite the reduction of imprisonment or because of it. A theoretical argument for the latter possibility is of course that the fewer the negative contacts with courts and prisons, the better for the juvenile.

There is a final point, which I wish to make and which concerns the *durability of the reduction.* The United Kingdom has had its periods of reduced prison populations (Rutherford, 1984, pp. 123 ff), but the use of imprisonment has always returned stronger than ever. And, as I have already indicated, West Germany, too, has seen periods of reduction before, but this reduction was eaten up by ever longer sentences. Chances are maybe a little better this time, because it is a reduction achieved not just by legislation, but by lawyers, judges and – last but not least – by prosecutors, many of whom seem to have learned something that should make a difference in the years to come: they have become profoundly disillusioned with prisons.

Another hopeful sign is the European 'competition' which I mentioned at the beginning of this chapter, because it aims at the right goals and makes us aware that other, in many ways similar, nations are doing a better job of reaching those goals. Still, even with respect to the Netherlands, Norway, Sweden and Greece, there is no certainty that the trend will not be reversed. As a matter of fact, there is a massive prison building programme presently underway in the Netherlands, of all places. Therefore, it will be of the utmost importance to consider and strive for conditions of lasting reduction, if not abolition, of the prison institution. Let me in conclusion offer the suggestion that the following two items might be among those conditions:

(a) replacing the belief system that prisons serve a useful purpose;
(b) solving some of the real problems that prisons do not solve.

Postscript (1991)

Three years after my original analysis, its results have been largely confirmed by others (Graham, 1990; Prowse *et al.*, 1990; Rutherford 1990): the reduction of the German prison population was due to changes in prosecutorial and judicial behaviour. The recent reduction in the prison population of England and Wales appears to follow the same pattern (Rutherford, 1990, p. 14).

But the decrease of the German prison population has meanwhile come to a virtual standstill and there is even a slight increase in the remand population (see Table 7.1). And at least with respect to adults, the number of prosecutions (Table 7.2) and convictions (Table 7.3) is rising again. Prowse *et al.* (1990, p. 39) are clearly right when they suggest 'that the term decarceration to describe the German experience since 1983 is, to say the least, premature . . . There are still powerful pressures for prison expansion.' One such pressure is the ever escalating war on drugs that is refilling the prisons at a fast rate.

Furthermore, it needs to be stressed that both the United

Table 7.1 Prison population (daily averages)

Year	Totals	Remand	Sent. Adult	Sent. Juv.	Other
1971	46 528	13 501	26 385	4887	1656
1972	51 054	15 123	28 586	5498	1847
1973	52 458	15 580	29 292	5695	1891
1974	52 820	15 731	29 731	5539	1819
1975	52 116	15 155	29 600	5535	1826
1976	52 392	14 405	30 451	5734	1802
1977	53 653	14 318	31 754	5840	1741
1978	54 452	13 603	33 099	6018	1732
1979	54 544	13 681	33 112	6024	1727
1980	55 949	14 553	33 685	5997	1714
1981	57 555	15 297	34 490	6046	1722
1982	61 336	16 365	36 721	6511	1739
1983	62 294	15 353	38 520	6710	1711
1984	60 985	13 855	39 197	6312	1621
1985	58 221	12 598	38 405	5782	1436
1986	53 744	11 626	35 601	5143	1374
1987	51 417	11 544	33 671	4734	1468
1988	51 272	11 813	33 413	4575	1453
1989	50 910	12 023	33 160	4233	1494

Source: Federal Ministry of Justice, unpublished statistics.

Table 7.2 Prosecutions by age groups

Year	Totals	14–17	18–21	21+
1970	738 141	68 113	94 460	575 568
1975	779 219	76 890	100 906	601 423
1980	928 906	123 390	123 390	676 294
1982	981 083	136 412	141 238	703 433
1984	966 339	120 367	134 862	711 110
1986	908 652	89 902	120 469	698 281
1987	890 666	78 417	116 230	696 019
1988	903 211	75 073	113 621	714 517

Source: Statistisches Bundesamt (1990) Fachserie 10, Reihe 3:
Strafverfolgung 1988, p.10.

Table 7.3 Convictions by age groups

Year	Totals	14–17	18–21	21+
1970	643 285	55 657	81 768	505 860
1975	664 536	58 750	84 599	521 187
1980	732 481	80 424	98 845	553 212
1982	772 194	87 476	106 820	577 898
1984	753 397	73 122	98 600	581 675
1986	705 348	53 753	86 532	565 063
1987	691 394	47 183	82 789	561 413
1988	702 794	44 479	80 271	578 044

Source: Statistisches Bundesamt (1990) Fachserie 10, Reihe 3:
Strafverfolgung 1988, p.10.

Kingdom and Germany (compared to the other Council of Europe
countries) are still in the uppermost ranges with respect to
detention rates (Tournier and Barre, 1990, p. 5).

References

Conti, G. and Macchia, A. (1989) *Il Nuovo Processo Penale. Lineamenti
della Riforma*, Roma, Buffetti.

Council of Europe (1980) *Report on Decriminalisation*, Strasbourg.

Council of Europe (1985) *Economic Crisis and Crime*, Strasbourg,
Council of Europe.

DVJJ (1987) *Und wenn es künftig weniger weden . . . Die Herausforder-
ung der geburtenschwachen Jahrgänge*, München, Deutsche Vereini-
gung für Jugendgerichte und Jugendgerichtshilfen e.V.

Feest, J. (1982) *Imprisonment and the Criminal Justice System in the Federal Republic of Germany*, Bremen, Universität.

Felstiner, W. (1979) 'Plea contracts in West Germany', *Law and Society Review*, vol. 13, pp. 309–25.

Graham, J. (1988) 'The declining prison population in the Federal Republic of Germany', *HORPU Research Bulletin*, pp. 47–52.

Graham, J. (1990) 'Decarceration in the Federal Republic of Germany: How Practitioners are Succeeding Where Policy Makers Have Failed', *British Journal of Criminology*, vol. 30, no. 2, pp. 150–170.

Jung, H. and Müller-Dietz, H. (1983) *Reform der Untersuchungshaft. Vorschläge und Materialien*, Bonn, Bundeszusammenschluß für Straffälligenhilfe e.V.

Pfeiffer, C. (1988) *Jugendkriminalität und jugendstrafrechtliche Praxiseine vergleichende Analyse zu Entwicklungstendenzen und regionalen Unterschieden*, Hannover, Kriminologisches Forschungsinstitut Niedersachsen.

Plemper, B. (1981) 'Haftentscheidungshilfe–Kommentierung aus sozialwissenschaftlicher Sicht', *Bewährungshilfe*, vol. 28, pp. 32 ff.

Prowse, R., Weber, H. and Wilson, C. (1990) *Reforming Remand Imrpisonment: Comparing Britain and Germany*, Paper presented to the Annual Conference of the European Group for the Study of Deviance and Social Control (unpublished).

Rutherford, A. (1984) *Prisons and the Process of Justice. The Reductionist Challenge*, London, Heinemann.

Rutherford, A. (1988) 'The English penal crisis. Paradox and possibilities', *Current Legal Problems*, vol. 41, pp. 93–113.

Rutherford, A. (1990) *Putting Practice into Policy. Some Hopeful Lessons* Address to Reaffirming Rehabilitation Conference. National Center for Institutions and Alternatives, Alexandria, Virginia (unpublished typescript).

Spalt, D. (1988) 'Gedanken nach der Praxis', in Schumann, K. F. *et al.* (1988) *Vom Ende des Strafvollzugs. Ein Leitfaden für Abolitionisten*, Bielfeld, AJZ Verlag.

Statistisches Bundesamt (1990) Fachserie 10, Rechtspflege, Reihe 3: *Strafverfolgung 1988*, Stuttgart, Metzler-Poeschel.

Stern, V. (1987), *Bricks of Shame. Britain's Prisons*, Harmondsworth, Penguin.

Tournier, P. (1987) 'Statistics on prison populations in the Member States of the Council of Europe', *Prison Information Bulletin*, no. 10, pp. 24–9.

Tournier, P. and Barre, M-D. (1990) 'Survey of prison systems in the Member States of the Council of Europe: Comparative prison demography', *Prison Information Bulletin*, no. 15, pp. 4–44.

Wolter, J. (1981) 'Untersuchungshaft, Vorbeugehaft und vorläufige Sanktionen', *Zeitschrift für die gesamte Strafrechtswissenschaft*, vol. 93, pp. 453 ff.

8

Correcting manifest wrongs? Prison grievance and inspection procedures in England and Wales, France, Germany and the Netherlands

Jon Vagg
Lecturer in Sociology, University of Hong Kong

> The care of a prison is too important to be left wholly to a gaoler; paid indeed for his attendance, but often tempted by his passions, or interest, to fail in his duty. To every prison there should be an inspector appointed; either by his colleagues in the magistracy, or by Parliament . . . He should speak with every prisoner; hear all complaints; and immediately correct what he finds manifestly wrong: what he doubts of he may refer to his brethren in office, at their next meeting. A good gaoler will be pleased with this scrutiny: it will do him honour, and confirm him in his station: in the case of a less worthy gaoler, the examination is more needful, in order to his being reprimanded; and, if he is incorrigible, he should be discharged
>
> (Howard, 1929, pp. 36–7, originally published 1777)

My aims in this chapter are mainly descriptive. The first part, on grievances, outlines the procedures in each of the four countries and makes a number of general points about the ways in which such systems operate. It concludes that grievance procedures cannot be effective without greater stress on inmate rights. The second and rather shorter part deals with inspections, and is

---

Source: Commissioned for this volume.

largely concerned with descriptions of who the inspectors are and what they do. It quickly concludes that, outside of the English system, inspectorates function mainly as technical advisers and not as an arm of public accountability. The final section of the chapter sounds some warning notes about the extent to which grievance procedures and inspections can bring about significant changes in prisons.[1]

Grievance procedures: some first thoughts

I have two mental pictures of prisoner complaints. In one, an English inmate appeared before the prison Board of Visitors to complain that he had been denied an extra amount of writing paper. The Board asked the prison governor for an explanation, which was that the inmate had been drawing on the writing paper he had been issued with; if he wished to draw, he should purchase drawing paper. The Board refused to uphold the complaint. In the second, a French inmate wrote to the wing governor (complaints must be in writing), asking for permission to have extra visits. He was called to the governor's office, where it was explained to him that since he was on remand, authority for visits lay with the examining magistrate and not the prison administration. The governor tore up the letter and threw it in the waste-paper bin before dismissing the inmate.

These are neither typical cases, nor very dramatic. But they serve to illustrate some general features of prison grievance mechanisms.

The English case demonstrates that complaints, however minor, are based on and adjudicated in terms of a set of legal rules and administrative regulations of startling complexity and, occasionally, pettiness. The English and French cases both illustrate a second point, which is that in almost every aspect of their lives, inmates are powerless. If we disregard for a moment the clandestine economy of contraband, inmates are dependent upon the authorities either to provide goods and services or to allow others, for example inmates' families, to provide them. With this restriction and control over even the most minor aspects of prison life, grievance procedures become, in principle at least, extremely significant. And indeed, complaints mechanisms within prisons are typically more elaborate and more often used than, for example, the equivalent procedures of other government bodies or public utilities.

The French case also illustrates the point that the term 'grievance procedures' covers a wide range of substantive issues. The French inmate was not, strictly speaking, making a complaint but a request. The procedure is, however, identical; and the same can be said of all the other jurisdictions discussed here.

One other point arises out of the French anecdote, since it makes the point that some aspects of prison life are outside the control of the administration and beyond the capacities of its internal complaints procedures. On the one hand there is a procedural chain starting with complaints to wing staff and moving on to the prison governor, and then headquarters, sometimes via a regional administration. For example, in England, pre-1990, complaints above the level of governor were handled by a single procedure, with only the subject matter differentiating between complaints handled at regional and headquarters levels. However, outside of the wing–governor–administration chain, grievance procedures are neither simple, unified nor straightforwardly hierarchical, and for good reason. In no European country would it now be accepted that inmates should not have free access to lawyers, the courts, and Members of Parliament. And in France, and in other countries influenced by the Napoleonic Code (Neville Brown and Garner, 1983; Vedel and Devolvé, 1984; David and Brierley, 1985) it has long been established that the examining magistrate, being in charge of the investigation, must have powers over remand inmates sufficient to prevent threats to witnesses, destruction of evidence, collusion of co-offenders, and so forth. Hence the issue in the French illustration above.

In order to describe the rather complex procedural arrangements for grievances in the four countries, I shall adopt a slightly idiosyncratic order of presentation. Rather than start with the lowest level of procedure and trace the routes that grievances can then take, I shall begin with the arrangements outside the prisons, and the wider legal frameworks within which they exist; and work 'upstream' to the internal procedures. Thus the context in which the internal procedures operate will have been described by the time the discussion of those procedures takes place.

Grievances: actors and procedures

Who, then, handles grievance procedures outside of the administrative hierarchy?

In *England*, the Boards of Visitors, Home Office-appointed outsiders with functions including the hearing of complaints, have been criticised as lacking in practice the independence from prisons that they have in theory (see Maguire and Vagg, 1984; Maguire *et al.*, 1985; Vagg, 1985). In addition, a number of rules and conventions screen out or delay consideration of complaints; for example Boards of Visitors will not usually entertain complaints which are also the subject of an unanswered petition. And since they act in a disciplinary capacity, they are barred from considering appeals against their own (or the governor's) disciplinary decisions – though they may consider the restoration of remission lost as a disciplinary measure, on the grounds of good behaviour. However, several major improvements were made to the complaints procedure in April 1989, the most significant being the abolition of Prison Rule 47(12), which had created a disciplinary offence of making a 'false and malicious' allegation against prison staff. It had been much criticized as a powerful deterrent to complainants, at Board of Visitors level as elsewhere, since virtually any complaint is at some level a complaint directed against staff. Further improvements followed in September 1990, and the impact of the two sets of changes also effectively redefined the role of Boards of Visitors as monitoring grievance procedures and replies within establishments, and reviewing and seeking to resolve complaints referred to them. This has a slightly stronger flavour of Dutch-style mediation, discussed in more detail below, than did the previous arrangements.

Outside of these channels, and given the freedom of communication described above, there are possibilities for inmates to initiate judicial reviews of administrative actions; for a Member of Parliament to take up an inmate's complaint with the Home Office; and for the MP to refer cases of alleged maladministration to the Parliamentary Commissioner for Administration (the ombudsman), though the PCA appears to deal with only seven or eight such cases each year (NACRO, 1990). Indeed, applications to the courts and to Members of Parliament are possible in all four countries, as are complaints to the ombudsman in all except West Germany (which has no ombudsman). However, the annual reports of the French ombudsman – unlike his English and Dutch counterparts – give no indication that any inmate complaints have been received.

In *France*, a judge, the *juge de l'application des peines* (JAP) has jurisdiction over matters affecting the actual time of imprisonment, including home leave and remission (though in the case of parole the JAP has undivided responsibility only for those sentenced to less than three years; where the sentence is longer, the JAP makes recommendations to the ministry). Such matters are thus out of the hands of the administration and its complaints procedures. And for inmates remanded in custody, the examining magistrate (*juge d'instruction*) determines a number of important issues, including whether inmates may be visited and may work. Interestingly, and presumably because they are judicial authorities, neither JAPS nor *juges d'instruction* appear to be regarded in the penal law as complaints bodies *per se* though inmates have the right of correspondence with them and the JAP must also be consulted on house rules applicable to individual establishments, transfer and administrative segregation (with 'letout' clauses permitting no consultation in emergencies), and a range of other measures including work programmes outside the prison (for further discussion of the role of JAP's see *Justice*, 1981; Couvrat, 1985).

Judicial reviews of administrative decisions are complicated by a law prohibiting the civil courts from hearing cases concerning the operation of the administration. Thus prison litigation is usually dealt with in the first instance by regional tribunals staffed by civil servants with judicial functions, and subsequently by the *Cours d'état*, again staffed by administrators acting in a judicial capacity.

In *West Germany*, all eleven prison systems prior to 1990 (one in each constituent state – there is no federal prison system) had their own internal regulations, similar in essentials though varying as to details. All eleven systems were, however, governed by the federal penal law (the *Strafvollzugsgesetz*), enacted in 1976 and coming into force in 1977. This law established specific courts for the hearing of prison matters including complaints, from which appeals are possible to the state and ultimately federal courts. Thus the courts became a routine part of the grievance procedure and not, as is the case in England, a comparatively rare resort.

Since the grievance procedure is a judicial one, the complaint must allege that the law (as opposed to the prison regulations) has been breached. Indeed, prison administrations have been faced with court decisions determining that their internal regulations were in breach of the penal law. In some states it appears that inmates are still required to ventilate grievances with the administration before complaints to the courts are possible. This is a matter of some controversy since the ECHR, in the *Golder* and *Silver* judgments, declared such practices inconsistent with the European Convention.[2]

The *Dutch* grievance system rests on prison 'visiting commissions', the *Commissies van toezicht*, which exist in each establishment. Their members are appointed from the local community, with the chairman always being an experienced lawyer (Kelk and de Jonge, 1982; Kelk, 1983; Nijboer and Ploeg, 1985). The commission appoints a subcommittee, the *beklagscommissie*, which hears inmate grievances and has wide-ranging powers both to substitute its own decision for that of the governor in any particular instance and to award compensation, either in cash or in the form of, for example, extra visits. In principle, complaints may concern only disciplinary measures, refusal to allow correspondence, refusal to allow visits, and measures denied which could be construed under the prison regulations as a right. In practice the first and fourth subjects are the most widely complained about, while the fourth, due to the phrasing of the regulations, covers almost all aspects of régimes (a separate body hears complaints about transfers between establishments, a matter often held in other jurisdictions as wholly within the discretion of the administration and not open to complaint). Both inmate and governor may appeal to a national advisory commission, the *Centrale Raad van Advies*, whose decision is final. None of this prejudices inmate rights to initiate litigation in the courts, or to approach the ombudsman, though clearly such complaints must allege breaches of law in the one case and maladministration in the other (Ybema and Wessel, 1978).

Grievances: underlying issues

The substantive issues in grievance procedures are straightforward and frequently discussed (see, for example, Austin and Ditchfield,

1985; Maguire *et al*, 1985; Home Office, 1989a; NACRO, 1990). In the main they have to do with procedural delays, and the suspicion that the low 'success rates' before 'independent' complaints mechanisms indicate their unwillingness or inability, by virtue of their powers or lack of expertise, to engage with the realities of prison life. There are, however, some significant but more general points to be made about the ways in which grievance procedures are structured.

An effective grievance system must be capable of hearing complaints about matters which are important to inmates, dealing with them in a fair and impartial manner, and providing effective remedies. A key issue in this connection is the linkage between grievances and prison régimes.

In England and France, prison conditions are on the whole rather poor. Much of the prison estate is old and overcrowding rife. Though the details differ between England and France, the reasons have to do in essence with the neglect of prisons through a succession of governments, coupled with trends in sentencing practices. The kinds of deprivations inmates might wish to complain about are thus in large part a function of recent political history and will take some years to correct, if indeed the political willingness is there to tackle them (King and McDermott, 1989). The situation in relation to régimes is slightly different, since key régime issues have to do with staff–inmate relations, the quality of management, and the provision of goods and services to inmates. The kinds of complaints registered in this regard can concern anything from changes in the arrangements for visits and recreation, to the prices and quality of goods in the prison shop, or the refusal of wing staff to listen to grievances. Like prison conditions, such matters affect large groups of inmates; but they are not necessarily easily or quickly corrected, since they often have their roots in more complex managerial problems such as the arrangement of staff shifts and contracts with outside suppliers.

As against this, grievance procedures are typically geared to complaints by individual inmates about matters affecting them personally. This conception of grievances means that matters affecting the whole of the inmate population are not treated as serious topics for complaint. Inmates do not typically use grievance procedures to complain about overcrowding – nor is it likely that they would receive serious attention if they did, unless they could demonstrate why they, as individuals, should be held in less crowded conditions. Thus far, litigation in European countries has not developed along the lines seen in America, where two significant steps resulted in the courts addressing questions of prison conditions. One was 'class actions', in which a number of similar cases are dealt with as a single case affecting a class of inmates; and the second was the willingness of the courts to consider the totality of prison conditions, rather than individual aspects of régimes, as a proper subject for complaint (cf. Jacobs, 1980; Morgan and Bronstein, 1985).

Grievance procedures are linked to prison conditions in a second way. Inmates in England or Germany may complain that they are not allowed to have televisions in their cells (in France and the Netherlands they do in fact have them). In all four countries, inmates in my own study complained about a wide range of matters including, for example, the lack of conjugal visits. But if there is no provision in the prison regulations for cell television (or conjugal visits), they will get short shrift. In essence, complaints need to assert that something provided for in the rules or the law was not done, that something was done contrary to such provisions, or that staff interpreted a rule or law wrongly. Even here, care needs to be taken; in England, the prison rules are subsidiary legislation and do not themselves have the force of law – though they, together with Standing Orders and Circular Instructions, have been cited in evidence in judicial reviews of decisions.

Thirdly, grievance procedures other than the courts tend on the whole to be quasi-inquisitorial in nature. Once a complaint is lodged, the adjudicating body asks for information from the administration, often in the form of a verbal briefing or memo from the governor. It is for the body hearing the complaint to determine whether the facts of the case were in conformity with the rules, but the evidence on which it makes its decision is often not based on detailed inquiry by staff of the complaints body – hence my description of the procedures as 'quasi' rather than fully inquisitorial. Once one reaches the courtroom, however, procedures are either fully inquisitorial (as in Germany and France) or accusatorial (as in England).

Often, there is little room either inside or outwith the prison for a 'half way' decision, or a determination that the inmate may have at least some justifiable grounds for complaint. The 1989–90 reforms in England did, to be sure, provide Boards of Visitors with more scope for mediation, though we have yet to see whether they will grasp this nettle in practice. As to internal complaints, in Austin and Ditchfield's (1985) study of petitions dealt with by regional or headquarters offices – which, of course, pre-dated the reforms – inmates' requests were granted or complaints upheld in only six out of 120 cases studied. And in the courtroom, where the litigant must demonstrate that a decision was wrong in law, the legal criteria that must be met are often rather strict. This probably accounts for the low success rates in prison litigation. In the West German system, for example, where the courts process several thousand cases each year, only about five per cent of inmates win their cases (Feest, 1988; Kaiser, Kerner and Schöch, 1983).

Grievances in the Netherlands

In the light of this it is instructive to look at the Dutch complaints mechanism.

The Dutch Penal Code explicitly refers to inmate rights. Prisoners have, *inter alia*, the right to half an hour per day in the open air (s11); to wear their own clothes (s18); to receive toiletries and other personal hygiene items (s20); to purchase items from the canteen weekly (s24); to smoke during exercise (s25); and to borrow items from the prison library once a week (s50). These rights can be withdrawn in the case of individual inmates (s15) or prison-wide (s16) for reasons for security, but the withdrawal must be in writing and signed by the prison governor; and it is possible to lodge complaints against such restrictions in exactly the same way as any other complaint may be made.

The processing of complaints by the *beklagscommissie* is more geared towards mediation than in the other three countries discussed here. A proportion of grievances seem to be dealt with informally, with members of the *commissie* acting as mediators between the inmate and the administration (Mante, personal communication). Of course, mediation is less likely at the appeal level of the system, but this approach is intended to maximise the possibility of resolving issues in the early stages of the procedure.

Statistics are probably not the best tools for evaluating complaints systems, but in the Dutch case they are rather interesting.

In round figures, about 15–18 per cent of complaints are found grounded by the *commissies*; about 25 per cent of all first-level decisions are appealed to the *Centrale Raad van Advies*, either by governors or inmates. The governors have a 'success rate' at appeal of about 65 per cent, and the inmates about 25 per cent. In terms of the final outcomes, and despite the high level of successful appeals by governors, inmates appear to be successful in about 10–12 per cent of their complaints – a much higher proportion than in the other three complaints systems, and a figure which, moreover, excludes the extent of informal mediation.

The possibility for mediation, however, depends crucially on the extent to which the dispute can be resolved through discussion between the inmate and the governor. This is most likely when they meet within a structure that sees them, broadly speaking, as equals. Power structures in prisons are typically weighted in favour of the administration. The complaints procedures in the Netherlands, then, depend crucially on the 'empowerment' of inmates through the recognition of a wide range of inmate rights – qualified rights, to be sure, but rights none the less. In the other three countries, prisoners are much less 'empowered' by legislation. Developments such as mediation, however desirable, cannot be given serious consideration until and unless there is a greater willingness to implement inmate rights.

Grievances and inmate rights

Since there is a substantial literature on prisoners' rights, it suffices here simply to paint a broad picture of the situation in the three countries I studied apart from the Netherlands[3]. In *England*, rights are on the whole only those established in common law and rely on issues of negligence, the duty of care, the concept of actions being *ultra vires*, the rules of natural justice and so forth. The development of rights has been *ad hoc*, depending upon the courts to set precedents. They have proven easiest to establish in relation to prison discipline, where the rules of natural justice (principally the concepts that all parties should be heard, and that no one should be prosecutor and judge in a case) have bitten hardest. In *France*, the law – the *Code de Procédure Pénale* – is rather detailed, making provisions of the kind often left to Standing

Orders in England. None the less it states no explicit inmate rights and only a few can be deduced from it. For example, Art D69 requires that correspondence with lawyers be left unopened, Art D94 requires that inmates are informed of institutional 'house rules' and Art D100 requires that sufficient productive work should be available to occupy an inmate's normal working day. However, the parlous state of many prisons has led to this last provision being honoured more in the breach than in reality. In *West Germany*, prison law is about as detailed as its French counterpart, and is thus more detailed than in England. It places a number of duties upon the administration, leading by implication to correlative inmate rights. Thus, since the law requires that inmates should be informed of their rights and duties (s5/2), and examined medically on reception (s5/3), inmates have specific rights in these areas. However, most provisions are hedged with qualifications. For example, inmates are entitled to send and receive letters and parcels, and make and receive telephone calls (ss28 *et seq.*), but there are maximum entitlements – for example, three parcels per year, containing only food or tobacco – and criteria by which they may be reduced or withdrawn – for example, when 'the security and order of the institution are immediately threatened' (s33/3).

In summary, these three jurisdictions are tardy about granting or recognising inmate rights; and those that have been recognised have tended to be procedural rather than substantive rights. That is, they are rights to have one's case considered, to make submissions or be represented, to be informed, and so on, rather than specific entitlements to certain goods and services. Moreover, in all three countries, even these rights have not been absolute; in various circumstances or for various reasons, it is possible for the administrations legitimately to refuse to recognise certain rights. Thus although effective complaints procedures depend crucially on the development of inmate rights, these have been slow in coming and burdened with heavy qualifications. In the Netherlands, it remains true that inmate rights are not full legal rights, but they are established by regulation and usage; they are rights because everyone treats them as though they are. Much of the effectiveness of the system relies on early and informal mediation; but this, too, has been made possible by the development of a formal complaints system which acknowledges inmate rights even though they are not rights in the full legal sense.

The inspectorates

Across the four countries discussed here, persons delegated to conduct inspections were involved in checking the humanity, effectiveness, efficiency, propriety and 'value for money' of prison régimes in general, and of specific aspects of prisons ranging from security to post-release aid to prisoners. They were dispatched to inquire into incidents, riots and escapes, and allegations of staff misconduct. They advised on proposed policy changes and were involved in the planning of new establishments and the renovation of old ones. They were consulted on new staff attendance systems and adjustments to staffing levels. In short, they were expected to look at anything that appeared to the prison administration as troublesome, and anything that was about to be changed; and, in addition, they were expected to keep a watching brief over the prison system.

The inspectorate in *England* is the largest and most complex of the four bodies discussed here. It comprises a Chief and Deputy Chief Inspector, two three-person inspection teams, and administrative and clerical support staff including the Chief Inspector's staff officer. Each inspection team consists of a prison governor and senior prison officer seconded from the prison service, and a third member with prior experience elsewhere in the civil service. In addition, the inspectorate can call on a number of specialist consultants (the number, and their specialisms, has changed over the years), and since 1983 a research officer has been either seconded to the inspectorate or directly employed by it.

The inspectorate was established in 1981, replacing an earlier 'in house' body. It is independent in that it reports to the Home Secretary, not the Director General of Prisons. Its major brief is to scrutinise prisons and their management and régimes in terms of humanity, propriety and value for money; and in line with the intentions behind its independence, its reports on establishments, including recommendations to the Home Secretary (but in the first years of its operation, excluding the comments on security), are published.

The English inspectorate is more ambitious in its mandate and rather better resourced than its French and Dutch counterparts. In *France*, one inspector and two assistant inspectors (plus secretarial support) deal with a prison system about the same size as the English system. The inspector, like most senior civil servants, is a trained lawyer and his assistants are prison governors on secondment. In the *Netherlands*, one inspector and two specialist consultants deal with an admittedly smaller, but no less complex, prison system (though at the time of my research, plans were under discussion to appoint a further three inspectors). The inspector had previous experience as a prison social worker rather than in a managerial position. In both cases the inspectorates are 'in-house', that is, organisationally part of the prison service and reporting to its director, with no publication of reports or findings.

Arrangements in *West Germany* are more complex, since they vary by state and are not necessarily separated from other aspects of administration. In Hessen, for example, two senior officials are designated as inspectors but their brief is largely concerned with security. In Baden-Württemberg, there is no inspectorate as such. Each senior official has one or two establishments that he is expected to visit regularly, and one or two system-wide functions (industry, discipline, education and so forth) that he has a special responsibility to oversee. Thus inspection becomes one of the tasks of the cadre of top administrators.

The nature of inspection

The English inspectorate inherited from its in-house predecessor a commitment to a rolling programme of visits to establishments. These are quite intensive; a three-person team spends a week in the establishment and typically produces two or three major and 50–100 minor recommendations. In addition, the inspectorate conducts one-day or half-day inspections, some completely unannounced. Although there was from the first an intention to conduct reviews of specific problem areas, it took several years before these 'thematic reviews' were properly established as a core element in the inspection process. These reviews which, like the institutional reports, are published, have dealt with matters ranging from prison suicides to sanitation and to categorisation and grievance procedures. They are seen by outside commentators as cogent and authoritative documents.

However, from 1981 to 1987 both inspections and reviews suffered a range of difficulties and delays. Morgan (1985) outlines the inspectorate's staffing problem in that period, and also catalogues the escapes and riots in the early 1980s that it was called upon to investigate. Subsequently, the latter part of 1986 and the first four months of 1987 were almost wholly taken up with inquiries into the widespread rioting in English prisons in April and May 1986. Only by late 1987 was it looking forward to a return to 'normal', scheduled, work.

In France, the inspectorate has largely been concerned with *missions d'enquête*, following escapes or incidents, and *missions de contrôle*, routine inspections of establishments. In addition, some inspections are described as *missions d'observation*, principally concerned with security; *missions d'étude*, often connected with policy reviews or organisational restructuring, and *missions du milieu ouvert*, studies relating to the fact that the French prison administration also has responsibilities for probation. Most inspections take only one or two days, and involve only one of the three inspectors. Hence the large number of inspections accomplished – usually around seventy each year, of which typically about one-third are in connection with incidents (Ministère de la Justice, 1986, 1987).

However, and unlike the English system in which outside inspectorates have a limited role, the French inspectorate is not alone in its prison 'missions'. The *Inspection Générale des Affaires Sociales*, which inspects health and sanitation, also conducts prison inspections and studies particular problem areas, including medical facilities and prescriptions.

In the Netherlands, although the inspector spends about half his time in the establishments, he does not conduct establishment inspections as such. Most of his work is connected with specific issues, be they staff malpractice, policy changes, or renovation and development plans for individual prisons. Thus on any one visit to an establishment, he deals primarily with the particular aspects of its functioning that demand attention at that time.

One point common across all the inspectorates was that despite attempts within prison systems to increase the flow of management information, documentary and statistical sources were regarded as essentially no more than an adjunct to the business of actually looking at establishments and talking to staff and inmates. The consensus was that only by physically going to instutitions and listening to people's views and complaints was it possible to discover what was really happening. Moreover, there was some scepticism about the value of explicit régime standards. The problem with standards was that they represented an attempt to quantify quality; although basic levels of provision (one inmate per cell, integral sanitation and so on) might be specified, many important régime factors were intangibles. The way that staff act towards inmates cannot easily be crunched into numbers without well-resourced social sciences research but is none the less easily visible to professional observers. While many critics of prisons (including me) have held out régime standards as a means of improving prison conditions, inspectors generally took a more cynical view. They were less optimistic about the prospect of drafting workable standards, and claimed that their own expertise provided adequate, if not quantifiable, yardsticks for studying régimes. In short, they saw their professionalism as an alternative to, and as more sophisticated than, explicit régime standards.

The results of inspection

These descriptions of what is inspected, and how, indicate that the business of 'correcting manifest wrongs' is only part of the inspectorate role; though it might also be fair to suggest that the more desk-bound parts of their work are in part to do with 'preventing manifest wrongs'. However, it is rather difficult to gauge how effective the inspectorates have been at either task.

The effectiveness of the inspectorate has been under discussion in England for some time, though in rather special terms. The point of instituting an independent inspectorate was to bring prison issues more fully into the public gaze. This it has done rather well, both in reports on individual establishments and in the Chief Inspector's annual reports. The result has been a catalogue of the chronic problems affecting the prison system, and Chief Inspectors since 1981 have not pulled their punches (e.g. HM Chief Inspector of Prisons, 1989a, 1989b). However, the production of the reports is only one part of the total process, since it is the Home Secretary's role to deal with the problems the inspectorate discovers, and this has proven the more difficult task. Some inspectorate reports have noted that even after a gap of two or three years, problems in specific institutions have still not been resolved. The major success to date, however, seems to have been the production and implementation of the new inmate grievance procedure in 1990 (discussed earlier) which originated out of the inspectorate's review of complaints (HM Chief Inspector of Prisons, 1987).

These thoughts prompt two assessments of the inspectorate's work. First, in terms of its mandate, it has quite clearly been effective. Both in terms of individual institutions, and increasingly in terms of policies and system-wide procedures and practices, it has brought to light a range of problems and offered workable recommendations as to how they can be addressed. A second and more global assessment, in terms of the objective that informed the inspectorate's mandate, would probably conclude that the purpose of having an independent inspectorate – namely, that it would be a step along the path towards more humane prisons – was an intelligent step. None the less, much of that path remains to be trodden.

In the other countries, inspectors are in-house advisers or, in the case of some West German states, are administrators first and foremost. Their role is not one of passing judgement on the prison system as a whole. They have specific and technical briefs, which reflect the concerns of senior administrators. In consequence, their contribution can only be measured in terms of, for example, what impact their work has had on the policy decisions made by top-level administrative committees. If hard evidence exists on this topic, it will be in the confidential minutes of meetings that took place behind closed doors. None the less, the impression one gets from speaking to the inspectors and other senior officials is that their voice is only one of many around the table, and that it does not necessarily prevail.

Conclusions

Taking a historical view of the current situation, the only real conclusion can be that inspectorates and grievance procedures alike have developed in a piecemeal and uncoordinated fashion. In England, grievance procedures have been influenced by the development of inmate rights, which have advanced unevenly, as new precedents have been set; and the move to an independent inspectorate was made according to the political exigencies of the time. In West Germany, the penal law was created anew in 1977 with new provisions for grievances, but individual administrations have largely been left to devise their own inspection procedures. Inspection was not touched upon in the law.

Grievances are primarily seen as the recourse of individual inmates, complaining about individual treatment. Inspections, whether external or in-house, are a means of monitoring the treatment of inmates in particular institutions, or in relation to specific problems or policy areas. The two ought to be complementary; but there is little sign of any official acknowledgement of this relationship, in any of the four countries discussed above.

Nevertheless, it seems to have 'just happened' that there is a relationship between the strengths of inspections and grievance procedures in and across the four countries, if inmate rights are taken as an index of the latter. England accords inmates the fewest rights, but has the most elaborate, and moreover independent, arrangements for inspection. The Netherlands offers the strongest rights, but has the smallest and least sophisticated inspection office. The French situation is midway between the two, and the West German falls roughly between the Dutch and the French, albeit with some variability in the ways inspections are performed.

An alternative view can be constructed by looking at the relationship between judicial and inspectoral oversight. In the Netherlands, one sees the smallest inspectorate and a grievance mechanism which, though not strictly judicial, not only behaves as though it is but also reaches far into the details of prison management. In West Germany, the courts dealing with inmate grievances are widely used; and although only a small proportion of inmates succeed in the courts, those successes are still numerous and, moreover, have a significant impact on prison administration. At the far end of the scale in terms of inspections, in England, judicial reviews of prisons are no longer rare, but advances have only been made in a limited number of fields. In this view the odd one out is France, which although possessing only a small inspectorate also has little to commend its handling of inmate grievances. The word of warning still applies, however; there is no evident reason why this relationship should exist, and it seems to have little to do with historical trends.

In the absence of a good theory, it is probably best to end with some more words of warning. Grievance procedures are about prison conditions and the quality of administrative decision-making. Improvement in conditions is largely a function of political willingness or legal clout, in particular in the form of substantive inmate rights. In the absence of these, grievance procedures cannot be an avenue for prison reform. Improvement in administration can be brought about by procedural inmate rights, but here, too, reform via inmate grievances and litigation has been piecemeal. So far as inspectorates are concerned, it must be remembered that, with the exception of England, their role is largely technical and advisory. They are hostage to the policy concerns of their masters. And in England, where the inspectorate has some distance from the administration, it can shout – admittedly rather loudly – but shouting does not, in itself, right wrongs. Inspection is only a preliminary to reform; a valuable preliminary, but not to be mistaken for the real thing.

Postscript: The Woolf Report

The Woolf Report (Woolf, 1991) sets out four requirements for grievance procedures: they should be straightforward, so inmates can understand them; expeditious, so remedies are timely; effective in providing remedies, as required; and independent. Woolf makes two pertinent observations and one major recommendation. First, he notes that inmates' 'confidential access' by sealed letter to the governor, senior officials and Boards of Visitors is flawed. Usually, the recipient of this letter can decide who needs to be told about it, but where complaints are made about staff, copies of the allegations are given to the staff concerned. Second, he proposes that the Boards of Visitors should: 'advise and assist' prisoners about grievances; investigate grievances is appropriate and make recommendations to the relevant officials; and, rather than making recommendations adverse to the inmate, simply inform the inmate that the Board could take no action. Third, Woolf recommends the creation of an independent arbitrator, the Complaints Adjudicator – in effect a prisons ombudsman. This post would be filled by an experienced barrister or solicitor, appointed by the Home Secretary, and making reports to Parliament in the way the inspectorate does to ensure parliamentary scrutiny of his work. This recommendation is to fulfil the requirement of an independent grievance system, which implies that the Boards of Visitors were not fulfilling the role. The tenor of Woolf's recommendation points towards mediation and negotiation as modes of dealing with inmates. Woolf thus moves towards recognising that prisoners have definite legitimate expectations (though not always strict legal rights). This would be a step in the direction of the more effective Dutch system.

Notes

1. I have concentrated on describing grievance and inspection systems, so some areas have received less comment than they deserve: e.g. the roles of ombudsmen, the European Council and Court of Human Rights for material these areas see Birkinshaw (1985a, b) and Reynaud (1986).
2. *Golder* v. *UK*: case 4451/70, judgment no. 18, 21 February 1975. *Silver and others* v. *UK*: case 2/1984/41/60–66, judgment no. 61, 25 March 1983.
3. A summary of the position across all four countries discussed here is in Vagg and Vossen (1988).

References

Austin, C. and Ditchfield, J. (1985) *A Study of Prisoners' Applications and Petitions*, Home Office Research and Planning Unit Papers, London, HMSO.

Birkinshaw, P. (1985a) 'An ombudsman for prisoners', in Maguire, M., Vagg, J. and Morgan, R. (eds) (1985).

Birkinshaw, P. (1985b) *Grievances, Remedies and the State*, London, Sweet and Maxwell.

Couvrat, P. (1985) 'Le recours contre les decisions du juge de l'application des peines', in *Rev Science Crim et de Droit Pen Comp*, No. 1, Jan–Mars.

David, R. and Brierley, J. (1985) *Major Legal Systems in the World Today*. 3rd edn, London, Stevens.

Feest, J. (1988) 'Prisoners' rights in Germany: legislation, implementation and evaluation', Paper presented at a Conference on 'Aspects of European Criminal and Penal Policy', Bristol, January 1988.

HM Chief Inspector of Prisons (1987) *A Review of Prisoners' Complaints*, London, Home Office.

HM Chief Inspector of Prisons (1989a) *Annual Report 1988*, London, HMSO.

HM Chief Inspector of Prisons (1989b) *HM Remand Centre Risley*, London, Home Office.

Home Office (1990) *Prison Disturbances April 1990* (The 'Woolf Report'), Cmnd 1456, London, HMSO.

Howard, J. (1929, first published 1777) *The State of the Prisons*, 3rd edn (abr.), London, Dent.

Jacobs, J. (1980) 'The prisoners' rights movement and its impacts, 1960–1980', in Morris, N. and Tonry, M. (eds) *Crime and Justice: An annual review of research, vol II*, Chicago, University of Chicago Press.

Justice (1981) 'Le juge de l'application des peines: peau de chagrin', in *Justice*, No. 84, Mars–Avril (author anonymous).

Kaiser G., Kerner, H-J. and Schöch, H. (1983) *Strafvollzug*, Heidelberg, C. F. Müller.

Kelk, C. (1983) 'The humanity of the Dutch prison system and the prisoners' consciousness of their legal rights', in *Contemporary Crises*, No. 2, April.

Kelk, C. and de Jonge, G. (1982) 'Le droit de plainte au Pays Bas', in *Deviance et Société*, vol. 6, no. 4, pp. 391–6.

King, R. and McDermott, K. (1989) 'British prisons 1970–1987: the ever-deepening crisis', in *British Journal of Criminology*, vol. 29, no. 2, Spring.

Maguire, M. and Vagg, J. (1984) *The Watchdog Role of Boards of Visitors*, London, Home Office.

Maguire, M., Vagg, J. and Morgan, R. (eds) (1985) *Accountability and Prisons: opening up a closed world*, London, Tavistock.

Ministère de la Justice (1986) *Direction de l'Administration Pénitentiaire: Rapport Général sur l'Exercice 1985*, Paris, Ministère de la Justice.

Ministère de la Justice (1987) *Direction de l'Administration Pénitentiaire: Rapport Général sur l'Exercice 1986*, Paris, Ministère de la Justice.

Morgan, R. (1985) 'Her Majesty's Inspectorate of Prisons', in Maguire, M., Vagg, J. and Morgan, R. (eds) (1985).

Morgan, R. and Bronstein, A. (1985) 'Prisoners and the courts: the US experience', in Maguire, M., Vagg, J. and Morgan, R. (eds) (1985).

NACRO (1990) *Grievance Procedures for Prisoners*, London, National Association for the Care and Resettlement of Offenders.

Neville Brown, L. and Garner, J. (1983) *French Administrative Law*, 3rd edn, London, Butterworths.

Nijboer, J. and Ploeg, G. (1985) 'Grievance procedures in the Netherlands', in Maguire, M., Vagg, J. and Morgan, R. (eds) (1985).

Reynaud, A. (1986) *Human Rights in Prisons*, Strasbourg, Council of Europe, Directorate of Human Rights.

Vagg, J. (1985) 'Independent inspection: the role of the Boards of Visitors', in Maguire, M., Vagg, J. and Morgan, R. (eds) (1985).

Vagg, J. and Vossen, R. (1988) 'Accountability and prisons: some European comparisons', Paper given to the 19th International Congress on Criminology, Hamburg, September 1988.

Vedel, G. and Devolvé, P. (1984) *Droit Administratif*, 9th edn, Paris, Presses Universitaires de France.

Ybema, S. and Wessel, J. (1978) 'Redress of grievances against administrative action', in Fokkema, D., Chorus, J., Hondius, E. and Lisser. E. (eds), *Introduction to Dutch Law for Foreign Lawyers*, Deventer, Kluwer.

9

The future of imprisonment in Scotland

Michael Adler and Brian Longhurst
Department of Social Policy and Social Work, University of Edinburgh.
Lecturer in Sociology, University of Salford

Introduction

Commentators have long lamented the lack of any coherent set of policies for the Scottish Prison Service. Ten years ago, the *Report of the Committee of Inquiry into the United Kingdom Prison Services* (the May Report) concluded that 'the rhetoric of treatment and training had had its day and should be replaced'. However, the Committee refused to espouse the concept of 'humane containment', which was favoured by most of the academic critics of rehabilitation, on the grounds that this concept was far too negative to serve as the aim of imprisonment, and instead advocated its own concept of 'positive custody'. The Report had far-reaching implications for the Scottish Prison Service and the Scottish Office set up a number of working parties to formulate detailed policies in the light of its recommendations. However, there appeared to be little sense of urgency and, after several years, few of the working parties had reached the stage of producing a final report. Some of the interim and draft reports were leaked to the press but there were no new policy initiatives.

Source: *Scottish Government Yearbook*, 1990, Edinburgh. Unit for the Study of Government in Scotland, pp. 226–7; and *Scottish Government Yearbook*, 1991, Edinburgh, Unit for the Study of Government in Scotland

Although this was a matter of considerable concern to a small band of prison reformers, political parties and the general public seemed largely indifferent.

This situation lasted until 1985 when the first of two separate developments created a crisis for Scottish prisons and encouraged the government to adopt a greater sense of urgency. In 1985, there was a sharp upsurge in the inmate population. Between 1973 and 1984, the average daily inmate population in Scottish penal establishments exceeded 5,000 in only two years (1978 and 1983). In 1985, receptions into custody were the highest on record (18,985 on remand and 24,532 under sentence) and the average daily population rose to 5,273. Per head of population, the number of receptions into prison was the highest in Europe and the prison population was second only to that of Northern Ireland. In 1986, the average daily population was the highest ever recorded (5,588) although the number of receptions into custody fell slightly below the 1985 levels. In 1987, there was a further drop (of 2.5 per cent) to 5,446 in the average daily population, with particularly sharp reductions in the number of remands, fine-defaulters and young offenders. However, the number of prisoners serving determinate sentences of three years or more and the number serving life sentences increased by 7 per cent to 1,247 and 356 respectively, the highest levels ever recorded.

The second set of developments made the crisis far worse and effectively forced the government to reformulate its prisons policy. In 1986 and 1987 there was an unprecedented series of roof-top incidents in which prison officers were taken hostage and substantial damage was done to the fabric of several establishments. Although roof-top protests and hostage-taking incidents are not new phenomena in Scottish prisons, the number and scale of these incidents attracted a considerable degree of public and media interest to which the government felt it had to respond.

Several factors eased the pressure of increased numbers on establishments. Between 1986 and 1987, an extra 675 places were provided with the completion of the refurbishment of Greenock Prison and the opening of Phase II of Shotts Prison. In addition, in 1987, the use of four establishments was changed to transfer under-utilised places in the male young offender institution (YOI) system to the hard-pressed establishments holding adult male long-term prisoners (LTPs). Under the plans known as 'Grand Design',

320 places were transferred to the adult LTP system when Gleno-chil and Noranside YOIs became adult prisons and Greenock and Dumfries prisons became YOIs. However, the nature of the problems confronting the prison service was such that a solution required more than a reallocation of establishments to the different sectors. In January 1988, the Secretary of State for Scotland announced his intention to publish plans for a new corporate philosophy for the Scottish Prison Service (SPS) and, in March 1988, the discussion paper *Custody and Care* (hereafter C & C),[1] which sets out a framework of aims and objectives for the future management of penal establishments in Scotland, was published. A second discussion paper *Assessment and Control* (hereafter A & C),[2] which sets out the approach of the Scottish Prison Service towards the particular problems of 'violent and disruptive inmates', was published in October 1988.

[. . .]

The government invited comments on C & C and A & C, the latter by 30 November 1988, and promised to take account of the comments received in developing its strategy which was to be announced 'early in 1989'. These plans were eventually revealed, some 15 months later than promised, in March 1990 in a new, and very professionally produced policy document entitled *Opportunity and Responsibility* (hereafter O & R)[3] which is available free of charge from the SPS. The O & R is a remarkable document, not only for the candour with which the SPS acknowledges the inadequacy of A & C and takes on board the criticisms which this provoked, but also for questioning many of the taken-for-granted assumptions and practices about prisons in Scotland and developing a positive and coherent philosophy of imprisonment. Although it is important not to confuse rhetoric with reality, O & R may well turn out to be a landmark in the development of penal policy in Scotland.

In this short note, we first provide a brief summary of the main features of O & R, drawing attention to the radical nature of the approach it adopts and the proposals it puts forward and to the differences between it and A & C. Having done so, we then subject the policy document to critical but, we hope, constructive scrutiny.

Summary of approach and proposals

O & R is divided into two parts. In the first (Chapters 2–4), the context for a review of policy is outlined, pressures for change are identified and recent developments in the prison system are described. In the second (Chapters 5–9), a framework for developing the long-term prison system is outlined. We shall briefly consider each part in turn.

It is significant that Part 1 begins with a review of penal philosophy and the aims of imprisonment. This is a welcome step as it recognises that agreement on aims and objectives is a prerequisite for developing a coherent strategy and a set of policies which will give effect to it. It accepts that the SPS found itself in a philosophical vacuum when confidence in the 'treatment model' declined but the 'justice model' failed to engender much enthusiasm. Rejecting the view of the May Committee,[4] which concluded in 1979 that 'no available philosophy provided an adequate basis for a new statement of the purpose of imprisonment', Chapter 2 outlines a new philosophy based on the twin assumptions that prisoners should be treated as responsible persons and that the prison system should aim to offer prisoners a full range of opportunities for personal development and the resolution of personal problems. The next chapter (Chapter 3) reviews the background against which the SPS was operating in the period up to 1988. Noting that many of those who commented on A & C felt that its analysis of the violent incidents which occurred in the period 1986–8 concentrated excessively on individual pathology, O & R identifies a number of external and internal factors, including overcrowding, 'Grand Design',[5] the differential liberalisation of régimes, drugs and deterrent sentencing, changes in parole policy and the role of Peterhead Prison in the system,[6] which contributed to the problems experienced in the mid-1980s. The approach adopted in O & R entails the almost total rejection of that adopted in A & C and no punches are pulled in admitting the extent to which the SPS unsettled its own house by some of its own policies and by the ideological difficulties which it encountered at that time. Chapter 4 examines some of the key developments since 1988, drawing attention to the 10 per cent reduction in the prison population, the fall in the number of prisoners held under Rule 36,[7] the reduced dependence on Peterhead for holding prisoners presenting what O & R refers to as 'management problems', and improvements in staff training.

Part 2 is more programmatic. Reacting to the views expressed by many of those who responded to A & C that it placed too much emphasis on the identification, segregation and containment of potentially disruptive prisoners, Chapter 5 makes it clear that the main solution for prisoners with difficulties lies in better quality mainstream establishments rather than in purpose-built control units. It reiterates the view, outlined above, that

> we should regard the offender as a person who is responsible, despite the fact that he or she may have acted irresponsibly many times over in the past, and that we should try to relate to the prisoner in ways which would encourage him or her to accept responsibility for their actions by providing him or her with opportunities for responsible choice, personal development and self-improvement. (p. 30)

Central to this approach are proposals for sentence planning which will allow the prisoner to participate at each stage in planning his or her sentence and the need to structure opportunities in a sensible and appropriate manner. Although this entails the retention of a system of progression, O & R suggests that it will be helpful to distinguish three aspects of régimes, namely the minimum elements a prisoner should receive by right ('the threshold quality of life', 'appropriate opportunities' and 'privileges') with what were previously regarded as privileges being progressively incorported into the basic threshold quality of life in prison.

Chapter 6 then spells out its own conception of normalisation, which is seen to entail the provision of 'régimes which allow prisoners the opportunity to live as normal lives as possible and as may be consistent with the requirements of security and order' (p. 37), and points to the need to review practices in three areas, namely, 'access to families', 'quality of life' and 'preparation for release'. Here O & R is at its most liberal, advocating increased home leave for most prisoners, promising to set up a working party to examine the possibility of providing 'family visits' for those prisoners who would not be eligible for home leave, and setting as policy objectives the provision to every prisoner of a room of his own and the abolition of 'slopping out'.

Chapter 7 makes it clear that security categorisation (introduced after the Mountbatten Report in 1966)[8] should only refer to security concerns and not to the prisoner's response to staff or to the stage reached in his or her sentence. In a particularly significant analysis of the need to achieve a balance between security, order and régime, it points out that 'an oversecure establishment will have pressure exerted on its control and regime elements' (p. 43), and suggests that more long-term prisoners should be placed in lower security categories from the beginning of their sentence.[9] The effect of this would be to alter the balance between the numbers of prisoners in Security Categories A–D. Moreover, by allocating prisoners to an appropriate hall rather than an appropriate establishment, the number of available options would be greatly increased.

The role of small régimes within the mainstream is considered in Chapter 8 and that of small units in Chapter 9. Chapter 8 proposes the eventual subdivision of existing accommodation into discrete small régimes and categorically rejects the extremely contentious proposals put forward in A & C to build a sixty-place maximum security complex at Shotts Prison. In place of A & C's expansionist aim of providing sufficient maximum security accommodation to accommodate all potentially violent and disruptive prisoners, O & R proposes as a 'rule of thumb' that roughly 1 per cent of inmates, i.e. about fifty at any one time should be accommodated in small units, whose 'value . . . lies as much in the ability to pioneer innovative approaches, the lessons of which can be applied to the mainstream generally, as in the capacity to provide for a limited number of prisoners who are having difficulty settling into their sentence' (p. 60).[10] With the commitment to establish another small unit for up to twelve difficult prisoners in Edinburgh, the proposals in O & R represent a reduction of about fifty maximum security places over the number proposed in A & C. One consequence of this is that Peterhead is to be retained 'in the medium term', i.e. for the forseeable future.

Critical assessment

In spite of its many positive features, there are a number of problems with O & R. We have argued elsewhere that the SPS is a site of power struggles which are expressed in, and effected by, different forms of discourse.[11] In the course of this analysis, we identified three discourses of substantive justice (concerned with the ends of imprisonment), viz rehabilitation, normalisation and control, and three discourses of administrative justice (concerned with the means of imprisonment) viz bureaucracy, professionalism and legality. It is clear that O & R represents, on the one hand, a confluence of normalisation and control discourses and, on the other, a fusion of bureaucratic and professional discourses. The latter should come as no surprise since the policy document was supposedly drafted by a civil servant and a prison governor. However, its failure to accommodate legal discourse is a matter of some considerable concern. It constitutes the basis of our first set of criticisms. Our second set of criticisms follow from the concept of normalisation which is utilised in O & R. The SPS' prior commitment to normalisation seems to us to be at odds with the thrust of some of the key proposals in the latest policy document. Finally, we identify a third set of criticisms which relate to omissions from, and internal inconsistencies in, O & R.

Although C & C outlined proposals for consolidating the Prisons (Scotland) Act 1952 and subsequent amending legislation and for revising and updating the Prison (Scotland) Rules, which likewise date from 1952 and the Standing Orders derived from them, O & R makes no reference to this and it is very much to be hoped that this does not represent a retreat from the earlier commitment. It is to be hoped, not only that the earlier commitment still stands but also that prisoners will have access to Standing Orders and other Government Circulars. Of equal concern is the fact that O & R makes few reference to prisoners' rights or the means by which they can be enforced. In accordance with prevailing government rhetoric, O & R emphasises prisoners' responsibilities, their need to make choices and to face the consequences of their decisions. This runs the risk that, in the absence of any reference to prisoners' rights, prisoners may find themselves in a very vulnerable position if and when they act 'irresponsibly' and take decisions that land them in trouble. In such circumstances, prisoners may still be moved, against their will, to a small unit or, *in extremis*, placed on Rule 36, or deprived of visits or of opportunities and other privileges without having any really effective means of redress. We are, in effect, invited to place our trust in the SPS to get things right by making the appropriate response to the prisoners' behaviour.

Although O & R does promise a review of its procedures for dealing with requests and grievances and this is certainly to be welcomed, its discussion of accountability is very disappointing.[12] The view conveyed that 'once all the developments proposed in O & R are introduced, prisoners will have no need to complain' is utopian in the extreme and it is to be hoped that the SPS will place as much emphasis on strengthening accountability as on developing new approaches to the management of long-term prisoners. In this connection it would have been reassuring if, in addition to examining the recommendations of the Home Office Working Party on Grievance Procedures,[13] the SPS had set up its own working party.

The definition of normalisation which is adopted in O & R (cited above) and its relationship to the provision of opportunities, also raises a number of problems. If the yardstick for living as normal a life as is consistent with the requirements of security and order is the kind of life the offender could lead outside prison, where few opportunities for personal development and self-improvement, education, training or employment may be available and where, in any case, little pressure may be exerted on the offender to take advantage of them, then this may not be consistent with the provision of opportunities and the encouragement which prisoners will need if they are to take advantage of them. In fact, the concept of normalisation may even be an impediment to the development of such opportunties.

Although the view of the May Committee that 'the notion of "treatment" or a "coerced cure" is a contradiction in terms and that a much more achievable goal is "facilitated change"' (p. 17), one positive feature of rehabilitation was its ability to command resources and the pressure it could bring to bear on prisoners. Whether O & R will be equally successful must remain to be seen. However, the absence of any reference to the need for effective external monitoring leaves the SPS at the mercy of the government of the day which may or may not supply the resources required to bring about improvements in prisoners' quality of life and in the opportunities necessary for personal development and self-improvement. It is thus of some concern that O & R makes no reference to the case for adopting a set of minimum standards or to strengthening the role of the Prisons Inspectorate so as to ensure that these standards are attained.

Sadly, O & R provides very little detail about the kinds of

opportunities that should be available for long-term prisoners and, in particular, for those with serious personal and personality problems. Likewise, it provides no indication of the roles which education, social work, psychology and psychiatry are expected to play. Moreover, its characterisation of the relationship between prison officers and prisoners as one of mutual interdependence and of the role of the prison officer as a facilitator, i.e. as a kind of 'social worker in the halls' is quite unsatisfactory, since it ignores the presence of power which lies at the heart of the relationship between prison officers and prisoners. More generally, power characterises the relationship between prisoners and all those in authority over them and it is precisely for this reason that prisoners need protection and that the neglect of prisoners' rights is of such significance.

In addition to the two sets of problems outlined above, there are a number of omissions and inconsistencies in O & R. The paucity of references to developments in other prison systems from which the SPS might learn and to innovations which it might wish to emulate is also disappointing. Apart from the reference to the Home Office Working Party on Grievance Procedures (see above), the only other comparative references are to the more generous provisions for home leaves and for family visits which are provided in many other countries.

The decision to retain the existing high-security prison at Peterhead will disappoint many people who would have liked to see it replaced either on the same site or, preferably, elsewhere. However, what particularly concerns us is the failure of O & R to address this question, although the various options were all set out in A & C.

Our final criticism refers to security categorisations, particularly in so far as they effect Shotts, the newest and largest establishment for long-term prisoners in Scotland. Although we welcome the fact that prisoners who do not constitute a security risk will no longer be held in high-security conditions, it would appear to be rather unsatisfactory for the large majority of Category B and Category C prisoners who are to be held in Shotts that security will have to be tightened for the very small numbers of Category A prisoners who are to be moved there from Peterhead, not least because O & R makes no reference to the possibility of reducing security levels in other establishments.

Conclusion

In spite of our criticisms, O & R deserves a warm welcome. It has many positive features and represents a major retreat from the worst excesses of control discourse which blighted the previous discussion paper A & C. Moreover, many of the defects we have identified in O & R are remediable. If the SPS continues to be as receptive to criticism as it has recently shown itself to be and responds to the shortcomings in its otherwise admirable policy document in a constructive manner, it could well find itself providing a model for other prison systems in the United Kingdom and elsewhere.

Notes

1. Scottish Prison Service (1988) *Custody and Care: Policy and Plans for the Scottish Prison Service*, Edinburgh, March.
2. Scottish Prison Service (1988) *Assessment and Control: the Management of Violent and Disruptive Prisoners*, Edinburgh, October.
3. Scottish Prison Service (1990) *Opportunity and Responsibility: Developing New Approaches to the Management of the Long-Term Prison System in Scotland*, Edinburgh, May.
4. Home Office (1979) *Report of the Committee of Inquiry into the United Kingdom Prison Services* (the May Report), Cmnd. 7673, London, HMSO.
5. 'Grand Design' was the rather grandiose name given to an essentially administrative measure designed to make better use of the prison estate by utilising spare capacity in young offenders' institutions (YOIs) for the relief of overcrowding in establishments holding adult long-term prisoners (LTPs). A total of 320 places were transferred from the YOI to the adult LTP system when Glenochil and Noranside YOIs became adult prisons and Dumfries and Greenock Prisons became YOIs in 1987.
6. For many years, the majority of convicted prisoners requiring maximum security conditions, and other long-term prisoners who were classified as 'untrainable', were held in Peterhead. However, it was also used as a dumping ground for inadequate and disturbed prisoners. This was an explosive mixture and Peterhead was the scene of some of the most violent prison disturbances. Critics of Peterhead attacked its failure to develop purposive régimes, the fact that it was considered 'the end of the road', the brutality of its staff and its isolation from the main centres of population.
7. Rule 36 of the Prison (Scotland) Rules 1952 states that 'if it is

desirable for the maintenance of good order and discipline, or in the interests of a prisoner, that he should not be employed in association with others', arrangements may be made 'for him to work in a cell and not in association'. However, in practice, Rule 36 is used to remove prisoners from all association. Following the series of violent disturbances which took place in Scottish prisons between 1986 and 1988, large numbers of prisoners in Peterhead were held on Rule 36 for long periods of time.

8. Home Office (1966) *Report of the Inquiry into Prison Escapes and Security* (the Mountbatten Report), Cmnd. 3175, London, HMSO.

9. All prisoners are assigned to one of four security categories, known as Categories A (maximum security) to D (minimum security). The prisoners' security category determines the amount of freedom they are allowed within the prison, as well as the prison to which they will be sent. Thus, for example, only Category D prisoners will be sent to an Open Prison. Irrespective of their security risk, it has been the practice of the SPS to place virtually all long-term prisoners in Category B at the start of their sentences and for them to spend most of their time in prison under Category B conditions. The three open establishments (Penninghame and Noranside Prisons and Castle Huntley YOI) can together accommodate only 344 detainees, i.e. between 6 and 7 per cent of the total population.

10. It should be noted that small units will provide accommodation over and above the specialist régimes for difficult prisoners and prisoners with special problems, e.g. sex offenders, which already exist in Peterhead and other mainstream establishments.

11. See Michael Adler and Brian Longhurst 'Power, Discourse and Justice: Prisons in Scotland Today', paper presented at the Annual Conference of Research Committee on Sociology of Law of the International Sociological Association, University of Bologna, June 1988 and 'Towards a New Sociology of Imprisonment: Prison Discourse Today', paper presented at the British Criminology Conference, Bristol Polytechnic, July 1989. This approach will be developed further in our forthcoming book entitled *Power, Discourse and Justice: Towards a New Sociology of Imprisonment*, London, Routledge.

12. For a fuller discussion of accountability, see Michael Adler and Brian Longhurst 'Accountability in Scottish Prisons', lecture to Howard League for Penal Reform (Scotland) Edinburgh, December 1989.

13. Home Office (1989) *An Improved System of Grievance Procedures for Prisoners' Complaints: Report of a Working Group*, London, HMSO, June.

10

The argument against building more prisons

Thomas Mathiesen
Professor of Sociology of Law, University of Oslo

The prison systems of a number of European countries are currently expanding. So are the various prison systems in the United States. The prison populations are increasing, and new prisons are being built, sometimes at an alarming rate.

During the first part of the 1970s, a decline of the prison population could be seen in several countries, such as England, Sweden, and various states within the US. The tendency, however, turned out not to be permanent. During the second part of the 1970s figures again began to rise. The rise continued in several countries, more or less at an accelerating rate, into the 1980s, with very significant overcrowding and/or increasing waiting lists – and new building programmes.

In England the completion of 14 new prisons is now in the programme, in addition to renovation of existing establishments. The programme is estimated to lead to an additional 10,000 to 11,000 new prison places by 1991, at a cost of £250 million (Home Office Working Paper, 1984). It has been characterised as the 'biggest-ever jail-building programme' in England (*The Standard*, 21 November 1983, p. 5).

For the United States, the situation has been characterised as

---

Source: Bishop, N. (ed.) *Scandinavian Criminal Policy and Criminology*, 1985, pp. 89–98, Scandinavian Research Council for Criminology, Copenhagen

follows by the reputable conservative magazine *Time* (5 December 1983): 'The major reason for bulging prison cells: a criminal-justice system that has become very punitive very fast. The rate of incarceration in this country was 93 per 100,000 population in 1972; it is now 177 per 100,000, the highest since the Government began keeping records in 1925.' These are, actually, minimum figures. A more correct estimate is probably 250 per 100,000 (see *Just the Facts*, American Institute of Criminal Justice). The magazine continued: 'New prisons cannot be built quickly enough to accomodate all of the new inmates . . . The construction bill alone is enormous: about $4.7 billion in prison and jail construction is planned across the country over the coming decade, including $1.2 billion for 16,500 new cells in California and $700 million for 8,000 in New York.'

With variations, a similar situation obtains in several other Western countries. The expansion of the prison systems cannot be interpreted as a mere automatic reflection of the crime rate. To repeat, the prison populations of several countries decreased significantly during the first part of the 1970s, whereupon they increased again. But the overall official crime rate increased throughout the decade. In other words, the prison figures and the official crime rate varied independently. Though the background of the expansion of the prison systems is complex, this historical example (and there are others) shows that criminal policy and the use of imprisonment is dependent on political inclination and choice on the part of political and legal authorities.

The fact that choice is being executed, the fact that the expansion of the prison systems is a political matter, makes the following question pertinent: is the expansion reasonable and necessary?

There is currently an international movement favouring abolition of prisons, or at least of a large majority of prisons. The abolitionist movement has its roots in the 1960s and 1970s, in the Scandinavian countries, England and other places. It has recently developed in Canada and the United States. Interestingly, among others the Quakers have been involved, arguing that since they once brought the inmates into the prisons, they must now see to it that they are brought out again. The First World Congress for the Abolition of Prisons was organised by the Quakers in Toronto in 1983, with international participation. The Second World Congress was held in Amsterdam in 1985, organised by the Institute of Criminology there.

My own conviction is that prisons should be abolished. Our society should be structured in such a way that prisons are unnecessary, perhaps excepting extreme cases. I also believe such a restructuring is sociologically possible, and I have tried elsewhere to describe some of its conditions and ramifications (see my *The Politics of Abolition*, Martin Robertson 1974, and *Law, Society and Political Action*, Academic Press 1980). Yet I am realistic enough to realize that the implementation of an abolitionist policy is not exactly imminent. A more modest and realistic goal to-day, and in the short-range and perhaps middle-range future, is *to curb and turn the rapid expansion of the prison system*, which is now in the process of making the prison a central core of the State's policy of social control.

What, then, are the main arguments against building more prisons? I see eight main arguments, which to my mind together constitute a forceful basis for advocating a policy of a permanent international ban on prison building.

In the first place, there is the argument of individual prevention. Over the past couple of decades, criminology and sociology have produced a large number of solid empirical studies showing, quite clearly, that the use of imprisonment does not improve the incarcerated law-breaker. For a long time, this fact has been used, irrationally, as a reason for building more prisons, and for using prisons more. The argument has been that since the amount of imprisonment has not helped, we need more of the same. Within the context of the right political climate, ineffective systems may thrive and expand for a long time on such an irrational reasoning. But, as I say, the reasoning *is* irrational. The large number of studies are a strong argument against prisons in general, and certainly against building more of them.

The fact that prisons are ineffective in terms of individual prevention is beginning to be realised even by state authorities. Thus, a Swedish government bill has the following to say about individual prevention (Government Bill 1982/1983: 85, p. 29, translated from the Swedish by the present author):

> What criminological research has presently taught us is, however, that the idea of improving the individual through deprivation of liberty in the form of imprisonment, is an illusion. On the contrary, it is presently generally accepted that such punishment leads to poor rehabilitation and high recidivism, in addition to the fact that it has a destructive effect on the personality.

The destructive effect pointed out here should especially be kept in mind.

In the second place, there is the argument of general prevention or deterrence in the larger society. We are here talking of the deterrent effect of prison. The question of the deterrent effect of prison is less easily amenable to empirical research, but it may be stated with considerable certainty that the effect is at least uncertain and definitely less significant in determining the development of crime in society than are features of social and economic policy. This is now also becoming recognised on the government level in various countries. As the above-mentioned Swedish government bill formulates it (p. 30, translated from the Swedish by the present author):

> The effects of imprisonment in this respect are, however, to a large extent uncertain.
>
> All available research as well as international comparisons thus show that the development of crime is not related in any definite way to the number of people imprisoned or the length of imprisonment which is maintained. In line with what the National Prison and Probation Administration has expressed in its statement, it is actually no exaggeration to say that the importance of criminal policy for the development of crime is in this respect rather subordinate when seen in relation to family and school policy, labour market and social policy, the organization and functioning in general of the judicial system, and of course the economic structure and view of man in society.

Above I have talked about the deterrent effect of prison in general terms. To this should be added that there is a difference between large-scale change of control systems, and minor changes. Large-scale alterations in the scale of punishment and official social control probably make a difference in terms of deterrence, while the finer nuances in punishment level probably make far less difference. The issue here is not large-scale change, not abolition, only a ban on a further development of the system. Such a ban may be instituted through a policy of minor changes in release practices and sentencing policy which makes the question of the deterrent effect of prison even less pressing (for a discussion of the distinction, in terms of likely effect, between major changes in control policy and minor nuances, see Nils Christie, 'Forskning om individualprevensjon og almenprevensjon', *Lov og Rett*, Oslo, 1971). This leads straight on to the third argument favouring a ban on the building of new prisons.

In the third place, there is the argument of the feasibility of a ban on prison building. The queues which are presently increasing, and the overcrowding which constitutes a problem in several prison systems in the Western world, have been used as arguments for new prisons. The queues and the overcrowding may be solved by going in a different direction, for instance by changing release practices, thus lowering the limit for release on parole, and/or by changing sentencing rules. Though Scandinavia has not escaped expansions, examples of alternative directions may be found there. In 1983 Sweden instituted new rules concerning release on parole, requiring mandatory release, for a large majority of inmates, after half-time. Only a few special categories of inmates are excluded from mandatory half-time release. The new release rules reduced the prison population by 13 per cent to 17 per cent between 1983 and 1984. The Swedish Council of Crime Prevention is presently undertaking a study of statistical long-term effects of the overall increased turnover in the prisons. Preliminary results suggest certain long-term increases in criminal activities, but the figures are very small compared to the total number of crimes reported to the police per year. In other words, the changed release rules will contribute only in a marginal way to the crime rate in Swedish society. In 1982 Denmark instituted reduced maximum punishments for a number of property crimes in addition to reducing the minimum time for release on parole and liberalising the rules concerning drunken driving. The reduced maximum sentences for property crimes was intended to reduce the general sentencing level by one-third. Pardoning has also been used extensively. It should be noted that the results of the Danish changes are less clear than those of the Swedish, because so much is left to the discretion of the courts. In a time of general prison expansion, new rules intending to reduce prison populations should be mandatory, not leaving discretionary power to decision-making bodies which may be subject to political pressure.

In the fourth place, there is the argument of the irreversible character of prison building. Once a prison is erected, it will not be torn down again quickly – rather, it will stand – and be used – for a long period of time. Let me briefly compare with a case concerning environmental protection in my own country, Norway. Some years ago, Norwegian authorities decided to build a 110 metre high dam in a large canyon in northern Norway. The dam was intended for the production of electricity. The changes it would create in the environment would be devastating to the local fishing and reindeer economies (as well as to the beauty of the surroundings) in the sub-arctic climate of the far north of Norway. Those of us who protested against the building of the dam argued that it would be irreversible: once built, the dam could and would never be 'undone' again. I am sorry to say that they are now building the dam. Similarly with prison building. Unless very special circumstances prevail, once built a prison will not be 'undone' for a long period of time. The architects behind the prisons built in Europe during the first part of the 1800s hardly imagined that their prisons would be in use during the mid- and late 1900s. But many of them are. The irreversible character of prison building, the fact that prison building in this sense should be seen as a part of a long-range historical process rather than as a short-term pragmatic measure, is in itself a major reason for not embarking on any construction programme to-day.

In the fifth place, and as a follow-up of the fourth argument, there is the argument of what I would call the expansionist character of the prison system. The prison system as a social institution is never satisfied – it is like an animal whose appetite increases with eating. More concretely: new prisons, even new prisons expressly intended as substitutes for, rather than as additions to, old prisons, in practice and fact tend to become additions. Though there are exceptions, the additive or expansionist character of the system is highly significant. It implies a momentum or political mechanism fostering enlargement rather than change once construction is started. Various social and political features outside and inside the system create this momentum – especially in periods of pressure on the prison system, like to-day. Thus, as *Time Magazine* put it in the above quote: 'New prisons cannot be built quickly enough to accomodate all of the new inmates . . . .'

In the sixth place, there is the humanitarian argument. To-day we know, beyond doubt, that prisons function as inhumane institutions, as inhumane social arrangements. A vast amount of information testifies to this. Reports from inmates, journalists, reporters, and social scientists testify to the degrading, humiliating, alienation-producing character of prison. The pains of imprisonment include the deprivation of liberty, the deprivation of goods and services of various kinds, the deprivation of heterosexual relations in most cases, the deprivation of autonomy, the deprivation of security. While there are variations in these respects between prisons, for example between open and closed prisons, it should be clearly recognised that to a large extent the pains of imprisonment are structurally produced, they are part and parcel of the structure of prisons. Therefore, though concrete material circumstances and prison organisation may alleviate the pains, they cannot be abolished. Among the deprivations most difficult to alleviate are the deprivation of autonomy and the deprivation of security. Inmates are subject to a régime implying a fundamental lack of clear-cut rights, and a vast amount of discretion on the part of prison officials which is intensely productive of a subjective feeling of lack of autonomy and security. Note in this context, again, that due to the expansionist character of the prison system, which is especially forceful in times of pressure on the system, old and deranged institutions are rarely abandoned in view of the coming of new prisons. Therefore, the humanitarian argument is not only an argument in general terms against building more prisons. Specifically, it is also an argument in the sense that building will, especially in times of pressure on the system, not imply the dismantling of the deranged and most obviously inhumane institutions.

In view of this, the rehabilitation of old institutions seems to be a more sensible policy from a humanitarian point of view than building. In addition, we should not take for granted that new sterile institutions function in a more humane way than old – rehabilitated – prisons.

In the seventh place, there is the argument of cultural values. The prison system is a system with cultural effects. Not only does it constitute a set of material institutions, and not only is it a complex social organisation. It is also a system which is symbolic of a way of thinking about people. As a way of thinking it emphasises violence and degradation as a method of solving inter-human conflicts. And when the system is expanded through new prisons, that symbolic effect is also enhanced. The building of new prisons implies, in the wider society, that the prison solution is a good solution – for who would build new prisons without believing in them? In actual fact, we know that politicians today advocate prison building without really believing much in them. This is another indication of the irrationality of today's penal policy. But to the general public, building necessarily signalises a positive value in building. This way, prison building solidifies the prison solution in our society. In the context of the first six reasons for not building new prisons, this is a major and – to my mind – forceful argument against prison construction.

In the eighth and final place, there is the obvious argument of economy. In my view, economy is not a relevant consideration alone. I would be willing to institute even very costly measures if they were humane and represented acceptable values. But in the context of the other arguments, the enormous costs of prison building become a very strong argument. There are, indeed, better ways of spending the money.

In short, the arguments of individual prevention, general deterrence, the feasibility of a ban, the irreversibility of building, the expansionist character of the prison system, humanitarianism, cultural values, and economy, all point away from building more prisons. The arguments function in conjunction. While one or some of them alone might not be sufficient as arguments, their sum strongly supports a lasting moratorium.

Let me, by way of conclusion, again emphasise the *political* nature of the issue of prison building.

Building is often seen as a technical question of architecture, construction, and short-term trends in inmate population. But the question is essentially political.

Politics is a question of deciding priorities of values. Therefore, the issue of prison building is a question of deciding priorities of values. Is this the way we want to treat fellow human beings? Is this how we want to meet the crime problem? These are some of the questions of value involved.

The arguments favour a policy of shrinking the prison system, by shortening sentences and increasing turnover in the system. Such a policy should be commenced immediately. The longer the expansive policy is pursued, the more difficult it will be to turn the tide. Several large countries are presently seeing an expansion of their prison systems exceeded only by the expansion at the beginning of the 1800s – which saw the beginning of prisons. Their example is currently spreading to other countries. Penologically, our times are therefore historical. It is high time to do something with that history.

PART 3

The imprisoned citizen in Europe

Introduction

The articles in this part of the book all concern the legal status and rights of people in prison, and the correlative duties which are owed to them by prison administrations. In particular we will be concerned with the ways in which these matters have developed (or not) under the influence of European agencies and institutions.

We thus begin by reprinting most of the *European Prison Rules* published in 1987 by the Council of Europe. This is followed by Kenneth Neale's commentary on the historical development and present scope of the Rules. Neale was instrumental in the drafting of the present Rules during his tenure as Chair of the Council of Europe's Committee for Co-operation in Prison Affairs. He is acknowledged as the leading (though naturally not entirely disinterested) expert on them. Neale accepts that there are some fairly severe limits on the efficacy of international rules both because of the compromises involved in reaching agreement between member states and because the Rules themselves are not enforceable or justiciable except where they are first incorporated into domestic law. This has provided the basis for considerable criticism and disappointment, and it should be noted that many commentators take a less optimistic view of the value of the Rules than Neale does. This is especially true in respect of recent debates over the necessity of legally enforceable minimum standards for penal establishments.

England and Wales are among the jurisdictions which have hitherto resisted the pressure for stated minimum standards, notwithstanding the convergence of opinion of penal reform groups, prison governors and the Prison Officers' Association on the issue. None the less, Neale argues that the Rules have at least provided a useful basis for informed criticism in prison reform debates. He also contends that the first six rules, the 'rules of basic principle', are in any case the most important. It would appear that the reform agenda emerging from Lord Justice Woolf's Enquiry into Prison Disturbances (initiated in the wake of the upheavals at Strangeways and elsewhere which rocked the English prison system in 1990) has been attentive to similar principles and seems likely to move the English Prison Service more into conformity with the spirit, if not the letter, of the Rules.

The access of prisoners to the courts and to legal redress was also among the concerns raised during the Woolf Enquiry. In his article Conor Gearty shows that, in the English case, such access has historically been very limited. Gearty shows that there have been some significant developments through prisoners' litigation in recent years, but these have not been such as to justify the flattering self-assessments of many lawyers that they and the courts (including the European Court of Human Rights) have been particularly successful in improving the quality of prisoners' daily lives. Matters of particular contention have included: the conduct of prison disciplinary proceedings; racial discrimination; the transfer of prisoners; and the questionable status of the powers of prison governors under Circular Instructions and the controversial Rule 43. Gearty takes a rather sober and pessimistic view of the development of prisoners' legal and practical position and advocates a much more activist form of legal intervention in prison life.

Of all the difficult legal issues surrounding penal practices, those affecting unconvicted prisoners are perhaps the most contentious. Although it is widely accepted that a person detained prior to conviction should forfeit no civil liberties except the freedoms of movement and association, in practice high rates of remanding in many European jurisdictions have often meant that the conditions of confinement for unconvicted prisoners have been materially worse than those for prisoners under sentence. By examining the position of unconvicted prisoners in a number of European countries Richard Vogler argues that the length and conditions of remand are closely linked to the nature of the pre-trial process. It is not only the material conditions of imprisonment but also the availability of information about the case, legal support and participation in the investigation itself which determine the extent to which incarceration of the unconvicted may be seen as legitimate.

Taken together these reflections begin the difficult task of outlining the tense relationship between the legal and social positions of prisoners and the ordinary obligations and entitlements of citizenship. This refers in the first instance to possibilities for extending the legal accountability of prison administrations (in the delivery of regimes and services on the one hand, and the protection of basic rights on the other). More broadly, it broaches the issue of the limits of incarceration and its degree of difference from other spheres of life. Many people go to prison at some time, but few (even among those who are imprisoned more than once) go there for more than a fraction of their lives. The desired outcome, to which most prison administrations are formally committed, of the return of the imprisoned to the status of 'citizens in good standing' demands attention to the continuity between the experience of imprisonment and the expectations which inhere in the concept of citizenship.

11

The European Prison Rules

Council of Europe, 1987

Preamble

The purposes of these rules are:

a. to establish a range of minimum standards for all those aspects of prison administration that are essential to humane conditions and positive treatment in modern and progressive systems;

b. to serve as a stimulus to prison administrations to develop policies and management style and practice based on good contemporary principles of purpose and equity;

c. to encourage in prison staffs professional attitudes that reflect the important social and moral qualities of their work and to create conditions in which they can optimise their own performance to the benefit of society in general, the prisoners in their care and their own vocational satisfaction;

d. to provide realistic basic criteria against which prison administrations and those responsible for inspecting the conditions and management of prisons can make valid judgments of performance and measure progress towards higher standards.

It is emphasised that the rules do not constitute a model system and that, in practice, many European prison services are already operating well above many of the standards set out in the rules and that others are striving, and will continue to strive, to do so. Wherever there are difficulties or practical problems to be overcome in the application of the rules, the Council of Europe has the machinery and the expertise available to assist with advice and the fruits of the experience of the various prison administrations within its sphere.

In these rules, renewed emphasis has been placed on the precepts of human dignity, the commitment of prison administrations to humane and positive treatment, the importance of staff roles and effective modern management approaches. They are set out to provide ready reference, encouragement and guidance to those who are working at all levels of prison administration. The explanatory memorandum that accompanies the rules is intended to ensure the understanding, acceptance and flexibility that are necessary to achieve the highest realistic level of implementation beyond the basic standards.

Part I

The basic principles

1. The deprivation of liberty shall be effected in material and moral conditions which ensure respect for human dignity and are in conformity with these rules.
2. The rules shall be applied impartially. There shall be no discrimination on grounds of race, colour, sex, language, religion, political or other opinion, national or social origin, birth, economic or other status. The religious beliefs and moral precepts of the group to which a prisoner belongs shall be respected.
3. The purposes of the treatment of persons in custody shall be such as to sustain their health and self-respect and, so far as the length of sentence permits, to develop their sense of responsibility and encourage those attitudes and skills that will assist them to return to society with the best chance of leading law-abiding and self-supporting lives after their release.
4. There shall be regular inspections of penal institutions and services by qualified and experienced inspectors appointed by a competent authority. Their task shall be, in particular, to monitor whether and to what extent these institutions are administered in accordance with existing laws and regulations, the objectives of the prison services and the requirements of these rules.
5. The protection of the individual rights of prisoners with special regard to the legality of the execution of detention measures shall be secured by means of a control carried out, according to national rules, by a judicial authority or other duly constituted body authorised to visit the prisoners and not belonging to the prison administration.

6. 1. These rules shall be made readily available to staff in the national languages;

2. They shall also be available to prisoners in the same languages and in other languages so far as is reasonable and practicable.
[. . .]

The allocation and classification of prisoners

11. 1. In allocating prisoners to different institutions or regimes, due account shall be taken of their judicial and legal situation (untried or convicted prisoner, first offender or habitual offender, short sentence or long sentence), of the special requirements of their treatment, of their medical needs, their sex and age.

2. Males and females shall in principle be detained separately, although they may participate together in organised activities as part of an established treatment programme.

3. In principle, untried prisoners shall be detained separately from convicted prisoners unless they consent to being accommodated or involved together in organised activities beneficial to them.

4. Young prisoners shall be detained under conditions which as far as possible protect them from harmful influences and which take account of the needs peculiar to their age.

12. The purposes of classification or re-classification of prisoners shall be:

a. to separate from others those prisoners who, by reasons of their criminal records or their personality, are likely to benefit from that or who may exercise a bad influence; and

b. to assist in allocating prisoners to facilitate their treatment and social resettlement taking into account the management and security requirements.

13. So far as possible separate institutions or separate sections of an institution shall be used to facilitate the management of different treatment regimes or the allocation of specific categories of prisoners.

Accommodation

14. 1. Prisoners shall normally be lodged during the night in individual cells except in cases where it is considered that there are advantages in sharing accommodation with other prisoners.

2. Where accommodation is shared it shall be occupied by prisoners suitable to associate with others in those conditions. There shall be supervision by night, in keeping with the nature of the institution.

15. The accommodation provided for prisoners, and in particular all

sleeping accommodation, shall meet the requirements of health and hygiene, due regard being paid to climatic conditions and especially the cubic content of air, a reasonable amount of space, lighting, heating and ventilation.

16. In all places where prisoners are required to live or work:

   a. the windows shall be large enough to enable the prisoners, *inter alia*, to read or work by natural light in normal conditions. They shall be so constructed that they can allow the entrance of fresh air except where there is an adequate air conditioning system. Moreover, the windows shall, with due regard to security requirements, present in their size, location and construction as normal an appearance as possible;

   b. artificial light shall satisfy recognised technical standards.

17. The sanitary installations and arrangement for access shall be adequate to enable every prisoner to comply with the needs of nature when necessary and in clean and decent conditions.

18. Adequate bathing and showering installations shall be provided so that every prisoner may be enabled and required to have a bath or shower, at a temperature suitable to the climate, as frequently as necessary for general hygiene according to season and geographical region, but at least once a week. Wherever possible there should be free access at all reasonable times.

19. All parts of an institution shall be properly maintained and kept clean at all times.

[. . .]

Medical services

26. 1. At every institution there shall be available the services of at least one qualified general practitioner. The medical services should be organised in close relation with the general health administration of the community or nation. They shall include a psychiatric service for the diagnosis and, in proper cases, the treatment of states of mental abnormality.

   2. Sick prisoners who require specialist treatment shall be transferred to specialised institutions or to civil hospitals. Where hospital facilities are provided in an institution, their equipment, furnishings and pharmaceutical supplies shall be suitable for the medical care and treatment of sick prisoners, and there shall be a staff of suitably trained officers.

   3. The services of a qualified dental officer shall be available to every prisoner.

27. Prisoners may not be submitted to any experiments which may result in physical or moral injury.

28. 1. Arrangements shall be made wherever practicable for children to be born in a hospital outside the institution. However, unless special arrangements are made, there shall in penal institutions be the necessary staff and accommodation for the confinement and post-natal care of pregnant women. If a child is born in prison, this fact shall not be mentioned in the birth certificate.

2. Where infants are allowed to remain in the institution with their mothers, special provision shall be made for a nursery staffed by qualified persons, where the infants shall be placed when they are not in the care of their mothers.

29. The medical officer shall see and examine every prisoner as soon as possible after admission and thereafter as necessary, with a view particularly to the discovery of physical or mental illness and the taking of all measures necessary for medical treatment; the segregation of prisoners suspected of infectious or contagious conditions; the noting of physical or mental defects which might impede resettlement after release; and the determination of the fitness of every prisoner to work.

30. 1. The medical officer shall have the care of the physical and mental health of the prisoners and shall see, under the conditions and with a frequency consistent with hospital standards, all sick prisoners, all who report illness or injury and any prisoner to whom attention is specially directed.

2. The medical officer shall report to the director whenever it is considered that a prisoner's physical or mental health has been or will be adversely affected by continued imprisonment or by any condition of imprisonment.

31. 1. The medical officer or a competent authority shall regularly inspect and advise the director upon:

   a. the quantity, quality, preparation and serving of food and water;
   b. the hygiene and cleanliness of the institution and prisoners;
   c. the sanitation, heating, lighting and ventilation of the institution;
   d. the suitability and cleanliness of the prisoners' clothing and bedding.

2. The director shall consider the reports and advice that the medical officer submits according to Rules 30, paragraph 2, and 31, paragraph 1, and, when in concurrence with the recommendations made, shall take immediate steps to give effect to those recommendations; if they are not within the director's competence or if the director does not concur with them, the director shall

immediately submit a personal report and the advice of the medical officer to higher authority.

32. The medical services of the institution shall seek to detect and shall treat any physical or mental illnesses or defects which may impede a prisoner's resettlement after release. All necessary medical, surgical and psychiatric services including those available in the community shall be provided to the prisoner to that end.

Discipline and punishment

33. Discipline and order shall be maintained in the interests of safe custody, ordered community life and the treatment objectives of the institution.

34. 1. No prisoner shall be employed, in the service of the institution, in any disciplinary capacity.

2. This rule shall not, however, impede the proper functioning of arrangements under which specified social, educational or sports activities or responsibilities are entrusted under supervision to prisoners who are formed into groups for the purposes of their participation in regime programmes.

35. The following shall be provided for and determined by the law or by the regulation of the competent authority:

    a. conduct constituting a disciplinary offence;

    b. the types and duration of punishment which may be imposed;

    c. the authority competent to impose such punishment;

    d. access to, and the authority of, the appellate process.

36. 1. No prisoner shall be punished except in accordance with the terms of such law or regulation, and never twice for the same act.

2. Reports of misconduct shall be presented promptly to the competent authority who shall decide on them without undue delay.

3. No prisoner shall be punished unless informed of the alleged offence and given a proper opportunity of presenting a defence.

4. Where necessary and practicable prisoners shall be allowed to make their defence through an interpreter.

37. Collective punishments, corporal punishment, punishment by placing in a dark cell, and all cruel, inhuman or degrading punishment shall be completely prohibited as punishments for disciplinary offences.

38. 1. Punishment by disciplinary confinement and any other punishment which might have an adverse effect on the physical or mental health of the prisoner shall only be imposed if the medical officer, after examination, certifies in writing that the prisoner is fit to sustain it.

2. In no case may such punishment be contrary to, or depart from, the principles stated in Rule 37.

3. The medical officer shall visit daily prisoners undergoing such punishment and shall advise the director if the termination or alteration of the punishment is considered necessary on grounds of physical or mental health.

Instruments of restraint

39. The use of chains and irons shall be prohibited. Handcuffs, restraint jackets and other body restraints shall never be applied as a punishment. They shall not be used except in the following circumstances:

a. if necessary, as a precaution against escape during a transfer, provided that they shall be removed when the prisoner appears before a judicial or administrative authority unless that authority decides otherwise;

b. on medical grounds by direction and under the supervision of the medical officer;

c. by order of the director, if other methods of control fail, in order to protect a prisoner from self-injury, injury to others or to prevent serious damage to property; in such instances the director shall at once consult the medical officer and report to the higher administrative authority.

40. The patterns and manner of use of the instruments of restraint authorised in the preceding paragraph shall be decided by law or regulation. Such instruments must not be applied for any longer time than is strictly necessary.

Information to, and complaints by, prisoners

41. 1. Every prisoner shall on admission be provided with written information about the regulations governing the treatment of prisoners of the relevant category, the disciplinary requirements of the institution, the authorised methods of seeking information and making complaints, and all such other matters as are necessary to understand the rights and obligations of prisoners and to adapt to the life of the institution.

2. If a prisoner cannot understand the written information provided, this information shall be explained orally.

42. 1. Every prisoner shall have the opportunity every day of making requests or complaints to the director of the institution or the officer authorised to act in that capacity.

2. A prisoner shall have the opportunity to talk to, or to make requests or complaints to, an inspector of prisons or to any other duly constituted authority entitled to visit the prison without the director or other members of the staff being present. However, appeals

against formal decisions may be restricted to the authorised procedures.

3. Every prisoner shall be allowed to make a request or complaint, under confidential cover, to the central prison administration, the judicial authority or other proper authorities.

4. Every request or complaint addressed or referred to a prison authority shall be promptly dealt with and replied to by this authority without undue delay.

Contact with the outside world

43. 1. Prisoners shall be allowed to communicate with their families and, subject to the needs of treatment, security and good order, persons or representatives of outside organisations and to receive visits from these persons as often as possible.

2. To encourage contact with the outside world there shall be a system of prison leave consistent with the treatment objectives in Part IV of these rules.

44. 1. Prisoners who are foreign nationals should be informed, without delay, of their right to request contact and be allowed reasonable facilities to communicate with the diplomatic or consular representative of the state to which they belong. The prison administrator should co-operate fully with such representatives in the interests of foreign nationals in prison who may have special needs.

2. Prisoners who are nationals of states without diplomatic or consular representation in the country and refugees or stateless persons shall be allowed similar facilities to communicate with the diplomatic representative of the state which takes charge of their interests or national or international authority whose task it is to serve the interests of such persons.

45. Prisoners shall be allowed to keep themselves informed regularly of the news by reading newspapers, periodicals and other publications, by radio or television transmissions, by lectures or by any similar means as authorised or controlled by the administration. Special arrangements should be made to meet the needs of foreign nationals with linguistic difficulties.

[. . .]

Part III

Personnel

51. In view of the fundamental importance of the prison staffs to the proper management of the institutions and the pursuit of their

organisational and treatment objectives, prison administrations shall give high priority to the fulfilment of the rules concerning personnel.

52. Prison staff shall be continually encouraged through training, consultative procedures and a positive management style to aspire to humane standards, higher efficiency and a committed approach to their duties.

53. The prison administration shall regard it as an important task continually to inform public opinion of the roles of the prison system and the work of the staff, so as to encourage public understanding of the importance of their contribution to society.

54. 1. The prison administration shall provide for the careful selection on recruitment or in subsequent appointments of all personnel. Special emphasis shall be given to their integrity, humanity, professional capacity and personal suitability for the work.

2. Personnel shall normally be appointed on a permanent basis as professional prison staff and have civil service status with security of tenure subject only to good conduct, efficiency, good physical and mental health and an adequate standard of education. Salaries shall be adequate to attract and retain suitable men and women; employment benefits and conditions of service shall be favourable in view of the exacting nature of the work.

3. Whenever it is necessary to employ part-time staff, these criteria should apply to them as far as that is appropriate.

55. 1. On recruitment or after an appropriate period of practical experience, the personnel shall be given a course of training in their general and specific duties and be required to pass theoretical and practical tests unless their professional qualifications make that unnecessary.

2. During their career, all personnel shall maintain and improve their knowledge and professional capacity by attending courses of in-service training to be organised by the administration at suitable intervals.

3. Arrangements should be made for wider experience and training for personnel whose professional capacity would be improved by this.

4. The training of all personnel should include instruction in the requirements and application of the European Prison Rules and the European Convention on Human Rights.

56. All members of the personnel shall be expected at all times so to conduct themselves and perform their duties as to influence the prisoners for good by their example and to command their respect.

[. . .]

Part IV

Treatment objectives and regimes

64. Imprisonment is by the deprivation of liberty a punishment in itself. The conditions of imprisonment and the prison regimes shall not, therefore, except as incidental to justifiable segregation or the maintenance of discipline, aggravate the suffering inherent in this.
65. Every effort shall be made to ensure that the regimes of the institutions are designed and managed so as:

    a. to ensure that the conditions of life are compatible with human dignity and acceptable standards in the community;

    b. to minimise the detrimental effects of imprisonment and the differences between prison life and life at liberty which tend to diminish the self-respect or sense of personal responsibility of prisoners;

    c. to sustain and strengthen those links with relatives and the outside community that will promote the best interests of prisoners and their families;

    d. to provide opportunities for prisoners to develop skills and aptitudes that will improve their prospects of successful resettlement after release.

66. To these ends all the remedial, educational, moral, spiritual and other resources that are appropriate should be made available and utilised in accordance with the individual treatment needs of prisoners. Thus the regimes should include:

    a. spiritual support and guidance and opportunities for relevant work, vocational guidance and training, education, physical education, the development of social skills, counselling, group and recreational activities;

    b. arrangements to ensure that these activities are organised, so far as possible, to increase contacts with and opportunities within the outside community so as to enhance the prospects for social resettlement after release;

    c. procedures for establishing and reviewing individual treatment and training programmes for prisoners after full consultations among the relevant staff and with individual prisoners who should be involved in these as far as is practicable;

    d. communications systems and a management style that will encourage appropriate and positive relationships between staff and prisoners that will improve the prospects for effective and supportive regimes and treatment programmes.

67. 1. Since the fulfilment of these objectives requires

individualisation of treatment and, for this purpose, a flexible system of allocation, prisoners should be placed in separate institutions or units where each can receive the appropriate treatment and training.

2. The type, size, organisation and capacity of these institutions or units should be determined essentially by the nature of the treatment to be provided.

3. It is necessary to ensure that prisoners are located with due regard to security and control but such measures should be the minimum compatible with safety and comprehend the special needs of the prisoner. Every effort should be made to place prisoners in institutions that are open in character or provide ample opportunities for contacts with the outside community. In the case of foreign nationals, links with people of their own nationality in the outside community are to be regarded as especially important.

68. As soon as possible after admission and after a study of the personality of each prisoner with a sentence of a suitable length, a programme of treatment in a suitable institution shall be prepared in the light of the knowledge obtained about individual needs, capacities and dispositions, especially proximity to relatives.

69. 1. Within the regimes, prisoners shall be given the opportunity to participate in activities of the institution likely to develop their sense of responsibility, self-reliance and to stimulate interest in their own treatment.

2. Efforts should be made to develop methods of encouraging co-operation with and the participation of the prisoners in their treatment. To this end prisoners shall be encouraged to assume, within the limits specified in Rule 34, responsibilities in certain sectors of the institution's activity.

70. 1. The preparation of prisoners for release should begin as soon as possible after reception in a penal institution. Thus, the treatment of prisoners should emphasise not their exclusion from the community but their continuing part in it. Community agencies and social workers should, therefore, be enlisted wherever possible to assist the staff of the institution in the task of social rehabilitation of the prisoners particularly maintaining and improving the relationships with their families, with other persons and with the social agencies. Steps should be taken to safeguard, to the maximum extent compatible with the law and the sentence, the rights relating to civil interests, social security rights and other social benefits of prisoners.

2. Treatment programmes should include provision for prison leave which should also be granted to the greatest extent possible on medical, educational, occupational, family and other social grounds.

3. Foreign nationals should not be excluded from arrangements

for prison leave solely on account of their nationality. Furthermore, every effort should be made to enable them to participate in regime activities together so as to alleviate their feelings of isolation.
[. . .]

Pre-release preparation

87. All prisoners should have the benefit of arrangements designed to assist them in returning to society, family life and employment after release. Procedures and special courses should be devised to this end.
88. In the case of those prisoners with longer sentences, steps should be taken to ensure a gradual return to life in society. This aim may be achieved, in particular, by a pre-release regime organised in the same institution or in another appropriate institution, or by conditional release under some kind of supervision combined with effective social support.
89. 1. Prison administrations should work closely with the social services and agencies that assist released prisoners to re-establish themselves in society, in particular with regard to family life and employment.

2. Steps must be taken to ensure that on release prisoners are provided, as necessary, with appropriate documents and identification papers, and assisted in finding suitable homes and work to go to. They should also be provided with immediate means of subsistence, be suitably and adequately clothed having regard to the climate and season, and have sufficient means to reach their destination.

3. The approved representatives of the social agencies or services should be afforded all necessary access to the institution and to prisoners with a view to making a full contribution to the preparation for release and after-care programme of the prisoner.

Part V

Additional rules for special categories

90. Prison administrations should be guided by the provisions of the rules as a whole so far as they can appropriately and in practice be applied for the benefit of those special categories of prisoners for which additional rules are provided hereafter.

Untried prisoners

91. Without prejudice to legal rules for the protection of individual

liberty or prescribing the procedure to be observed in respect of untried prisoners, these prisoners, who are presumed to be innocent until they are found guilty, shall be afforded the benefits that may derive from Rule 90 and treated without restrictions other than those necessary for the penal procedure and the security of the institution.

92. 1. Untried prisoners shall be allowed to inform their families of their detention immediately and given all reasonable facilities for communication with family and friends and persons with whom it is in their legitimate interest to enter into contact.

2. They shall also be allowed to receive visits from them under humane conditions subject only to such restrictions and supervision as are necessary in the interests of the administration of justice and of the security and good order of the institution.

3. If an untried prisoner does not wish to inform any of these persons, the prison administration should not do so on its own initiative unless there are good overriding reasons as, for instance, the age, state of mind or any other incapacity of the prisoner.

93. Untried prisoners shall be entitled, as soon as imprisoned, to choose a legal representative, or shall be allowed to apply for free legal aid where such aid is available and to receive visits from that legal adviser with a view to their defence and to prepare and hand to the legal adviser, and to receive, confidential instructions. On request, they shall be given all necessary facilities for this purpose. In particular, they shall be given the free assistance of an interpreter for all essential contacts with the administration and for their defence. Interviews between prisoners and their legal advisers may be within sight but not within hearing, either direct or indirect, of the police or institution staff. The allocation of untried prisoners shall be in conformity with the provisions of Rule 11, paragraph 3.

94. Except where there are circumstances that make it undesirable, untried prisoners shall be given the opportunity of having separate rooms.

95. 1. Untried prisoners shall be given the opportunity of wearing their own clothing if it is clean and suitable.

2. Prisoners who do not avail themselves of this opportunity, shall be supplied with suitable dress.

3. If they have no suitable clothing of their own, untried prisoners shall be provided with civilian clothing in good condition in which to appear in court or on authorised outings.

96. Untried prisoners shall, whenever possible, be offered the opportunity to work but shall not be required to work. Those who choose to work shall be paid as other prisoners. If educational or trade training is available, untried prisoners shall be encouraged to avail themselves of these opportunities.

97. Untried prisoners shall be allowed to procure at their own expense or at the expense of a third party such books, newspapers, writing materials and other means of occupation as are compatible with the interests of the administration of justice and the security and good order of the institution.

98. Untried prisoners shall be given the opportunity of being visited and treated by their own doctor or dentist if there is reasonable ground for the application. Reasons should be given if the application is refused. Such costs as are incurred shall not be the responsibility of the prison administration.

[. . .]

Insane and mentally abnormal prisoners

100. 1. Persons who are found to be insane should not be detained in prisons and arrangements shall be made to remove them to appropriate establishments for the mentally ill as soon as possible.

2. Specialised institutions or sections under medical management should be available for the observation and treatment of prisoners suffering gravely from other mental disease or abnormality.

3. The medical or psychiatric service of the penal institutions shall provide for the psychiatric treatment of all prisoners who are in need of such treatment.

4. Action should be taken, by arrangement with the appropriate community agencies, to ensure where necessary the continuation of psychiatric treatment after release and the provision of social psychiatric after-care.

12

The European Prison Rules: Contextual, philosophical and practical aspects

Kenneth Neale
Formerly Chair of European Committee for Co-operation in Prison Affairs (1981–4), consultant in penal matters for The Council of Europe.

A great deal of pioneering zeal and faith has been invested in the validity of international prison standards and rules for almost a hundred years. The successive formulations have inspired, and themselves been informed by, a broad philosophical approach to the design and management of prison régimes based on humane standards and a respect for human dignity. However, contemporary problems in penal systems throughout the world, as evidenced, for example, in the disruption at Strangeways (Manchester) in 1990 have posed serious challenges and raised fundamental questions. These confront not only political policy and prison management, but also the faith that has buttressed the prison rules to which most governments across the world are committed morally, politically and, in some cases, legally. There are thus doubts about the efficacy of international prison rules. Yet, increasingly, the European Prison Rules are being cited as a yardstick against which to test prison conditions. That is an essential role for the Rules as the all too prevalent decay to be found in most prison systems is, it seems, one of the major factors underlying the poverty in prison régimes, tension and incipient disruption in prisons. There is pressure also for the adoption of more stringent and specific codes than those in the present international Rules, in order to support

Source: Commissioned for this volume

the drive for physical improvements in the prison estates and to create a framework of reference within which legal processes and sanctions can be brought to bear on the problem. Prison systems are complex and difficult to describe let alone operate, and most are burdened with decades of past neglect and a pervasive indifference in society at large. As Judge Stephen Tumim, the Chief Inspector of Prisons in the United Kingdom, was reported to have said following the Strangeways riot: 'Bluntly, you can't have minimum standards without drains.'[1]

This commentary attempts, within the limits of scale, to explain and discuss the provenance and content of the international Rules, in particular the most modern version, the European Prison Rules; how far they have been influential; whether the faith that has promoted them has been justified; and how their unique status has been misunderstood. It is helpful, in order to put this discussion into a historical and realistic dimension, first to adumbrate the origins, philosophical and contextual development and eventual adoption of the European Prison Rules.

The historical background and evolution of the Rules

There is now a long tradition behind the international exchange of information and experience in penal matters. Within that tradition, an impetus for penal reform and improvement towards the end of the nineteenth century led naturally to the spread of common standards. This process eventually matured in the formulation and adoption of internationally agreed rules designed to ensure minimum standards in prison conditions and treatment.[2] By the turn of the century international gatherings at which penal topics were debated had become a regular feature of international co-operation in this field. One result was the establishment of the International Penal and Penitentiary Commission (IPPC) which, as part of a wider interest in penal matters, drew up the first, somewhat speculative but commendably comprehensive, code of Standard Minimum Rules for the Treatment of Prisoners (SMRTP). This code achieved international status when it was recommended to member governments by the Assembly of the League of Nations at its Fifteenth Ordinary Session in September 1934. This was formalised at the Sixteenth Ordinary Session on 28 September

1935 in a Resolution which requested governments accepting the Rules to promulgate and promote their application in prison systems. It was an important stage in the development of the Rules for, although not seen as a definitive model, the criteria that derive from minimum standards and humanitarian principles were unambiguously enshrined in this and all subsequent approaches. In context the original version was concerned, albeit lacking a conspicuous focus, with the same priorities and principles that have persisted in later codes.

The trauma of the war of 1939–45 led to fundamental social renewal across Europe and an urgent interest at international level in human rights and the treatment of prisoners. Both these emotive topics were charged by the experience of millions of people who had been imprisoned or suffered as a result of the excesses that are the inevitable concomitant of war. The new postwar organisations, the United Nations (1945) and the Council of Europe (1949) put the protection and guarantee of human rights high on their priorities. The Universal Declaration of Human Rights (1948) (UDHR) and the United Nations SMRTP (1955) were followed by broadly similar enactments in 1953 and 1973[3] in the Council of Europe. Below, I shall consider briefly the differences in application of these instruments under the auspices of the world and regional organisations.

As had happened globally, the development and co-operation in penal matters in Europe led to the perceived need for a regional formulation of the Rules. This was envisaged as giving them a European emphasis and reflecting the particular need and circumstances of the prison systems of the member states of the Council of Europe. The European version was adopted by the Committee of Ministers in Strasbourg in the Resolution that came into force on 19 January 1973. This urged the member states to be guided, in legislation and practice, by the principles of the Rules and, importantly, to report to the Secretary General every five years on progress with implementation. It was a valuable step but, in form and substance, only a modest adaption of the United Nations text. There was thus, from its inception, a body of opinion in the Council of Europe that aspired to a new, more creative and distinctively European model. That view was reinforced as developments in penal policy and prison practice exposed those areas of the existing codes that were inadequate, incompatible, even irrelevant, in terms of current and foreseeable trends. The quin-quennial review of 1978 led, therefore, to the appointment of a European Select Committee which was instructed, when reporting on the results of the review, to advise also on a revision of the European Rules and, significantly, on the difficult problems of international oversight and effective application in the member states. Its report[4] and conclusions were approved by the Council of Europe in 1980 and were followed by two important measures.

The first was the establishment in 1981 of the European Committee for Co-operation in Prison Affairs (CCPA), which was given a wide remit in penological matters and, specifically, special responsibility for the application of the SMRTP in Europe. The second was the commissioning, under the authority of the European Committee on Crime Problems (ECCP), of the drafting of new European rules. That initiative was supported by the Parliamentary Assembly of the Council of Europe (R. 914 (1981)) and gained wide support from the member states. After the approval of the new draft rules by the CCPA and the ECCP, they were adopted by the Committee of Ministers in February 1987.[5]

The philosophy of the Rules

The decision of the Council of Europe to promote new rules should be seen against the background of major post-war phenomena of a social and political nature, as well as the impact of the developing thought and practice that had occurred in the penal field. The serious disruption of societies and economies that was the manifest legacy of war was mirrored by the perception of new and threatening changes in social behaviour. In the prisons cherished and comfortable treatment roles of supportive and caring staff were undermined to the point of fragility by pressure, change, technical innovation and the disquieting results of research. The routines of those in custodial roles yielded to increasing and changing demands of management and the expectations of prisoners. At the level of European penology several basic strands of thought can now be seen as moulding the emerging philosophical strategy as the Council of Europe and the prison administrations of the member states grappled with these issues. They may be conveniently summarised as follows:

(a)   that in punishment involving the deprivation of liberty, this should be seen as the sole instrument of punishment;

(b)   that treatment régimes must be aimed principally at the re-education and re-socialisation of the offender;

(c)   that the administration of prisons must show respect for the fundamental rights of individuals, and at all times uphold the values that nourish human dignity.

European penal philosophy had become concerned less with the retributive aspects of punishment than with the social and penal prevention of crime and the social rehabilitation of offenders.

The penological approach to the new Rules sought to comprehend the intellectual, moral and operational challenges that flowed from all this. New themes were required and priorities had to be changed. Above all, those concerned were conscious that the United Nations SMR (and, therefore, the modified European version) were vulnerable to the criticism that they were not only out of date, but lacked a compelling underlying rationale and were thus diminished in application and in the influence they exerted on penal thought and practice. In particular, there were lacunae in the Rules of general application in regard, for example, to the ethic of human dignity, a rather surprising omission in view of the emphasis on this in Article I of the UDHR. The new Rules in Europe were expected to remedy that. There was also little support in the earlier versions for the roles of prison inspection, a vital aspect of the Rules. That meant a significant departure from the parallel text of the United Nations Rules which was a matter of principle with political overtones that had to be faced. Efforts made to initiate a process of change in the United Nations had always foundered as there was insufficient commitment to it; and, procedurally, there was the further difficulty in the United Nations of establishing compliance when only a small and diminishing number of its member states responded to periodic United Nations requests for information. It was decided, therefore, that the Council of Europe would itself undertake a major revision and this was announced and described to the Sixth United Nations Congress on the Prevention of Crime and the Treatment of Offenders in Caracas in 1980.[6] This divergence illustrates the ability of a smaller, more cohesive regional organisation to make progress in sensitive areas of international co-operation and agreement that are more difficult, if not almost impossible, on a global basis. It is difficult to foresee an agreed revision of the United Nations Rules, so future progress will be based on regional versions, a point to which I shall return.

The European Prison Rules (1987)

The process of drawing up a new set of Rules, or a similar document of international status, promoted by the Council of Europe, may be carried out, as has been noted, by means of a Select Committee, or as in this case, the appointment of a consultant to prepare the first drafts for presentation to the appropriate standing committees and eventual approval by the Committee of Ministers. In the work of drafting, account was taken of the experience in the implementation of the existing Rules, the views and proposals of the member states, the results of studies of specific aspects of penal treatment and administration carried out by the Council of Europe and the information and ideas which could be culled from relevant work by academic and professional experts, as well as political and public opinion. In the case of the European Prison Rules of 1987, the main influences of a general character flowed from social and economic change, new developments in treatment theory and techniques, changing patterns of criminality, the introduction into prison management of modern technology and increasingly difficult operational circumstances. The need to define a relevant and progressive framework to accommodate these changes and, in doing so, to offer new approaches, was a primary consideration. It was also apparent that there was scope for considerable textual improvements of a technical and presentational nature. Above all, important moral imperatives were needed, as also were means of strengthening the effectiveness and influence of the Rules in practice.

Changes in the presentational aspects of the Rules were seen as means of elevating the moral criteria on which the Rules are based and establishing essential priorities. It was also thought desirable to achieve a more logical sequence of the main components. Thus the old Rules 1–4 (which were not really cast as rules at all) were transferred to an enhanced Preamble which set out the overall purposes and defined the scope of the Rules. A valuable consequence of this was that it made it possible to devote Part I of the new rules to six Rules of basic principle of which Rule I 'The deprivation of liberty shall be effected in material and moral conditions which ensure respect for human dignity and are in conformity with these rules', is described in the Explanatory Memorandum as establishing the authority and priority of the Rules in all aspects. The memorandum also insists, in reference to the six Rules of basic principle that they are

> the most important, being fundamental to the philosophy and management of any prison system that is based on those principles of humanity, morality, justice and respect for human dignity that are essential to a modern civilized society. In no circumstances should any departure from these rules, or compromise in interpreting them, be accepted. They are intended to endow all the other rules with overriding standards to which all prison administrations that adopt the European Prison Rules will subscribe without reservation.

The Rules of basic principle also strengthen the role of inspection to include the requirements of the Rules as formal criteria in their assessments. Thereafter, the Rules deal successively with the management of prison systems, personnel, treatment objectives and régimes and the Rules which are specific to the situation of prisoners in special categories. In the process more positive expression was given to the text, the wording of every Rule was changed, a few were dropped and some new Rules included, especially where it was considered necessary to strengthen a particular requirement or to introduce Rules concerned with new developments. In order to promote a better understanding of the Rules and to facilitate their application in practice the Explanatory Memorandum, already quoted above, was associated with the Rules. This sets out at greater length the general approach to each part of the Rules, the purport of each individual Rule and, as necessary, offers some further guidance in regard to possible difficulties. The inclusion of the Explanatory Memorandum also made it possible to refine the purposes and detailed implications of the individual Rules more usefully than the astringent quasi-legal language, in which the Rules themselves are inevitably cast, would have allowed. Also included in the Council of Europe publications in which the Rules are promulgated is a paper dealing with their historical background, philosophy and development which is intended to establish the international context and status of the Rules since their inception. The addition of the Explanatory

Memorandum and the background paper (neither of which is printed with the Rules above) has given the Rules a stronger philosophical base and a more credible operational validity. It is also worth noting that the change from the ponderous designation of the Council of Europe Standard Minimum Rules for the Treatment of Prisoners to the shorter, more explicit title of the European Prison Rules has given them a more convenient and dynamic image. The Rules are manifestly European and they can now be seen to extend also to areas of vital importance to the care of prisoners such as personnel, management and the community aspects of treatment, all of which have been given greater emphasis in the new version.

The status of the Rules

Almost all international agreements are vulnerable to the charge that they exhibit less than ideal standards and arrangements or that they are weakened by 'loopholes' that permit compliance at barely minimum levels. The international prison Rules are no exception and, in terms of the current conditions in prisons in the United Kingdom and many other European countries, have been criticised as such. That criticism, although frequently valid in a strict sense, does not comprehend the necessity, in reaching agreement across the international spectrum, for compromise and flexibility. Without these two debilitative but enabling attributes there would be few effective agreements at all. It is appropriate, therefore, to evaluate the European Prison Rules, in concept and practice, in that perspective.

The European Prison Rules are widely accepted, with virtually no reservations.[7] That is because they set standards which provide a threshold that satisfies basic considerations of humanity without imposing unacceptable burdens upon governments which are themselves constrained by resource considerations and political priorities. Inherent also is the flexibility to accommodate the widely differing circumstances to be found in a regional grouping, even one that is as coherent as Europe, that now includes twenty-five member countries and extends to a number of others that adhere to the European code. Experience has endorsed the view that the Rules, although not binding in international law, are influential because they impose political obligations and exercise a moral sanction on national authorities. Where, as in some countries, they are embodied in domestic law and are thus justiciable they are most effective. In those other countries that accept the Rules, these are reflected in penal policy and local regulations. That means that the philosophy and standards that inspire them influence penal thinking and practice and impose definable obligations on the administering authorities. They do not confer rights upon prisoners, who cannot normally cite the Rules in pursuing a formal complaint either in regard to individual treatment or concerning general conditions.

In the international sphere the influence of the Rules can be seen in the drafting of conventions and other agreements that govern activity (labour, transfer, etc.) of relevance to the treatment of prisoners. As regards human rights there is no machinery in the United Nations for the enforcement of the UDHR but the European Convention on Human Rights is effective in this respect and specially sensitive, in the nature of its requirements, to the situation of prisoners from whom numerous applications alleging breaches of the Convention have been received. The European Directorate of Human Rights has acknowledged the influence of the European Rules. Although it is not a definitive legal interpretation, the Directorate has stated that whereas the Court and the Commission have no jurisdiction to examine the conditions of detention except in so far as they involve a breach of a right guaranteed by the Convention, and that there is no specific provision on the treatment of prisoners in it, in the experience of the Commission there is now a corpus of law on this subject. The Rules are acknowledged as constituting 'a virtual code for the treatment of prisoners'. The point is that although prison conditions may fall short of the standards required by the European Prison Rules, this does not necessarily constitute inhuman or degrading treatment such as to violate the Human Rights Convention. The influence of the Rules in this fundamental area is evident.

It is a mistake and a misunderstanding of the international status and the explicit purposes of the Rules to underestimate the moral and practical influence they exert. Their increasing authority in the inspection services, reinforced, as we shall see below, by the Council of Europe's own machinery has made them a valid force for humanising prisons. It is through the influence that stems from agreement and the national and international procedures for compliance that their role has been optimised. An idealistic formulation, honoured only in rhetoric and not in practice, is not an attractive or viable alternative. It is nevertheless true, as the Chief Inspector of Prisons in the United Kingdom (then Sir James Hennessy) noted in his report in 1985, that there are deficiencies in that many prisons satisfy the Rules only to a limited extent. The quinquennial returns to the Council of Europe confirm that it is true also of many of the prisons in the rest of Europe. In some areas the level of compliance is barely above the minimum and there are, inevitably, shortfalls in application in some of the Rules, though such are usually technical or peripheral in detail. Nevertheless, the Rules have, as those assessments show, defined the standards and given authority to the inspecting authorities to challenge the responsible prison administrations. The moral is that the international code needs to be reinforced by local, specified and justiciable standards, an approach that is examined more closely below.

An important additional dimension to the practical influence of the Rules in Europe is the procedural machinery established by the Council of Europe. This is intended to promote the philosophical concepts embodied in them and to encourage the implementation of the Rules in the prison systems of the member states and the other administrations that follow the European version. When the earlier European Rules were adopted in 1973, the biennial meetings of the Directors of Prison Administrations in Europe were given formal responsibility in regard to the Rules. Specifically, they were charged to report on implementation in their own countries and, collectively, to consider how to remedy any difficulties that may have arisen in practice. Additionally, the Council requested its members to report every five years on a formal basis, the returns from which were studied in the Select Committee whose report is referred to earlier in this paper. These regular evaluations enable the Council and the prison administrations to keep themselves informed on progress and of any weaknesses in application. But there was no capacity to develop this process or to exert any further influence until the establishment of the CCPA following the report of the Select Committee of 1980. The formulation of the new Rules of 1987 took full account of this strengthening of the procedural arrangements for monitoring and more effective implementation.

The CCPA, which was formed in 1981, is comprised of five members, elected in their own right, not as representatives of their own countries, for a five-year term of office by the ECCP, to which parent committee the prison committee owes its responsibility. It was conceived as having a broad remit in prison affairs so as to enable it to follow developments in penal treatment and administration generally throughout the member states of the Council of Europe. Within that overall role it was expected to provide a forum for the collection and dissemination of information and data concerning the prison field; the regular *Prison Information Bulletins* of the Council of Europe are a product of that. The CCPA also prepares the agendas for the biennial meetings of the European Prison Directors. Importantly, and of central relevance to this commentary, it is required to give oversight to the application of the European Prison Rules and to identify and deal with specific problems that may arise in a particular country or, more generally, in the case of a Rule which may prove difficult to implement in practice. Through co-operation with the authorities concerned, the Committee is expected to bring its influence to bear so as to ensure conformity with the requirements of the Rules. It was considered that the promotion of the Council of Europe's policies in regard to the Rules would be better served in a forum of specialists of this kind, with a broadly based responsibility for prison affairs, than to attempt to establish specific procedures and an administrative capacity concerned only with the application, or rather non-application, of the Rules themselves. The whole notion of international oversight and compliance arrangements is, of course, of considerable delicacy and it was necessary to find a formula that would be acceptable and, more importantly, effective in practice. It was the first ever international procedure to be established for the active promotion of the Rules and the formal monitoring of non-compliance with arrangements for co-operation to achieve remedies where problems occurred. As such, and in practice, it has proved to be a useful and symbolic measure of progress. It is difficult to imagine that any such process could be agreed at global level and is thus another valuable example of what can be achieved regionally when the motivation and agreed philosophical framework already exists. The arrangements in Europe have certainly enhanced the status of the European Prison Rules and underline the important place that they have in the regulation of prison administration. Without the international

Rules there would be no common standards, only the general ground of moral and political philosophy. Certainly there would be no acceptable framework for enforceable standards to which this commentary now turns.

Enforceable standards

'There is no bigger disgrace to Britain than its prisons.'[8] In that unambiguous assertion *The Times* epitomised the challenge to a penal policy that has for decades been impoverished by philosophical doubt, public apathy and political reticence. Inspired thinking, dedicated staff and administrators, as well as courageous and passionate reformers, have all been frustrated in that web of confusion and tentative purpose. The question that arises in this essay is whether the European Prison Rules, reinforced at national level by the provision of more specific standards enforceable in law, can provide the framework and moral authority for an effective approach to this insistent problem. There is growing pressure for this which comes from a wide range of people and organisations engaged in the prison field. Penal reform groups, encouraged by various developments in this direction abroad, notably at federal, state and local levels in the United States and Australia, have been in the forefront. The organisations representing prison governors and prison officers have lent their experience and authority to the campaign for enforceable standards in the United Kingdom. They have been supported in this in Parliament and by the reports and informed views of the Prison Inspectorate, which has unique access to the prisons, which makes it the most qualified of independent observers to comment. The same proposals have more recently been re-echoed in the Inquiry conducted by Lord Justice Woolf following the Strangeways riot. Even the government at one time, in 1981, seemed to have decided to introduce such a code and some work was done on this. Little progress was made and the code has not so far materialised. Why, it may be asked, is that so; and why is it that the European Prison Rules themselves do not specify standards in quantifiable and enforceable terms?

In her trenchant evaluation of the prison system Vivien Stern,[9] the Director of NACRO, has written 'The European Standard Minimum Rules set out high standards for imprisonment . . . Unfortunately they also allow lower standards to continue.' She is justified in making that comment, but it is necessary and helpful to appreciate that the issues are not quite as simple as that selective quotation might suggest. For reasons of complexity, the diversity of circumstances in subscribing states and in the nature of international agreements, it would be impracticable and, in fact, ineffective to use international Rules themselves as the immediate vehicle for the establishment of a detailed enforceable code. It would be futile to attempt to draw up complicated measurable standards for all those aspects of prison administration that would need to embrace such concepts as accommodation standards, dietary schedules and the varied cultural elements of prison régimes. Such specific standards could not be consistent and sensibly enforceable in the disparate conditions that prevail in, for example, France, Iceland or Turkey, among many other adherents to the European Rules. The new European Prison Rules do, it would be reasonable to argue, embody and seek to construct a humane and progressive philosophy that should satisfy all but the most idealistic or eccentric campaigners. Of parallel importance is the comprehensive practical framework of minimum and essential standards they offer within which can, and should, be constructed detailed national codes that would prescribe specific standards. Under such a code, conditions in prison systems would be measured on a defined and comprehensive basis of assessment and regulation. A serviceable model for such a code which advanced measurable standards for cell dimensions, lighting, heating, ventilation, personal hygiene, food and exercise, was published by NACRO in outline in 1984.[10] The schedules in that code, carefully thought out, were in fact limited in scope and do not, for example, offer standards in relation to staff or régimes, both of which are significant components of the European Prison Rules and need to be buttressed by a broadly similar approach to be fully effective at national level. But the NACRO code would have provided a valuable starting point.

It ought to be reiterated here that in some European countries where the European Prison Rules have been integrated into national legislation and regulating instruments, they are, naturally, enforceable in law. That is not, of course, a quantifiable approach in the sense that a specific code of detailed standards could be, but it is important to the status of the Rules and as a means of ensuring compliance. Any measurable code would have to have a legal or quasi-legal status to be enforceable in some forum or another. The situation in regard to action under the Human Rights Convention has already been mentioned. We are concerned here with the reasons why, except in the examples already quoted where comprehensive codes have been drawn up and enacted abroad, not without difficulty, enforceable standards have not been adopted. They are not always, as critics might suppose, due to lack of purpose or the absence of caring attitudes. Many of the standards that would be the essential ingredients of such a code do, in fact, exist in many systems, including the United Kingdom, in regulations and, more obviously, in management instructions, manuals and operational formulae for treatment, buildings and régimes, especially in regard to new construction or development. What is lacking is a discrete codification and the means of enforcement. These pose genuine problems for resources of all kinds. So far as physical circumstances and financial resources are concerned the difficulty is readily apparent. What is not so obvious, but in reality could be formidable in present circumstances, is the administrative, managerial and legal burdens that could arise in practice, especially in the early stages, in dealing with and resolving the deficiencies that would be exposed by inspection or complaint. Almost certainly, if the political decision were to be taken to formulate and enact a comprehensive enforceable code in the United Kingdom, it would be necessary to stage its application or place temporary constraints on its enforcement in certain areas of the prison system. That should be an acceptable approach and could indeed be an important means of building the credibility, and thus the confidence, needed to make a success of such a code. In the longer term a more positive level of compliance would result. Certainly the European Prison Rules in the modern formulation provide a suitable basis for this approach. This is especially so in view of their insistence on immutable general standards, the scope they offer for specific coding to suit the social, cultural and climatic needs of all the participating states, and comprehensive coverage of wide aspects of prison treatment and administration.

Future developments

The European Prison Rules, with the associated philosophical papers, arguably represent the most important international document in the field of prison affairs. They are not likely to be superseded for many years in Europe or elsewhere. They will remain, therefore, for the foreseeable future as an authoritative and agreed basis for the development of modern prison administration and treatment régimes. Progress, built on that foundation may be seen, broadly speaking, as likely to be made in three areas.

First, there will be the political and geographical extension of the applicability of the European Prison Rules. Already, all the twenty-five member states of the Council of Europe have accepted the Rules, which have been translated into all member states' national languages; the formal version, as approved in Strasbourg, is couched in the two official languages of the Council of Europe, namely English and French. Following the historic political realignments in Central Europe and fundamental reappraisals of penal policies there, Hungary became a member in November 1990, Czechoslovakia in February 1991, Poland and Yugoslavia have applied to join the Council of Europe and the translation of the Rules into their languages is being undertaken. Other European countries, Bulgaria and Romania in particular, are likely to follow. It can also be reasonably expected that the Soviet Union, or some of its constituent republics, will associate closely with or become members of the Council of Europe in due course. A Russian translation of the European Prison Rules has already been prepared in the Soviet Union. It is also probable that the European Prison Rules will be adopted, or at least will inspire new codes, in some of the observer states of the Council of Europe and even further afield in countries seeking a model of contemporary validity. Rules governing the detention of people in circumstances other than imprisonment, based on a similar philosophy, are also to be expected.

Second, it can be expected that bodies with responsibility for examining the conditions of prisons or adjudicating the complaints and petitions of individual prisoners will make increasing use of the Rules as providing practical criteria for their assessments. These authorities include the national prison inspection services, the Commission and Court of Human Rights and such inspectorial teams as those that have been established under the European Convention for the Prevention of Torture which have already carried out an inspection of some of the English and European prisons.

Finally, it now seems inevitable that more countries, including it is to be hoped the United Kingdom, will draw up systematic specifications in the form of a code of standards that will rely on the ultimate authority of the European Prison Rules. These codes will necessarily have some arrangements for enforcement even if, at the early stages of implementation, they are constrained in practice for a transitional period.

With the increasing public anxiety about the state of the prisons and its consequentially higher priority in the political agendas, progress in this field is inevitable. If it is to be effective and valid in its human aspects, in social policy, and if it is to be coherent and measurable, an enforceable code of standards is essential. The European Prison Rules establish the moral climate and provide a pragmatic framework for that.

Notes

1. *The Times*, 22 May 1990.
2. Space forbids that this essay should attempt yet another definition of 'treatment'. The author is content to rely on that accepted by the Council of Europe for the purposes of the European Prison Rules (1987); namely, 'to indicate in the broadest sense all those measures (work, social training, education, vocational training, physical education and preparation for release, etc.), employed to maintain or recover the physical and psychiatric health of prisoners, their social re-integration and the general conditions of their imprisonment'.
3. Resolution of the Committee of Ministers (73)5 of 19 January 1973.
4. Report of Select Committee of Experts PC-R-RM(80)1 of 15 February 1980.
5. Recommendation of the Committee of Ministers R(87)3 of 12 February 1987.
6. United Nations (1981) Report on the Sixth United Nations Congress for the Prevention of Crime and the Treatment of Offenders 1980, New York, United Nations.
7. In the case of the European Prison Rules, for practical reasons Denmark reserved the right not to comply with Rule 38.3, and France Rule 54.2 for technical reasons.
8. *The Times*, 28 July 1990.
9. V. Stern (1989) *Bricks of Shame: Britain's prisons*, Harmondsworth Penguin.
10. S. Casale (1984) *Measurable Standards for Prison Establishments*, London, NACRO.

13

The prisons and the courts

Conor Gearty
Senior Lecturer in Law, Kings College, University of London

The appointment of Lord Justice Woolf to inquire into the Strangeways prison riot of April 1990 is a reminder of the confidence that the executive – and by extension perhaps the general public – place in the senior judiciary in times of crisis. The most well-known reports of the 1980s have been those by Lord Justice Taylor into the Hillsborough disaster[1] and Lord Scarman into the Brixton disorders,[2] but these are no more than two examples of what has for years been accepted by the judges as a difficult but legitimate part of their duties. Indeed, the prison service has already been reviewed by a committee headed by a judge[3] and, partly as a result of a recommendation from that body, it is now under the constant supervision of a Chief Inspector who happens presently to be drawn from the ranks of the judiciary.[4] What makes the prison system different from other areas of judicial inquiry, however, is that one of its main problems, overcrowding, results not from executive action but, rather, from the remand and sentencing decisions of various courts across the country. This leads some to argue that the courts are part of the problem which Lord Justice Woolf has been asked to address.

While this may be true, it fails to distinguish between the lower courts – responsible for imprisoning offenders – and the divisional

Source: Commissioned for this volume

and appellate courts, which are concerned with addressing the grievances of prisoners through the process of judicial review. The verdict on the contribution of the courts in this latter area is, by common consent, a positive one. Textbooks on civil liberties and human rights which are otherwise quite critical of the judicial record in the United Kingdom exempt the senior judges when it comes to their involvement in prison law. Thus, one leading casebook refers to the courts' 'remarkable and quite unexpected willingness to involve themselves in the control of prison administration'.[5] One case was described by Geoffrey Robertson as a 'welcome reminder of an often forgotten power in the courts to protect all those in detention against inhumane treatment'.[6] It is generally agreed that this past decade has seen an unparalleled level of judicial intervention in this area.

Indeed, there may be no area of public life in greater need of reform than our prison system. As the Whitaker Report demonstrated for the Republic of Ireland,[7] and routine condemnations from the Chief Inspector of Prisons and the Boards of Visitors of various prisons confirm for the United Kingdom, there is a crisis of major proportions afflicting the jails of these islands.[8] In 1988, the average population of persons in custody, including those held in police cells, was about 49,950. In that year the United Kingdom had a rate of 98 prisoners per 100,000 of the population, substantially higher than the Council of Europe average of 78 per 100,000. Even by the Government's own standards, overcrowding was very high, with the system suffering from a 15 per cent overcapacity by 1987.[9] By the middle of 1990, the prison population had been reduced to 45,500, though whether the 1991 Criminal Justice Bill, with its attempt to direct the sentencing practices of the judges more clearly, will reverse this downward trend remains to be seen. The United Kingdom imprisons a higher proportion of its population than does any other major Western European country. More than 20 per cent of the inmates are untried or unsentenced, a percentage that is not far out of line with Europe, though the absolute total of prisoners involved is of course much higher. Of those convicted and sentenced, no more than 40 per cent are imprisoned for an offence of personal violence (including robbery and sexual assaults). It would appear that UK judges are deeply committed to jailing many of the criminals that come before them, regardless, it would seem, of the pleas for alternatives that emanate from Government[10] and the strain that their action is placing on already stretched resources.

The situation is compounded by antiquated facilities, poorly thought out routines and often the entire collapse of staff morale. The result has been overcrowding, rioting, suicides and disgruntlement on a very large scale. Between April 1987 and March 1988, a thousand prisoners injured themselves intentionally and 300 attempted suicide – another thirteen succeeded. In the year to the end of March 1989, there were thirty-two suicides.[11] Sir James Hennessy, the former Chief Inspector of Prisons in England and Wales, warned in his last report before retirement that 'overcrowding, with its consequential effects on physical conditions and regimes, contributed to the creation of the climate of discontent among inmates'.[12] Some prisons provided 'seriously impoverished regimes'.[13] In one prison, for example, between sixty and ninety inmates shared two WCs and one urinal;[14] the inspectorate found that 'three inmates sharing a cell did not even have the minimal comfort of a chair each'.[15] One Board of Visitors described how many inmates at their prison

> have no proper exercise, no fresh air or natural light. They are kept in cramped surroundings with inadequate sanitation and washing facilities. In many cases, they have been in the same clothes for up to twenty-one days. Sometimes their families do not know where they are; in some locations, social visits are impossible or in unsuitable conditions. Their solicitors have difficulty in locating them.[16]

The Board of Visitors at another prison has been reported as describing their jail as 'humiliating and disgusting'.[17] The new Chief Inspector, Judge Tumim, has used such words as 'intolerable', 'squalid', 'shabby', 'dirty' and 'dilapidated' to sum up some of the places he has had to visit; he has described how in many establishments 'cell windows and outside walls [are] smeared with excrement, and . . . parcels of faeces – wrapped in newspaper or in items of clothing – litter the ground outside'.[18]

There is an obvious paradox in all this. These descriptions come not from 1980, but, rather, from 1987 to 1989. In other words, they reflect the reality of prison life after a decade of what is supposed to have been unparalleled judicial intervention on the prisoners' behalf. So what have the higher courts been doing? As we shall see, the answer is that a great deal of litigious energy has been expended in the procedural area, but that decisions compelling improvements in the actual conditions within prisons have been few and far between. In the background, adding its own impetus for reform, has been the European Court of Human Rights and we shall see how this tribunal has affected the development of the local law. The European Prison Rules have only recently emerged as a possible source of relevant law. Two important Court of Appeal decisions in 1990 indicate that the trend against judicial involvement in the quality of prison life may be on the verge of a dramatic reversal.

The active judiciary

The starting point is *R.* v. *Board of Visitors of Hull Prison, ex parte St. Germain*.[19] In the summer of 1976, very serious rioting took place in Hull prison. A great deal of damage was done to prison property and a number of inmates participated in a rooftop protest. When the furore died down, the authorities exacted their retribution: 180 prisoners were brought before the prison's Board of Visitors to face disciplinary charges. Loss of remission was the severest penalty meted out; in one case of this type, a man had 720 days added to his period of detention. Five prisoners challenged the procedure before the Board; hearsay evidence had been relied upon; they had not been allowed to cross-examine witnesses or to call alibis to prove that they were uninvolved in the disorder; they argued that these restrictions were so unfair as to amount to a breach of natural justice. The Board of Visitors denied that the courts had any jurisdiction to examine the way they went about disciplining their prisoners. This argument succeeded before a Divisional Court presided over by the then Lord Chief Justice, Lord Widgery, but that decision was overturned by the Court of Appeal. Shaw LJ declared that '[t]he courts are in general the ultimate custodians of the rights and liberties of the subject whatever his status and however attenuated those rights and liberties may be as the result of some punitive or other process.'[20] An 'essential characteristic of the right of a subject is that it carries with it a right of recourse to the courts unless some statute decrees otherwise' and 'to deny jurisdiction on the grounds of expediency seems . . . tantamount to abdicating a primary function of the judiciary.'[21]

This was strong stuff and it marked a turning point in the courts' approach to prison discipline. In the important case of *O'Reilly* v. *Mackman*, decided four years later, Lord Diplock described the conclusion on jurisdiction in *St. Germain* as 'clearly right'.[22] The decision on the facts eventually led to the five prisoners having their findings of guilt quashed and their remission restored to them.[23] Subsequent cases give a flavour of the positive influence on procedure that the courts soon began to have. In one instance, a Board of Visitors found a serious charge against a prisoner unproven, but went on to direct that a charge of a lesser offence, arising out of the same incident, should be brought against him. The Court of Appeal held that the Board had no power to act in this arbitrary way.[24] Similarly, the Divisional Court has quashed an adjudication by a Board which misinterpreted the Prison Rules to the detriment of a prisoner,[25] and has declared it to be desirable in the interests of justice that a welfare report relevant to a prisoner's disciplinary case be shown to him even if he has not asked to see it.[26] One of the strongest decisions is *R.* v. *Blundeston Prison Board of Visitors, ex parte Fox-Taylor*.[27] The Board of Visitors awarded ninety days loss of remission against a prisoner for an offence against discipline, namely committing an assault. Another inmate had seen the incident which gave rise to the charge but his availability as a witness, though known to at least one of the prison officers, was drawn to the attention of neither the prisoner nor the Board of Visitors. Phillips J quashed the ninety days award, holding that there had been a breach of natural justice which had been neither trivial nor trifling. The prisoner had 'suffered a real and substantial detriment because somebody else, in effect [had] decided for him what witnesses are to be called, and he [had] been deprived of the opportunity of calling, if the Board of Visitors did not do so, a witness whom he might well have regarded, and probably would have, as material.'[28]

The jurisdiction has on the whole been so successful that the House of Lords has recently felt emboldened to extend the due process tentacles of the law right into the prison itself – into the disciplinary awards of the prison governor.[29] Their Lordships had 'heard no suggestion of any adverse effects flowing from the exercise of the courts' supervisory jurisdiction over proceedings before boards of visitors.'[30] Furthermore, there seemed

> no reason to doubt that, so far from fulfilling the fear expressed in argument for the respondents in *St. Germain's* case that 'the subjecting of disciplinary proceedings to scrutiny by the courts would have inevitably adverse affects on the discipline and morale of prisoners and staff alike', the courts' infrequent interventions have improved the quality of justice administered by boards of visitors.[31]

Disciplinary decisions by governors were part of a 'public function which affects . . . liberty' and as such were subject to 'the general common law principle which imposes a duty of procedural fairness when a public authority makes a decision not of a legislative nature affecting the rights, privileges and interests of individuals'.[32] There was as little reason to believe the scare stories about hordes of disgruntled prisoners waiting to launch spurious actions as there had been when this spectre had first been dragged out, during argument in *St. Germain*.

Not all the fleshing out of the breakthrough in *St. Germain* has been to the advantage of the prisoner. Even as the House of Lords was expanding the oversight of the courts into the realm of the governor, it was emphasising that the need to obtain leave to apply for judicial review and the discretionary nature of public law remedies remained as two obstacles to a decision in an applicant's favour. In *R. v. Board of Visitors of Frankland Prison, ex parte Lewis*,[33] Woolf J declined an opportunity to use the rules of natural justice to force a division between the administrative and disciplinary sides of the work of Boards of Visitors. There has been a great deal of public debate over the unfortunate consequences that flow from requiring Boards to do both these jobs,[34] but change has been slow, on account both of the cost and of the administrative inconvenience involved in any alteration.[35] Would it not have been a valid exercise of judicial discretion to have forced such a reform upon our reluctant policy-makers?

The courts have also not been prepared to contemplate a fully fledged rule allowing legal representation before Boards of Visitors. We now have the authority of a unanimous House of Lords for the proposition that this is not available to a prisoner as of right.[36] According to Lord Goff, such an entitlement 'would result in wholly unnecessary delays in many cases, to the detriment of all

concerned including the prisoner charged, and to wholly unnecessary waste of time and money contrary to the public interest.'[37]
Their Lordships were not convinced by the argument in favour of
representation which pointed out that proceedings before such
Boards were sophisticated hearings, involving complex procedure,
and possibly resulting in deprivation of liberty (in the shape of lost
remission) greater than anything which could be meted out by a
Magistrates' Court. Already, this has led to a decision by the
Court of Appeal that legal representation need not be allowed
where the charge has what the Board in question determines to
be a straightforward factual basis.[38] Whether this flexible approach
is reconcilable with the European Convention of Human Rights
has yet to be clarified, though there is certainly room for argument
that the Strasbourg court has adopted a much less equivocal line.
Thus in *Campbell and Fell*,[39] the European Court held that the
inability of one of the applicants to consult a lawyer before and to
be legally represented at the Board's hearing constituted a
violation of Article 6:1.

British prisoners have been frequent supplicants in Strasbourg,
far more so than their counterparts in other European countries and
it is the European Court which has underpinned the second area
of prison life in which the judges have had a major impact. This
relates to the access to the courts enjoyed by potential litigants
among the prison population. In *Golder* v. *United Kingdom*,[40] it
was alleged that the applicant had been involved in serious
offences against discipline arising out of a disturbance at Parkhurst
Prison on the Isle of Wight. When it emerged that he had a good
alibi for the relevant evening, no charges were preferred against
him. The fact that disciplinary proceedings had been considered
remained on his prison record and subsequently seems to have
prevented him from making a successful application for parole.
When Golder learned of this latter fact, he set out to sue for libel
the officer who had made the original allegation against him. The
Home Secretary, acting under the then Prison Rules, refused him
permission to consult a lawyer with a view to launching such
proceedings. The European Court of Human Rights was unanimous
that this veto on contacts with Golder's lawyer amounted to an
unwarranted breach of Article 8(1) of the Convention, which
guarantees, among other things, that 'Everyone has the right to
respect for his . . . correspondence.' The Court remarked that

'[i]mpeding someone from even initiating correspondence constitutes the most far-reaching form of "interference".'[41] Despite
'having regard to the power of appreciation left to the Contracting
States', the Court could not discern how these restrictions were
'necessary in a democratic society', as the exceptions in Article
8(2) uniformly require.[42] A majority also considered that the
refusal to allow contact with Golder's lawyer was tantamount to
denying him access to the courts and that this was a breach of
Article 6(1).

As can be imagined, the implementation of *Golder* required a
thoroughgoing overhaul of many of the Prison Rules.[43] One
regulation which continued to inhibit litigation was the requirement
that, before an applicant could pursue a matter relating to the
prison through the courts, he or she had first to make a complaint
to the prison authorities and then await the outcome of the
internal investigation that followed. This 'prior ventilation' rule
was condemned by the House of Lords in March 1982.[44] Lord
Bridge thought it an infringement of the 'basic . . . right to
unimpeded access to the courts'.[45] Lord Wilberforce emphasised
that 'under English law, a convicted prisoner, in spite of his
imprisonment, retains all civil rights which are not taken away
expressly or by necessary implication.'[46] Similar reasoning was
employed by Robert Goff LJ in the following year when the
Divisional Court struck down the 'simultaneous ventilation' rule
which was brought in by the Home Office as their replacement for
the rule which had been castigated in the House of Lords. This
required only that the prisoner initiate the internal procedure
before starting the litigation, but even this milder approach was
not satisfactory:

> [T]he simultaneous ventilation rule constitutes an impediment to the
> right of access to a solicitor, because it requires the inmate to do
> something, unnecessary for the purpose of enabling him to see his
> solicitor, which otherwise he could not be required to do. No inmate
> can be compelled to make an internal complaint against a member of
> the prison staff, and it is possible to envisage circumstances of a
> controversial nature in which an inmate may hesitate to make an
> internal complaint for fear that he may be accused of committing the
> disciplinary offence of making a false and malicious allegation against
> a member of the prison staff – an offence which, if found proved
> against him, may result in his suffering punishment in the form of loss
> of privileges or loss of remission.[47]

The passive judiciary

It is clear that these various decisions represent a substantial breakthrough in a hitherto neglected area of the law. The issues successfully resolved in them appear, however, somewhat peripheral, particularly when the terrible state of British prisons referred to earlier is taken into account. The case law on access to the courts, for instance, begs the question of the extent to which such access has improved the lot of the prisoner. Until 1990, the answer would appear to have been that very little had been achieved outside the narrow area of disciplinary proceedings. The record shows that the courts matched their enthusiasm for procedural reform with a reluctance to engage in judicial law-making where the quality of life in prison was concerned. Before examining the recent breakthroughs that may presage a change in this approach, we should review this sequence of earlier cases.

The first point to note is that a breach of prison rules does not in itself give a prisoner any right of action. This restriction was first established in a case in 1942 involving plaintiffs detained under the well-known regulation 18(b) of the Defence (General) Regulations 1939.[48] In 1972, the Court of Appeal unanimously took the same approach, with Lord Denning remarking that if 'the courts were to entertain actions by disgruntled prisoners, the governor's life would be made intolerable' and the 'discipline of the prison would be undermined'.[49] In giving the leading judgment in *ex parte St. Germain (No. 1)*, Megaw LJ went out of his way to preserve this rule from the reforms in other areas of the prison law which he and his colleagues in the Court of Appeal were then effecting.[50] Lord Denning's comments have an old-fashioned ring about them today and, as we have seen, similar sentiments were decisively rejected by the House of Lords in 1988 when it extended the jurisdiction of the courts over the disciplinary decisions of governors.

A second area of judicial inactivity has been in relation to discretionary decision-making affecting prisoners. Our starting point is *Payne* v. *Home Office*, an unreported decision in 1977, but one which was later summarised in the following terms by Tudor Evans J:

> That . . . was a case in which the plaintiff sought to invoke the principles of natural justice in relation to his classification as a

Category A prisoner. He submitted that he ought to have been informed of what was being alleged against him and allowed to put his own case.

Having considered all the cases, . . . the legislative framework in which the legislator was working and the scope and objective of the proceedings, Cantley J held that it was inappropriate that a prisoner should have the right to be heard in relation to classification. He held that the legislation did not contemplate that a prisoner should be given the details relevant to his classification or to make representations as to how he should be classified. The duty was, in the circumstances, confined to acting fairly when classifying prisoners.[51]

Classifications like these have far-reaching implications for the quality of life in jail; they can mean the difference between dispersal conditions and a less secure environment. Similarly important are decisions about the movement of inmates from prison to prison. Sudden and frequent changes of this nature can make visiting very difficult and may also affect the quality of a prisoner's defence case where he or she is being held on remand pending full trial. Both these points were made in *R. v. Secretary of State for the Home Department, ex parte McAvoy*.[52] Webster J considered such decisions to be 'reviewable in principle if it is shown that [the Minister] has misdirected himself in law'.[53] However, the occasions for judicial intervention could well be 'rare and exceptional' and, even where well-founded, the judge would have a discretionary power not to grant any remedy. In this case, the Home Office justified their sudden move of McAvoy from Brixton to Winchester on 'operational and security' grounds. No further information was volunteered. Webster J considered it

undesirable, if not impossible, for this court to examine operational reasons . . . and to examine security reasons for decisions . . . could . . . be dangerous and contrary to the policy of [the relevant] statutory provision, which is to confer an absolute discretion, within the law, on the Secretary of State to make such executive decisions as he thinks fit for operational and security reasons.[54]

Given the nature of the subject matter, it will not be difficult for the Home Office, quite fairly, to characterise all movement of prisoners as being for either operational or security reasons. Indeed, so broad are these criteria that it is hard to visualise such a move being made on any other basis. The advance in *ex parte McAvoy* would appear to be more apparent than real.

The governor's power to order the segregation of a prisoner under Rule 43 has also been judicially considered recently. Since the improvements in the fairness of disciplinary proceedings, this power has become controversial, since it has been alleged that it is being used by the authorities as a way of punishing inmates without having to prefer formal charges.[55] This would be quite improper since the regulations are specific that Rule 43 is to be employed solely for the maintenance of good order or discipline or in the interests of the prisoner. In *R.* v. *Deputy Governor of Parkhurst Prison, ex parte Hague*,[56] the applicant was segregated at Parkhurst and was subsequently transferred to Wormwood Scrubs where his isolation was continued for a further twenty-eight days. In the Divisional Court, the prisoner alleged that the order was made for the improper purpose of punishing him. The Court, while accepting the availability in principle of judicial review of a governor's decisions about segregation and transfer, nevertheless denied him relief. If the governor 'considered that the preferring of a charge against a prisoner who was properly regarded as a disruptive trouble-maker, would result in embarrassment of prison officers, he was entitled to treat that as a reason for not preferring a charge.'[57]

Furthermore, there was

> no obligation on a prison governor to prefer a disciplinary charge as a precondition of acting on information, which demonstrated commission by a prisoner of an offence against discipline, before he might act on that information as a ground for placing the prisoner on rule 43 . . . Fairness did not require that a prisoner be given the right to be heard before a decision affecting him was made under rule 43.[58]

The prisoner had a right to be given the reasons for his segregation, but even this was 'subject to the limitation that the governor could not be required to include any material which should be withheld in the interests of security' and 'failure to give reasons did not in every case render the decision void'.[59] In the Court of Appeal, the allegation that Rule 43 had been used as an indirect form of punishment was dropped, and the applicant succeeded in establishing that the transfer procedure was an unlawful fetter on the discretion of the governor to whose prison he had been sent. However, the Court of Appeal decided that natural justice played no part in the application of Rule 43 and, furthermore, disagreeing with the Divisional Court on this point, that prisoners do not have a legal right to be given reasons for their segregation.[60]

Other cases involving discretionary powers tell a similar story. A recent change in the Prison Rules removed from unconvicted prisoners an entitlement to receive food provided at their own expense or those of their friends.[61] Section 47(4) of the Prison Act 1952 provides *inter alia* that 'Rules made under this section shall provide for the special treatment of . . . any . . . person detained in prison, not being a person serving a sentence.' In proceedings for judicial review, the change was held by the Divisional Court to be *intra vires* this provision. According to Mann LJ, the Act required only that 'there should be "some" special treatment for unconvicted prisoners'. The section 'did not predicate what the treatment should be.' This was 'a matter for the judgment of the Home Secretary and his judgment could only be impugned if it was perverse which it was not in the present case.'[62] Two decisions have dealt with the sensitive matter of parole. In *Payne* v. *Lord Harris*,[63] the appellant was an 'exceptionally well-behaved' and 'model' prisoner who had nevertheless had his applications for release on licence rejected on many occasions, without any reasons being given to him as to why he was failing with such regularity. The Court of Appeal held that the Parole Board was under no obligation to tell a prisoner why they were turning down a request for parole. This was 'in the interests of society at large – including the due administration of the parole system'.[64] Shaw LJ considered that 'no constraints or pressures should weigh upon the Parole Board in coming to what must in the end be a decision in which expediency must be an important influence.'[65] In a later case, the Divisional Court confirmed that the Board was exercising an administrative rather than a judicial function and that it was as a result under no obligation to give a prisoner an opportunity to be heard or to disclose documents to him or her.[66] This was despite the interests of the prisoner 'as a human being facing indefinite detention' as Lord Denning had described Payne in the first of the two decisions.[67]

Cases that directly tackled the conditions in British jails were similarly unsuccessful. In *Williams* v. *Home Office (No.2)*,[68] the plaintiff had spent 180 days in a control unit in Wakefield Prison. It was a programme specifically designed to deal with difficult prisoners, and was explained in the following terms by Tudor Evans J:

[T]he regime was divided into two stages. Originally . . . each stage
was to last for three months, but these periods were amended . . . to
90 days each. At stage 1, the prisoner did not associate with other
prisoners, save when he had one hour's exercise a day. In fact . . . the
plaintiff exercised alone for the first month. The prisoners were not
obliged to work . . . [and] . . . refusal to work was not to be treated
as a disciplinary offence, because this would lead to a confrontation
between the prisoner and the staff which the regime was designed to
avoid. If the prisoner worked he was paid for it, but if he did not, time
did not start to run. He could only qualify for stage 2 if he worked.

At stage 2 the prisoner was allowed a degree of association with
other prisoners in the unit. He was allowed to associate at work and
for leisure or educational purposes . . . At stage 2 if the prisoner failed
to work or attempted to cause trouble, he reverted to stage 1, and he
was then required to start again and to complete a further continuous
period of 90 days good behaviour before qualifying for entry into stage
2.[69]

The plaintiff's argument that this game of penal snakes and ladders
amounted to a tortuous false imprisonment fell at the first hurdle.
The detention itself was lawful and there was 'no authority in
modern law to support the . . . submission that . . . it can become
unlawful if the nature (meaning the conditions) of the imprisonment changes'.[70] Such conditions were 'a matter for the Secretary
of State' to whom a prisoner could complain if he was not satisfied.
Moreover, there was 'in the administration of prisons of this
country ample safeguard against abuse'.[71]

More interestingly, the plaintiff also pinned his case on the Bill
of Rights 1688, arguing that the way he was being detained
amounted to the infliction of 'cruell and unusuall punishments'.
Tudor Evans J resisted the temptation to use this old phrase as
the basis for an assertion of judicial control over prison conditions.
The regime was 'not unusual when compared with other regimes
in the English penal system'.[72] Furthermore, it was not cruel since
it did not 'fall below the irreducible minimum, judged by contemporary standards, of public morality'.[73] Later cases have hinted
that this provision of the Bill of Rights might be more creatively
employed. In *R.* v. *Secretary of State for the Home Department,
ex parte Herbage (No.2)*,[74] leave to apply for judicial review was
granted on the basis of an allegation of cruel and unusual punishment in respect of a physically disabled but mentally sound man
being detained in the hospital wing of a prison in close proximity
to mentally disturbed inmates. Purchas LJ considered that the case

raised an issue of a 'fundamental right' which went 'far beyond the ambit of the Prison rules'.[75] It was

> generally held to be unacceptable that persons, supposedly of normal
> mentality, should be detained in psychiatric institutions as is said to
> occur in certain parts of the world . . . [I]f it were to be established
> that the applicant as a sane person was, for purely administrative
> purposes, being subjected in the psychiatric wing to the stress of being
> exposed to the disturbance caused by the behaviour of mentally ill and
> disturbed prisoners, this might well be considered as a 'cruel and
> unusual punishment' and one which was not deserved.[76]

Other judges have been less willing to enter this field, McNeill J commenting in one case that a 'practice of including an averment of breach of the Bill of Rights would be viewed strictly – at any rate in any case which became before me – unless the averment was well-founded.'[77]

The European dimension

The European record is also not particularly dramatic when it is examined from the point of view of the direct impact it has had on the quality of prison life. Here we can see the contrast between the judicial approach of the European Court and the administrative reforms suggested by the European Prison Rules. The decisions of the former have the important advantage of being self-executing in the particular case and of imposing an international law obligation of compliance on the State against whom judgment has been de'ivered. The Rules, in contrast, need to jump through the democratic hoops of consultation, consensus and incorporation before having the chance of improving the lot of the prisoner. There have been notable achievements in the European Court, such as the relaxation in the rules on correspondence signalled by the *Silver* case[78] and the enactment of the Marriage Act 1983 following the Commission's finding in favour of a prisoner's right to marry in *Hamer*.[79] However, the overall impression is that, except where discipline and access to lawyers and the courts is concerned, the European Convention on Human Rights has not had so great an influence as might have been supposed, especially in view of the high reputation enjoyed by the Court in this area. Thus, in *Boyle and Rice* v. *United Kingdom*,[80] a concerted challenge to many of the United Kingdom's restrictive rules on correspondence, prison visits and compassionate leave ended in failure. The Court emphasised that the Convention had to be read in the light of 'the ordinary and reasonable requirements of imprisonment'[81] and that this meant that a considerable amount of discretion was inevitably vested in the national authorities.[82] Even in the otherwise extremely assertive decision in *Campbell and Fell*,[83] in which the Court delivered a strong judgment on access to legal advice and on procedural fairness in the context of disciplinary hearings before a Board of Visitors, the Commission had earlier decided that Article 6 gave no 'automatic right to medical examination whenever a prisoner considers that he might have a cause of action'. This question was not pursued before the Court.

Indeed, the Commission siphons out many prisoners' rights cases in much the same way as does the application for leave procedure in domestic law. Thus, the Commission has rejected as manifestly ill-founded both an application to relax the rules on visitors in a specific case[84] and an argument that the method of classifying prisoners infringes the Convention.[85] It has also rejected arguments against solitary confinement based on Article 3 (prohibiting 'inhuman or degrading treatment or punishment')[86] and dismissed a series of complaints arising out of conditions in The Maze Prison in Northern Ireland in the late 1970s.[87] The Convention's lack of relevance to the core problems afflicting the prison system is nowhere better illustrated than in the Commission's decision in the poignant case of *Hilton* v. *United Kingdom*.[88] The subject matter of the case was summarised as follows:

> The applicant maintained all his allegations of ill-treatment which in his submission amounted to a breach of Article 3 of the Convention. The alleged assaults and abuse from prison staff, he claimed, constituted mental and physical torture. Furthermore, he submitted that his detention removed from association with other prisoners under rule 43 of the Prison Rules was not for his own protection but was 'undue, unjust and unjustified punishment,' inordinately long, consisting of 23 hours a day solitary confinement, involving loss of privileges and causing him severe mental strain and degradation.
>
> Finally, he contended that the cumulative effect of solitary confinement, alleged ill-treatment deliberately inflicted, the refusal by all concerned to investigate, or cause to be investigated, the complaints of brutality he was making against prison officers, the incessant

complaints that were made against him and subsequent disciplinary proceedings which allegedly ignored the rules of natural justice and the continuous loss of privileges, resulted in his total degradation and constituted a breach of Article 3 of the Convention.[89]

The Commission recognised that 'such factors as the conditions of overcrowding and understaffing disclosed by this application and the rigorous, impersonal application of disciplinary measures, on occasions to the point of absurdity (for example, the applicant's punishment for putting his hands in his pockets) all had their depressing and discouraging effect upon the applicant.'[90] Moreover, 'there were, and still are, regrettable limitations on normal prisons, because of understaffing and overcrowding which make it difficult to give special attention to an individual prisoner's problems.'[91] Nevertheless, the Commission's conclusion was that the treatment of the applicant, 'although extremely unsatisfactory in all the circumstances of the case, did not amount to degrading treatment contrary to Article 3 of the Convention.'[92] Four members of the Commission disagreed and filed a joint dissenting opinion:

> We are not denying that the applicant became an uncooperative, difficult prisoner. It is clear that he had genuine problems, but also that he was not essentially bad or evil or out to cause trouble. He was emotionally and psychologically disturbed and unable to cope with his situation . . . The inflexibility of the prison staff in their rigorous insistence that the applicant conform to the Prison Rules, the isolation of the applicant under rule 43 from other prisoners and from contact with outside help, such as from lawyers, the lack of facilities in the prison concerned, the understaffing and overcrowding, all took their toll on the applicant . . . We find it inadmissible that a prison system should reduce a prisoner to an 'animal-like state,' to use the phrase frequently mentioned in this case, whatever his difficulties.[93]

Conclusion: a new approach?

As we have seen, European and national courts are at their best when tackling such subjects as discipline and access to the courts. These are issues that, for all their importance, are not central to the core problems facing prisons today. Is it possible for these courts to do more? The answer is clearly yes, and two recent decisions in the UK courts demonstrate that this is the case. In

Weldon v. *Home Office*,[94] the plaintiff prisoner alleged that he had been assaulted by prison officers and held overnight in a strip cell where his clothes had been removed from him. On these facts, which were accepted as true for the purposes of the hearing, the Court of Appeal ruled that the tort of false imprisonment was in principle available. The reasoning in *Williams* v. *Home Office (No.2)*[95] was 'not conclusive'. A couple of earlier cases dealing with a remand prisoner and a suspect detained by the police had hinted that there might be a minimum standard of habitability below which lawful detention could not fall and Ralph Gibson LJ used such dicta to underpin a general principle: '[T]he legislative intention is that a prisoner should, subject to any lawful order given to him and to any rules laid down in the prison, enjoy such liberty – his residual liberty – within prison as is left to him.'[96]

It followed from this that the tort of false imprisonment was available where the authorities stepped out of line. But how wide-ranging was this remedy to be? Counsel for the applicant argued that it covered every imprisonment falling below the standards set by the Prison Rules, the European Prison Rules and the European Convention on Human Rights and Fundamental Freedoms, 'whether the breach be in respect of the physical conditions of confinement or of standards of treatment, for example, with reference to the quality of food, facilities for religious observance, or access to educational facilities'.[97] Without ruling conclusively on the issue, Ralph Gibson LJ thought such a submission 'unsustainably wide'.[98] It was clear that the 'difficulties which could arise in the administration of prisons and in the maintenance of order within prisons' were very real.[99] The solution was to stress that the tort arose here because of the 'intolerable conditions of detention'[100] to which the applicant had been subjected by prison officers who had – crucially – also been acting in bad faith. Ralph Gibson LJ saw this concept of bad faith as an important control on an otherwise potentially explosive tort. It applied to those officers who 'intentionally deprive a prisoner of his residual liberty within the prison and who do so without reasonable cause and with knowledge that they have no reasonable cause.'[101]

In the second recent Court of Appeal decision, *R.* v. *Deputy Governor of Parkhurst Prison and others, ex parte Hague*,[102] it was confirmed that breach of the Prison Rules could not in itself defeat a defence of lawful authority to a false imprisonment action, and that the gist of the action lay in establishing intolerable conditions. Taylor LJ did not probe further into this important phrase, but Nicholls LJ limited his version of it to physical circumstances. It covered conditions which were 'seriously dangerous to health' but did not encompass segregation under Rule 43 or transfer to another prison, for both of which other remedies were available.[103] The Court was agreed that the bad faith criterion introduced in *ex parte Weldon* should be jettisoned. It would 'alter the tort of false imprisonment and in effect create a new tort special to prisons and prisoners.'[104]

In both *Weldon* and *Hague*, leave to appeal to the House of Lords was granted. The judicial activism that could now be released by two authoritative decisions from their Lordships can be seen by looking at the United States. The Federal Courts there have involved themselves in the familiar territory of due process and fair play.[105] But, led by the Supreme Court,[106] many circuit judges have also steeled themselves to confront the key issues of overcrowding and bad conditions in their prison system. Three cases may be used as examples.[107] The first is *Toussaint* v. *Yockey*,[108] where the Court of Appeals for the Ninth Circuit upheld a District Court injunction limiting the double celling of inmates in small cells at four California state prisons. The Court found unconstitutional the double celling of prisoners in windowless cells approximately six feet wide and eight to nine feet long. It ordered that involuntary double celling be limited to thirty days per year and that it should, in any event, only take place in cells of fifty square feet in area. Critical to the Court's decision was its finding that double celling in these prisons had been found to cause violence, tension and psychiatric problems. The Court also found that the denial of exercise to segregated prisoners constituted a cruel and unusual punishment.

In a similar vein is *French* v. *Owens*.[109] The District Court had found that the prison involved here housed over twice its intended capacity and that 40 per cent of the prisoners in double cells spent twenty to twenty-three hours per day in rooms with only twenty-four square feet of available space. On this basis, it ordered a reduction in the number of inmates by almost 400. The Circuit Court affirmed this decision, and noted that conditions at the institution amounted to cruel and unusual punishment of the inmates. Even more startling to our eyes is *Mitchell* v. *Cuomo*,[110] where the Circuit Court prohibited the New York authorities from closing a prison on the ground that the knock-on effect of such a move would lead to a drastic increase in overcrowding in the rest of the State's prisons. J. Pratt put it succinctly:

> In view of the tragic consequences of past disturbances in New York's prison system and the likely relationship between these disturbances and overcrowding, we cannot find an abuse of discretion in the district justice's hesitation to permit still greater overcrowding of the correctional system under the particular circumstances of this case.[111]

It may be that American prison conditions are sometimes much worse than those that pertain on this side of the Atlantic. This should not stop us asking whether an Irish or UK judge could be capable of taking such a robust line? Could the European Court of Human Rights? In all these jurisdictions, such an approach is possible. The European Convention prohibits 'inhuman or degrading treatment or punishment'. The Republic of Ireland includes privacy and bodily integrity among the personal rights protected by its Constitution. *Weldon* and *Hague* have demonstrated the potential offered by the tort of false imprisonment. For once, English judges cannot wriggle out of the moral dilemma by complacent invocation of the sovereignty of Parliament and the non-applicability of the European Convention in domestic law. In this area, if in no other, the United Kingdom has a Bill of Rights and it prohibits cruel and unusual punishments just as clearly as the American Constitution does. Parliament may have spoken a long time ago – but at least it has spoken.

The ability of the courts to involve themselves directly in the task of improving the conditions within prisons resolves itself into a matter of judicial discretion – and judicial courage. There are strong arguments for action. The prisons are a shameful disaster area, not only because judges continue to fill them with every sort of criminal but also because the Government finds it impossible to care sufficiently for those who end up in their squalid cells. The Chief Inspector, Boards of Visitors and prison officers up and down the country are in despair because of the paucity of resources made available to remedy the degradation that is a daily part of their prisoners' lives. New prisons in the future are no answer to the problems of today. (And no doubt they will be overfilled by enthusiastic judges as soon as they come on stream; new prisons, like new motorways, are never uncrowded for long.) In any event, by appearing to compel new buildings, the courts may embolden the Government to contemplate more dramatic innovations. There is a need for minimal standards, based on the European Prison Rules, within our penal system, but these are rarely warmly welcomed by government, for whom prisons represent an unwelcome and unpopular call upon scarce resources. The only group that can force the human rights of prisoners up the agenda, and compel such minimum standards, is the senior judiciary. At the very least, judicial review leads to a public ventilation of the inadequacies of our prison system and forces each sector within society to confront the policy implications of imprisoning more and more people in deteriorating conditions. If the House of Lords were to follow up and develop further the more robust line signalled by the Court of Appeal in *Weldon* and *Hague*, it would be a partial remedy for the excesses of their sentencing brethren; and it would help to end this frustrating paradox of judicial activism in an area of underfunded squalor, a state of affairs which is a reproach to all lawyers who believe that courts matter.

Notes

1. *The Hillsborough Stadium Disaster, 15 April 1989*, Cmnd 962 (1990).
2. *The Brixton Disorders, April 10–12, 1981*, Cmnd. 8427 (1981).
3. *Report of the [May] Committee of Inquiry into the UK Prison Service*, Cmnd. 7673, (1979).
4. Judge Tumim. For his annual report, see *post*, n.12.
5. S. H. Bailey, D. J. Harris and B. L. Jones, *Civil Liberties. Cases and Materials* (2nd edn, London, Butterworths, 1985), p. 526.
6. G. Robertson, *Freedom, the Individual and the Law* (6th edn, Harmondsworth, 1989), p. 342. The case referred to in these terms was *ex parte Herbage*, on which see *post*, n. 74.
7. *Report of the Committee of Inquiry into the Penal System (The Whitaker Report)*, Pl. 3391 (Dublin, 1985).
8. See generally V. Stern, *Bricks of Shame. Britain's Prisons* (2nd edn, London, 1989). See also M. Maguire, J. Vagg and R. Morgan (eds.), *Accountability and Prisons. Opening up a Closed World* (London, 1985); Richardson, 'Time to Take Prisoners' Rights Seriously' (1984) *Journal of Law and Society*, vol. 11, p. 1.

9. See V. Stern, *Imprisoned by Our Prisons. What Needs to be Done* (London, 1989), p. 25.

10. These various figures come from *Prison Statistics for England and Wales*, Cmnd. 825 (1989). For the Government's approach to sentencing, see *Punishment, Custody and the Community*, Cmnd. 424, (1988) and *Crime, Justice and Protecting the Public*, Cmnd. 965, (1990).

11. *Report on the Work of the Prison Service*, Cmnd. 835, (1989), p. 84. For the 1987/88 figures, see Stern, *op. cit.*, p. 19.

12. *Annual Report of the Chief Inspector of Prisons for England and Wales for 1986*, HC (1987–88) 428, para. 4.01.

13. *Ibid.*, para. 3.01.

14. *Ibid.*, para. 4.02.

15. *Ibid.*, para. 3.02.

16. *The Independent*, 21 April 1988. Another prison was said to have 'a kitchen and dining hall alive with birds, vermin, cockroaches, mould, grease, and swill', (1989) *Howard Journal of Criminal Justice*, vol. 28, p. 317.

17. *The Independent*, 2 May 1988.

18. *Annual Report of the Chief Inspector of Prisons for England and Wales for 1988*, HC (1988–89) 491, para. 2.05. See also *Annual Report of the Chief Inspector of Prisons for England and Wales for 1987*, HC (1987–88) 670. For a strong attack on the state of British prisons, see Glazebrook at [1989] CLJ 539.

19. [1978] QB 678 (QBD); [1979] QB 425 (CA).

20. [1979] QB 425, at p. 455.

21. *Ibid.*

22. [1983] 2 AC 237, at p. 274.

23. *R. v. Board of Visitors of Hull Prison, ex parte St. Germain (No.2)* [1979] 1 WLR 1401.

24. *R. v. Board of Visitors of Dartmoor Prison, ex parte Smith* [1986] 3 WLR 61.

25. *R. v. Board of Visitors of Thorp Arch Prison, ex parte De Houghton, The Times*, 22 October 1987. See also *R. v. Board of Visitors of Dartmoor Prison, ex parte Seray-Wurie, The Times*, 5 February 1982, where the Governor's interpretation of the prison rules was upheld.

26. *R. v. Board of Visitors of Wandsworth Prison, ex parte Raymond, The Times*, 17 June 1985.

27. [1982] 1 All ER 646. See also *R. v. Board of Visitors at Gartree Prison, ex parte Mealy, The Times*, 14 November 1981.

28. *Ibid.* at p. 649. See also *R. v. Liverpool Prison Board of Visitors, ex parte Davies, The Times*, 6 October 1982.

29. *Leech v. Deputy Governor of Parkhurst Prison, Prevot v. Deputy Governor of Long Lartin Prison* [1988] AC 533, overruling *R. v. Deputy Governor of Camphill Prison, ex parte King* [1985] QB 735 and following the line adopted by the Northern Irish Court of Appeal in *R. v. Governor of the Maze Prison, ex parte McKiernan* (1985) 6 NIJB 6.

30. [1988] AC 533, at p. 557, *per* Lord Bridge.

31. *Ibid.*

32. *Ibid.*, at p. 578, *per* Lord Oliver.

33. [1986] 1 WLR 130.

34. *Report of the Committee on the Prison Disciplinary System*, Cmnd. 9641 (1985).

35. *The Prison Disciplinary System in England and Wales*, Cmnd. 9920 (1986). See The Prison (Amendment) Rules 1989, SI No. 330.

36. *R.* v. *Board of Visitors of HM Prison, The Maze, ex parte Hone and McCartan* [1988] AC 379. See also *Fraser* v. *Mudge* [1975] 1 WLR 1132; *R.* v. *Secretary of State for the Home Department, ex parte Tarrant* [1985] QB 251.

37. *Ibid.*, at p. 392.

38. *R.* v. *Board of Visitors of HM Remand Centre Risley, ex parte Draper, The Times*, 24 May 1988.

39. *Campbell and Fell* v. *United Kingdom* (1985) 7 EHRR 165.

40. (1975) 1 EHRR 524.

41. *Ibid.*, para. 43.

42. *Ibid.*, para. 45.

43. The case was applied in *Hilton* v. *United Kingdom* (1978) 3 EHRR 104 (European Commission of Human Rights); *Silver* v. *United Kingdom* (1983) 5 EHRR 347 (European Court of Human Rights); and *Campbell and Fell* v. *United Kingdom* (1985) 7 EHRR 165 (European Court of Human Rights).

44. *Raymond* v. *Honey* [1983] 1 AC 1.

45. *Ibid.*, at p. 14. See also *Silver* v. *United Kingdom, op. cit.*, para. 99; and *Campbell and Fell* v. *United Kingdom, op. cit.*, para. 110. (See note 43.)

46. *Ibid.*, at p. 10.

47. *R.* v. *Secretary of State for the Home Department, ex parte Anderson* [1984] 2 WLR 725, at pp. 734–5.

48. *Arbon* v. *Anderson* [1943] KB 252.

49. *Becker* v. *Home Office* [1972] 2 QB 407, at p. 418. See *R.* v. *Deputy Governor of Parkhurst Prison, ex parte Hague, The Independent*, 11 August 1989, on which see Bradley, 'Judicial Review, the Prison Rules and the Segregation of Prisoners' [1989] PL 521.

50. See [1979] QB 425, at p. 449.

51. *Williams* v. *Home Office (No. 2)* [1981] 1 All ER 1211, at p. 1247.

52. [1984] 3 All ER 417. This case was followed in Scotland: *Thompson, Petitioner*, 1989 SLT 343.

53. *Ibid.*, at p. 422.

54. *Ibid.*, at p. 423.

55. See generally Sir James Hennessy's report, *A Review of the Segregation of Prisoners under Rule 43* (Home Office, 1985).

56. *The Independent*, 11 August 1989. See Bradley, 'Judicial Review, the Prison Rules and the Segregation of Prisoners' [1989] PL 521.

57. *Ibid.*, *per* Ralph Gibson LJ.

58. *Ibid.*

59. *Ibid.*
60. [1990] 3 All ER 687, at p. 699, *per* Taylor LJ.
61. Prison (Amendment) Rules 1988, S.I. No. 89.
62. R. v. *Secretary of State for the Home Department, ex parte Simmons*, *The Times*, 25 October 1988. See also R. v. *Secretary of State for the Home Department, ex parte Hickling, The Times*, 7 November 1985.
63. [1981] 1 WLR 754.
64. *Ibid., per* Lord Denning at p. 759.
65. *Ibid.*, at p. 764.
66. R. v. *Secretary of State for the Home Department, ex parte Gunnell* [1984] Crim. LR 170. See also R. v. *Secretary of State for the Home Department, ex parte Benson, The Independent*, 16 November 1988; *re Hales, The Times*, 8 May 1990; R. v. *Parole Board, ex parte Bradley, The Times*, 16 April 1990.
67. [1981] 1 WLR 754 at p. 759.
68. [1981] 1 All ER 1211.
69. *Ibid.*, at p. 1216.
70. *Ibid.*, at p. 1227.
71. *Ibid.*, at p. 1241. In R. v. *Board of Visitors of Gartree Prison, ex parte Sears, The Times*, 20 March 1985, the Divisional Court held that variations in the conditions of a lawful imprisonment could not make the detention unlawful for the purposes of the tort of false imprisonment.
72. *Ibid.*, at p. 1244.
73. *Ibid.*, at p. 1245.
74. [1987] 2 WLR 226. See R. v. *Secretary of State for the Home Department, ex parte Herbage (No. 1)* [1986] 3 WLR 504.
75. *Ibid.*, at p. 241.
76. *Ibid.*, at p. 242. The case does not appear to have proceeded to trial.
77. R. v. *Secretary of State for the Home Department, ex parte Dew* [1987] 1 WLR 881, at p. 890. The Republic of Ireland's written constitution has also not been very much help to prisoners trying to improve their conditions, despite the numerous relevant rights that – in other contexts – the judges have held to be implicitly contained within it: *Murray and Murray* v. *Ireland and the Attorney General* [1985] IR 532 [ban on conjugal relations between married prisoners upheld]; *Kearney* v. *Minister for Justice, Ireland and the Attorney-General* [1986] IR 116 [restrictions on correspondence upheld]; *The State (Boyle)* v. *Governor of the Military Detention Barracks*, Unreported Supreme Court decision, 3 March 1981 [transfer of prisoner to military custody an unreviewable administrative power]; *The State (Gallagher)* v. *Governor of Portlaoise Prison* [1987] ILRM 45 [restrictions on visits upheld].
78. *Silver* v. *United Kingdom* (1983)5 EHRR 347. See also *McCallum* v. *UK, The Times*, 16 October 1990.
79. *Hamer* v. *United Kingdom* (1979) 4 EHRR 139.
80. (1988) 10 EHRR 425.
81. *Ibid.*, para. 74.

82. *Ibid.*, para. 81.
83. (1985) 7 EHRR 165. The Report of the Commission is at (1983) 5 EHRR 207.
84. *X* v. *United Kingdom* (1983) 5 EHRR 260.
85. *Brady* v. *United Kingdom* (1979) 3 EHRR 297.
86. Application 9282/81 summarised at (1983) 5 EHRR 283. Application 9813/82 summarised at (1983) 5 EHRR 513.
87. *McFeeley* v. *United Kingdom* (1980) 3 EHRR 161.
88. (1978) 3 EHRR 104.
89. *Ibid.*, paras. 72, 73.
90. *Ibid.*, para. 97.
91. *Ibid.*, para. 101.
92. *Ibid.*, para. 102
93. *Ibid.*, paras. 3, 4 and 7 of the dissenting opinion.
94. [1990] 3 WLR 465.
95. *Supra*, n.51.
96. [1990] 3 WLR 465, at p. 473. The two cases relied on by the Court were *Middleweek* v. *Chief Constable of Merseyside*, a 1985 decision noted at [1990]3 WLR 481 and *R.* v. *Metropolitan Police Commissioner, ex parte Nahar, The Times*, 28 May 1983.
97. *Ibid.*, at p. 479.
98. *Ibid.*
99. *Ibid.*, at p. 474.
100. *Ibid.*, at p. 479.
101. *Ibid.*
102. [1990] 3 All ER 687.
103. *Ibid.*, at pp. 709–10.
104. *Ibid.*, at p. 707, *per* Taylor LJ.
105. Recent Supreme Court cases of importance include *Turner* v. *Safley* 107 S. Ct. 2254 (1987); *O'Lone* v. *Shabazz* 107 S. Ct. 2400 (1987); *Kentucky Department of Corrections* v. *Thompson* 104 L. Ed. 2d 506 (1989); *Thornburgh* v. *Abbot* 104 L. Ed. 2d 459 (1989). A useful summary is Cohen, 'The law of prisoners' rights: An overview' (1988) *Criminal Law Bulletin*, vol. 24, 321.
106. In *Rhodes* v. *Chapman* 452 US 337 (1981).
107. I had drawn these cases from Kessel, 'Prisoners' rights: unconstitutional prison overcrowding' [1986] *Annual Survey of American Law* 737, an article which provides an excellent overall picture of this area of judicial activity. See also Morgan and Bronstein, 'Prisoners and the courts: the US experience' in Maguire, Vagg and Morgan (eds), *op. cit.* (See note 8.)
108. 722 F. 2d 1490 (9th Circuit, 1985).
109. 777 F. 2d 1250 (7th Circuit, 1985).
110. 748 F. 2d 804 (2d Circuit, 1984).
111. *Ibid.*, at p. 808. For the problems that occasionally attend the implementation of these decisions, see Morgan and Bronstein, *op. cit.* (See note 107.)

14

The remand prisoner and European penal procedures

Richard Vogler
Lecturer in Law, University of Sussex

Approximately one-third of all prisoners currently within the European prison system are on remand awaiting trial. Favoured by legal codes which offer them a privileged status, in reality they suffer conditions which are universally more bleak and restrictive than those of serving prisoners. More than any other group of prisoners, their existence is governed by the actions of agencies which operate wholly outside the walls of their institutions. These agencies – the remanding courts – in their widely differing policies and practices, may have a dramatic impact upon the nature of the imprisonment.

The predicted length of the remand, the degree of personal involvement in the pre-trial, the amount and the quality of the information available, are all crucial to the well-being of the unconvicted prisoner. However, the practices of courts in these crucial areas vary from country to country. It is the aim of this short article to suggest that the *purpose* of remand differs significantly across national boundaries and that these differences have an important bearing upon the situation of unconvicted prisoners. For this reason it is particularly difficult to establish common standards for remands in a European context.

It is no accident that, among comparable prison populations,

Source: Commissioned for this volume

the unconvicted account for 44.3 per cent of the total in France, 43.7 per cent in Spain, but only 20 per cent in England and Wales and 22.4 per cent in Germany.[1] The explanation lies simply in the policies adopted by the remanding institutions in each case. Attempts to establish European standards for the treatment of prisoners as part of a wider harmonisation of criminal justice institutions in the region must take account of this problem. The reasons for a particular penal practice may be determined by the character of the national legal system, and the contradictions between such systems are often intractable.

For example, in advance of the abolition of border controls within the European Community after 1 January 1993, the signatories to the Schengen Convention (France, Germany and the Benelux countries) of 1985, agreed on 'compensatory measures' to offset any potential loss of security. These involved increased supra-national police co-operation, the harmonisation of criminal law legislation and the simplification of criminal procedure under letters rogatory. Even such modest reforms have proved difficult and the failure to implement the agreement on time is clearly not unconnected with differences in national criminal justice practices (Kattau, 1990; Spencer, 1990, pp. 32–7).

Much more problematic will be any attempt to harmonise penal practices across the major European fault line between the common law and the civil law countries. An explanation of the differences in the function of remand among the various countries in the region requires certain broad characteristics. Generally speaking, the position of the remand prisoner under a common law (adversarial) system is quite unlike that of the prisoner under a civil law (inquisitorial) system. Before going on to look at remand practices in the four European countries mentioned above, it is therefore necessary to consider briefly the nature of the two overarching systems of criminal justice and the functions of the pre-trial phase in each.

The inquisitorial and adversarial systems compared

It would be misleading to suggest that any European system of criminal justice fell neatly into one or other of these categories. All are, to a greater or lesser extent, hybrids. However, it is still possible to detect the dominance of a particular mode within a jurisdiction. A criminal justice system such as that of England and Wales, for example, is clearly characterised by the common law or adversarial method. It is essentially one which is set in motion and driven by the actions of the parties. In effect this means the actions of the Crown Prosecution Service, acting on behalf of the police, on the one hand, and the defence group of lawyers (usually solicitor and barrister), acting on behalf of the prisoner, on the other. Pre-trial investigation is entirely in the hands of these parties, whose abilities to deploy the fruits of their enquiries by way of evidence is strictly limited by a highly restrictive and rigidly enforced code of rules of evidence. The defendant must be given, at an early stage, full written details of the totality of the prosecution case. The court itself is intended to provide merely a neutral terrain in which these two contrasting accounts may be dramatised and tested as the parties wish. The judge essentially takes a passive role, ensuring fairness and scrupulous adherence to the rules of evidence. For better or worse, the outcome depends upon the immediate effectiveness of the oral presentation of evidence during the short period (often a matter of hours only) allocated for the trial. Judgment is given, typically by a group of lay assessors (magistrates or jury) and without reasons or justification. The opportunities for appeal are extremely limited. It is a relatively quick, dramatic and final process, with little opportunity for extended or detailed pre-trial consideration of evidence (Smith and Bailey, 1984, pp. 477–527; Spencer, 1989, pp. 213–71).

The civil law or inquisitorial method, as practised in France and Spain and other continental countries, however, is markedly different. Central to the procedure is the pre-trial investigator, the 'Examining Magistrate' who supervises the collection of evidence from all sources over an extended period. His role is to interview all the witnesses, including the defendant, to oversee the police investigation and to compile a *dossier* of evidence for transmission to the trial court (Merryman, 1969, pp. 132–48; Stein, 1984, pp. 36–8; Farrar and Dugdale, 1990, pp. 62–73).

In the inquisitorial process, the remand prisoner is at the service of the court and its investigation. He or she may be called before the Examining Magistrate for interrogation at any time until the *dossier* is completed. The remand prisoner under a common law system is not available in this way. He is at the service only of his or her own defence and may not be subjected to interrogation or surveillance before trial. If the prosecution have not successfully obtained the confession evidence that they require by the time the defendant first appears in court for remand, they can have no further access. The primary purpose of remand under a common law system is merely to ensure attendance at an eventual trial. The primary purpose of remand in a civil law system is to maintain the availability of the defendant and the control and surveillance of his or her activities throughout the instruction process. In order to understand this unfamiliar relationship between the continental judge and the remand prisoner, it will be helpful to look in more detail at the principles of *Instruction*.

Instruction and the remand prisoner

The purpose of Instruction is to provide a more thorough examination of the case than is possible in open court. It is also intended to weed out the weak cases without the embarrassment and cost of a public trial. Proceedings are secret and inquisitorial. Under the French system, which may be adopted as a model of the procedure, the Examining Magistrate (*Juge d'Instruction*) assumes a central position and his powers are extensive.

Although they are often young, these officers have been described as 'the most powerful men and women in France' and their authority over remand prisoners is total. Whereas serving prisoners in France are under the general supervision of an independent 'Prison Magistrate' (*Juge de l'Application des Peines*), who is responsible for their welfare and treatment, remand prisoners are answerable directly to the Examining Magistrate in their case. All important decisions regarding welfare or conduct will therefore be brought before him or her. Similarly, mail to and from the prisoner may be examined and censored as part of the *Instruction* process. The conduct of the prisoner during the remand, the content of any correspondence he may have and the identity of any visitors, can all be treated as evidence for the *dossier*. In short, the separation which exists in the adversarial process between the remand prison and the court is entirely absent here.

Clearly, one of the central functions of *Instruction* is the formal and detailed examination of the defendant. However, the scope of the examination is much wider, and further investigations of all kinds may be commissioned by the Magistrate from the police and other agencies. A general enquiry commission (*Commission Rogatoire*) requiring the police to take 'all steps necessary to establish the truth' may be issued.

Individual sessions with the defendant may last for several hours, but rarely take more than half a day when a defendant is in custody, since police escorts have to be booked in advance. The Examining Magistrate sits at his desk in a smallish office, faced by the defendant with his police escort (in a custody case) behind. Usually handcuffs are removed. The lawyer sits next to the defendant and, unlike the Magistrate, will be robed. It is most unusual for the Prosecutor to be present; at one side of the room will sit the clerk (*greffier*) before a typewriter.

The Examining Magistrate will begin proceedings by summarising the case as he or she sees it, and, having invited comments from the defence, will then open his interrogation.

He or she is completely unrestricted in the questions which can be asked, and the rules of evidence (as understood in common law courts) do not apply. The Examining Magistrate will ask the defendant to comment on contradictory evidence and may even read other witnesses' statements to him or her. Each Magistrate has a characteristic style, and may use sarcasm, irony or apparent astonishment in order to produce the responses that are sought. Some Magistrates may use anger and aggression, whereas others may adopt a mild and friendly approach. The examination will proceed on the basis of a short session of question and answer. At the end of each sequence of questions, the Magistrate will dictate a summary of the defendant's answers (*sur interpellation*) to the clerk, who will type them out on a sheet of paper in the form of a statement. The defendant will be asked to confirm that the summary is correct. At intervals, the lawyer will be asked for his or her 'observations and questions', although it is rare for a lawyer to make any. The main purpose of his or her presence is to ensure that the proceedings are conducted fairly and not to participate in the examination. Indeed, the lawyer has no right to ask questions unless invited to do so by the Magistrate. At the close of the session, all present will be asked to sign the statement.

The defendant may be called back for as many as six or seven sessions, especially if new evidence or technical information has become available. In serious cases there may be a separate session for the Examining Magistrate to take details of the defendant's background and personal history. Defendants can expect fairly detailed questioning about their family, education, marital situation, health, finances and interests, etc. Any psychiatric or medical reports will probably be read to him or her for comments. Both parties have a right to examine the file at any time and to take copies, although the defendant will be obliged to do this through his or her lawyer, and the duplication costs in some cases can be beyond the prisoner's means.

It will be obvious that this is a painstaking and extended process and that the care taken to examine the facts independently from every angle accounts for the length of the French pre-trial and the long periods of remand which it necessitates. Although in larger courts there may be more than one Examining Magistrate, and in Paris, for example, there are sixty-eight, their workload is heavy (50–200 cases at a time). Therefore imprisoned defendants likely to receive lengthy custodial sentences often go to the bottom of the lists. Most Examining Magistrates aim to complete the process within two to three months, but serious cases take longer, and delays of a year or more are not uncommon.

In three ways, therefore, the remand prisoner under an inquisitorial system is at a disadvantage in comparison with a similar prisoner under an adversarial system. First, the period of incarceration will be significantly longer. Second, the amount of information about the case will be much more limited and difficult to obtain. Finally, since the decision on bail or custody is traditionally made by the Examining Magistrate conducting the *Instruction*, and not by an independent body, it can be used as a device to encourage confession. The means adopted to overcome these difficulties, by the use of time limits as we shall see, and the introduction of limited adversarial procedures, have varied from country to country.

It is now necessary to consider the relative disadvantages suffered by the remand prisoner in a common law pre-trial process. Here the remand is almost completely uncoupled from the progress of the investigation and this may open up the possibility of the imprisonment being used for other purposes such as containment or pre-emptive detention.

The remand prisoner in the English and Welsh system

For well over a century, penal legislation in England and Wales has marked a 'clear difference'[2] between the remand prisoner and the serving prisoner. The Prison Act 1952 requires the Secretary of State to make special rules to protect the position of remand prisoners[3] and their status is preserved in the Prison Rules 1964 which provide that 'unconvicted prisoners shall be kept out of contact with convicted prisoners as far as this can reasonably be done'.[4]

A number of important privileges are available. In contrast to the very restrictive régime for serving prisoners, remands may send and receive as many letters as they wish and enjoy as many visits as they wish.[5] They are entitled to full access to books, newspapers and writing materials. Although, as a result of fears about the importation of drugs, the right to receive food or drink from outside was withdrawn in 1988,[6] remand prisoners may still wear their own clothing and arrange for this to be cleaned and sent in by friends or family.[7] They cannot be required to work and they may call on the services of their own doctor or dentist provided that the fees are paid and the agreement of the governor is obtained.[8] All these rights and privileges are, of course, stated to be subject to any restrictions which the Home Secretary may think appropriate to apply (Plotnikoff, 1986; Treverton-Jones, 1989, pp. 37–40).

Despite these advantages, the 'privileged' status of the remand prisoner in England and Wales exists more in jurisprudential theory than in reality. Casale and Plotnikoff (1990) have noted the variations in remand régimes from institution to institution and, in particular, the difficulties for unconvicted prisoners in obtaining access to legal facilities and resources. Moreover, overcrowding and cell sharing have been concentrated by the Home Office on the remand populations in order to provide relatively more civilised conditions for longer-serving prisoners (Morgan and King, 1977; Prison Reform Trust, 1985). In 1984 the Home Office Home Affairs Committee found that 'overcrowding is at its worst, and conditions are at their most squalid in the local prisons and remand centres in which the remand prisoners are housed.'[9] Following the 1989 disturbances at Risley Remand Centre, a facility described by the Chief Inspector of Prisons as 'both barbarous and squalid',[10] the concept of the exclusive remand prison was abandoned. However, as the 1990 Strangeways riot demonstrated, the situation for remand prisoners is little better in the local prisons.[11] These are evidently not the 'clear differences' in treatment which were envisaged by the early legislation.

Nevertheless, the right to free visits and correspondence is an essential feature of the remand. Under a common law system, the pre-trial defendant is a party to the proceedings with important functions to perform. Thus, remand in custody has always been regarded with suspicion. Potentially it represents an inhibition on the free operation of the adversarial process, or, as Lord Hailsham has put it, 'the solitary exception to Magna Carta'.[12] Therefore, at least until committal for trial to the Crown Court, the unconvicted prisoner is accommodated on a strict weekly basis only, travelling every seven days back to the remanding court for a further opportunity to apply for bail. On each application the prosecution must convince a bench of magistrates, who will also hear submissions from the defence that a further remand in custody is necessary (Smith and Bailey, 1984, pp. 492–500; Spencer, 1989, pp. 248–54; Ingham, 1990, pp. 105–10). Although this right has been eroded in recent years (see below), the weekly tenure emphasises the temporary, provisional character of remand and the exclusion from the central functions of the prison system.

Remand in custody was therefore seen as a device of last resort where there was no other way to secure attendance at trial. According to Lord Russell in 1898: 'It cannot be too strongly impressed on the magistracy that bail is not to be withheld as a punishment but that the requirements as to bail are merely to secure the attendance of the prisoner at his trial.'[13] In accordance with this principle, the Anglo-American system had developed a bail system based upon a pre-trial contract for the payment of a variable amount of money-bail, relating to the seriousness of the offence and the likelihood of abscondence. Remand prisoners, where they were unable to find the sum proposed by the Court, were notionally being held for debt.

This private contract system was swept away in England and Wales by the Bail Act 1976 which established a new presumption in favour of bail to be enforced by the Court. This right is not absolute, but is hedged around with restrictions. Under Section

4(1) the right is excluded and replaced with a discretion to be exercised by the Court, where any of the Schedule 1, Part 1 conditions apply. These include substantial grounds for believing that the defendant will fail to surrender to custody, commit an offence while on bail or interfere with witnesses or otherwise obstruct the course of justice. The revolutionary new system proposed by the Act was intended to: 'Enable courts to release more prisoners on bail . . . without significantly . . . diminishing the protection afforded to the public.'[14]

The results of this liberalising measure were certainly spectacular, but not in the way that its sponsors had intended. Whereas in 1976 the remand population stood at 8 per cent of the entire prison population, by 1984 the figure had risen to 16.5 per cent and, in 1988, to 23 per cent. The proportion of remand prisoners in the prison system had therefore nearly trebled during the first twelve years of operation of the new Act.

Two explanations may be put forward for this explosion in the remand population during the last two decades. The first is that progressive attempts have been made to weaken the effect of the Act by cutting back the number of occasions on which an application for bail may be made. The second relates to the creation of a new role for pre-trial remand as preventative detention.

In 1980, the Divisional Court reduced the number of permitted applications for bail from a weekly basis throughout the remand in custody, to a maximum of two only, in the absence of 'a change of circumstances' justifying a further opportunity.[15] This restriction was ultimately given statutory force by Section 154 of the Criminal Justice Act 1988. Nevertheless, prisoners still had to be brought to the remanding court each week, despite having lost the right to ask for their freedom after the initial applications. The spectacle of large numbers of remand prisoners being ferried backwards and forwards for no conceivable purpose was clearly absurd and the logical next step was to allow them the right to waive their attendance at court each week. Eventually courts were given the power, in certain circumstances, to remand for twenty-eight days instead of the usual maximum of eight.[16]

The concept of pre-trial remand in custody as an exceptional infringement of a right, subject to repeated testing before different tribunals operating under adversarial principles, has thus given way to a single (or at best double) consideration of complete finality (Hayes, 1981).[17] Such a system compares unfavourably with the automatic periodical reviews available under many continental European systems.

A second factor in the increase in the percentage of remand prisoners within the prison population is the development of the use of interim custody as a means of preventing future offending. The central position of this concept has become a characteristic of the English and Welsh system and one which marks it off from comparable remand systems across the Channel. It rests upon the assumption that offending can be predicted with some accuracy and that pre-trial remand in custody is a legitimate weapon to prevent such offending.

The idea was developed largely on the initiative of the Court of Criminal Appeal under Lord Goddard in the 1950s (Vogler, 1983). As we have seen, 'the likelihood of further offences' was adopted as a ground for the refusal of bail in the 1976 Act. Figures released by the Home Office in 1978[18] indicated that the possibility of a defendant committing further offences while on bail had become the major reason for a remand in custody in 63 per cent of all custodial remands and, although the contemporary data is not available, there is evidence to suggest that this remains the primary ground for bail refusal.

Clearly, the remanding court is in no position and lacks the evidence to make actuarial predictions about the possibility of offences being committed between the time of remand and the trial. The continental approach, with its stress on the requirements of the investigation, seems at least to offer a more logical justification for remanding an unconvicted defendant.

Despite these serious inroads into the concept of adversarial procedure and the escalating population of remand prisoners, the percentage figures of remands are still low in comparison with other European jurisdictions. As has already been indicated, the major factor in this favourable relative rate is the rapidity of the pre-trial phase under an adversarial system. Although the length of time spent on custodial remand in England and Wales has increased from an average of twenty-seven days in 1977 to fifty-seven days in 1988,[19] these figures do not compare with continental waiting times. It is clearly unacceptable that 100 UK prisoners in 1988 had been waiting in excess of a year for trial, and 850 had been waiting over six months, but these exceptional delays can perhaps be avoided by the imposition of maximum time limits on the lines of the Scottish model.[20] Quite simply, the major advantage enjoyed by a remand prisoner in England and Wales over his or her continental counterpart is the rapidity of the pre-trial phase. Moreover, a further benefit of the common law pre-trial is that it involves the remand prisoner in decision-making about his or her own case. It also permits a regular flow of information, protection from institutional surveillance and (despite recent derogations from the principle) repeated contact with the remanding court in order to ensure sensitivity to changes in circumstances. It is these advantageous features of the system which would be lost if an inquisitorial mode of pre-trial were to be adopted.

The remand prisoner in the French system

The dangers of the *Instruction* running on at excessive length while a defendant waits in prison are met in most cases by the imposition of a clear system of time limits. In France, the length of time that a remand prisoner can be held before trial is determined by the gravity of the offence. For the highest category of offences (*crimes*), carrying penalties of five years and upwards, there is no maximum period of remand. However, a prisoner facing a charge characterised as a *délit* (less than five years' sentence) is entitled to an automatic review of his or her detention every four months (Article 145) and at the close of the *Instruction*. It is, of course, not unheard of for *crimes* to be charged initially, rather than *délits*, to avoid the necessity for the four-monthly decision-making process. Full hearings on the renewal applications are not obligatory until the total pre-trial custody exceeds twelve months. Despite the absence of any maximum term for pre-trial detention, Article 145 provides that a prisoner of good previous character facing a charge categorised as a *délit*, cannot be held for longer than a period of six months (two months after the first unsuccessful review).

Remand prisoners in France are entitled to separate accommodation in a remand centre (*maison d'arrêt*). There is a total of over 169 penal institutions in France, and the system is organised on a regional basis. Remand centres often form part of larger prisons and again overcrowding is concentrated on these populations.[21] However, conditions in French prisons, including remand prisons, are considerably better than in their English and Welsh counterparts. Sanitation is usually available in the cells and the whole régime is more relaxed and less militaristic. All prisoners are permitted to wear their own clothes and less time is spent locked up and more in association.

The rights of remand and other prisoners enshrined in the European Minimum Rules on the Treatment of Prisoners have all been adopted verbatim in the Prison Regulations in the 5th book of the Criminal Procedural Code, and the European Convention on Human Rights has also been incorporated into procedural law. Nevertheless, many of the domestic regulations regarding the right to a single cell, the absence of any obligation to work, and the complete liberty to correspond, have been denied in practice, and the régime for unconvicted prisoners is considerably more harsh than that for convicted offenders. Many of the extra restrictions relate to the role of the prisoner himself or herself in the evidence-gathering procedures of the *Instruction*.

As has already been noted, remand prisoners are under the direct authority of the Examining Magistrate sitting in their case, rather than the Prison Judge, and there has been considerable controversy regarding this relationship. He or she must censor all incoming and outgoing mail and may seize letters which may be of use as evidence for the *dossier* (Art. D65). There is no duty to inform the prisoner of the reasons for confiscation but correspondence with a prisoner's lawyer (Art. D419), and Consulate (Art. D244) may not be intercepted. Since the Magistrate must usually sanction visits, these are often rather more difficult to arrange than for serving prisoners (in contrast to the position in England and Wales). Telephone calls, which are sometimes available for serving prisoners, may not be made by remand prisoners. The Examining Magistrate is also responsible for complaints but is usually reluctant to interfere in the prison régime.

The remand prisoner in the Spanish system

Spain has the smallest prison population of any major European country and one of the highest proportions of unconvicted prisoners within that population. Prisoners in the Spanish system are distributed among seventy-four prisons, some with up to 560 inmates, such as *El Dueso* and some with as few as twenty-seven, such as *Ste Cruz de la Palma*. Over 50 per cent of the prison population is concentrated in the Catalan, Andalucian and Madrid provinces.

Despite the requirements of Regulation 14 of the *Reglamento Penitenciario*, which brings into operation the precepts of Article 24 of the 1978 Spanish Constitution and which insists on the strict separation of remand and serving prisoners, by no means all unconvicted detainees are held in separate remand prisons (*Establecimientos de Preventivos*). Crowded dormitory facilities in ordinary prisons (*Establecimientos de Cumplimiento de Penas*) often house a heterogeneous population ranging from the mentally ill to serious drug offenders. Remand prisoners cannot be subjected to any criminological observation or treatment and are not obliged to work.

The Spanish remand prisoner facing a serious charge must participate in an *Instruction* process (known as *sumario*) not dissimilar to that which operates in France. The powers and authority of the Examining Magistrate (*Juez de Instruccion*) are also comparable. Some prisoners can be ordered to be held *incommunicado* for up to five days (Art. 506) if the Magistrate feels that there is a likelihood of interference with the course of justice. The amount of correspondence permitted to a remand prisoner is in any event considerably less than that of a serving prisoner, again in contrast to the position in England and Wales.

The Spanish Penal Procedural Code (Art. 504) requires that all pre-trial matters must be dealt with by the prosecution and the court authorities as quickly as possible (*de forma prioritia y con especial diligencia*) where a defendant is in custody. Usually the court file in these cases is marked with a red sticker *causa con preso*. In theory, the *Instruction* must last no longer than a month and if the work is not done by this time, the Examining Magistrate must provide regular reports to the trial court (*Audiencia Provincial*) explaining the reasons for the delay. However, in practice these limits are regularly exceeded. Moreover, as in France, a system of formal time limits is imposed by the Penal Procedural Code, based upon the nature of the offence charged. For example, a defendant charged with an offence carrying a penalty of up to six months maximum (*arresto mayor*) cannot be held for more than three months on remand. Similarly, the remand of a defendant who faces a sentence of *prisión menor* (six months and one day, up to six years) cannot exceed one year. Finally, two years is the maximum period of remand for prisoners facing longer terms (*prisión mayor* and above).

However, under Art. 504, the time limits for *prisión menor* and *prisión mayor* can be extended (and frequently are extended) to two and four years, respectively, after a prosecution application to the effect that the case is a complicated one. Needless to say, the cases of individuals facing long prison sentences are rarely given priority and delays of up to several years are not unheard of.

Again, the general position and welfare of the remand prisoner is the responsibility of the Examining Magistrate who is obliged to make weekly unannounced visits in the company of the prosecutor to prisons in his area. He or she must find out everything possible regarding the situation of those detained and do what can be done to remedy problems (Art. 526).

The remand prisoner in the German system

Although the German trial system is essentially inquisitorial, it does not employ the extended pre-trial *Instruction* phase familiar from the French and Spanish models. Since the focus is on the trial itself, the pre-trial is much abbreviated and this is reflected in the percentage of remands in the prison population. German prison facilities are generally not so severely crowded as those in other European countries, and the population of 53,039, which has been declining for some years, is dispersed among 168 prisons with a total capacity in excess of the actual numbers incarcerated. The principle that remand prisoners should be treated in a 'more dignified, just and humane' manner (Remand Prisoners Code, Art. 18) is accorded more respect than in some other jurisdictions. The health of remand prisoners is regarded as being of special concern since it might inhibit their chances of standing trial. They are allowed special medical facilities and may be taken under escort for outside medical treatment.

However, remand prisoners are subject to the same degree of surveillance as those in France and Spain. The pre-trial judge (*Hafrichter*) again has a supervisory responsibility and will (together with the prosecutor) censor mail coming in and out. Letters which are considered relevant as evidence may be produced at trial.

Where possible, prisoners are kept in a single cell during remand and it has often been suggested that this policy may be intended to encourage a desire to talk and confess.

Remand prisoners are allowed to keep their own rings and watches (unless this interferes with prison order) and can have their own bedding, cutlery and tablecloth, etc. Clothing and other linen can only be sent in if it is collected regularly for washing. Remand prisoners are not obliged to work and cannot be punished as severely as serving prisoners for disciplinary offences. It is not possible, for example, for shopping rights (*Einkauf*) to be taken away. The pre-trial judge has ultimate authority to overrule the prison regulations in the interests of a fair trial or the prisoner's health. Friends and relatives who feel aggrieved by restrictions on communication can also lodge appeals with the court.

The scope of pre-trial remand in German courts again depends critically on the nature of the offence charged and the penalty anticipated. A defendant suspected of a minor offence (*Vergehen*) is unlikely to face detention unless the pre-trial judge takes the view that he will abscond. This view must be based on a previous abscondence, an immediate threat of abscondence, no fixed address or a failure to establish identity. Beyond these exceptions, no defendant charged with a minor offence may be held.

With regard to more serious offences (*Verbrechen*), on the other hand, the discretion is wider. As an alternative to the likelihood of abscondence (*Fluchtgefahr*), the likelihood of interference with evidence or the witnesses will suffice, under Article 112 of the Penal Procedural Code, to deny bail. However, detention is governed by the principle of proportionality to the offence (*Verhältnismäszigkeit*). This means that the pre-trial judge must look at the seriousness of the crime and weigh that against the defendant's background, including his employment, family situation and residence.

There are, however, two main exceptions to these general principles which reflect the position in England and Wales. The first is that where a defendant is charged with an offence carrying a penalty in excess of two years' imprisonment and there is danger of repetition of the offence, he is likely to lose his liberty. This provision, under Art. 112 III will only be invoked where a defendant has been imprisoned for a similar offence during the past five years.

The second exception relates to very grave offences, where none of the usual restrictions on custody applies. Such offences would include murder, serious bodily harm, genocide, explosives and terrorist cases.

There are no overall time limits on custody. However, appeals may be lodged with the Local State Court (*Amtsgericht*) at any time and there is a regular system of reviews. The Local State Court must review the detention after three months and, unless the prosecution applies for an extension, the preliminary detention order will be vacated by the Regional State Court (*Landgericht*) after six months (Art. 121 I). If the prosecution seek further detention and their decision is opposed, there will be a defended adversarial hearing before the Regional State Court (Art. 122 I), during which the court must decide whether or not the complexity of the case, or some other significant reason, is preventing the case from coming to trial and justifies further detention. It may order successive three-monthly periods of detention.

Although remand prisoners under the German system are not subject to a classic *Instruction* process, they must still undergo the restrictions on communication and access which normally accompany it. The extent to which the superior material conditions within German prisons compensate for this imposition is difficult to say.

Pre-trial remand is surely the most stressful and demanding period of a prison sentence and the suicide rate is then at its highest. Remand populations are volatile, often unsegregated and outside the settled patterns of prison life. Since they occupy a no-man's land between criminal jurisprudence and penal theory, their plight is not always given the attention that it deserves.

The aim of this article has been to indicate that the most pressing problems for remand prisoners are not simply those which relate to the material conditions and the control régimes under which they live. What may be of equal importance is the purpose of the remand, and clarity in this matter is essential. Already, attempts are being made to harmonise aspects of the pre-trial phase across European national boundaries, and this should not be attempted unless clear guidelines on the treatment of the unconvicted are established. On 18 July 1990, Sir Peter Imbert, the Metropolitan Chief Commissioner of London, suggested the adoption in Britain of a continental pre-trial system under the supervision of an Examining Magistrate.[22] This view is shared by a number of senior British judges including Lord Scarman[23] and was established as a specific issue to be considered by the 1991 Royal Commission on Criminal Justice.[24] Similarly, in France, proposals have been put forward to adopt an adversarial mode of procedure on bail applications, similar to that operated by English and Welsh courts. Under this proposal, the powers of Examining Magistrates over remand prisoners would be considerably weakened (Levasseur, Chavanne & Montreuil, 1988, pp. 185–6).

Such proposals open up the possibility of a European minimum standards régime relating to the specific needs of remand prisoners, to match those which operate in the area of prison conditions and rights of procedural fairness at trial generally. These might include minimum standards of access to information for prisoners, minimum rights of involvement in the pre-trial and maximum lengths of remand incarceration throughout Europe.

Notes

1. Council of Europe (1990) *Prison Information Bulletin*, June, p. 8.
2. See Prison Act 1877, s.39.
3. See s.47(4)(d) of the 1952 Act.
4. Rule 3(2).
5. Rule 34(1).
6. SI No.89.
7. Rule 20(1).
8. Rule 17(4).
9. First Report from the Home Affairs Committee, Session 1983–4, *Remands in Custody*, vol. 1, HMSO, 1984, para. 1. See also Woolf (1991) p. 26.
10. *New Law Journal*, 12 May 1989, p. 633.
11. Over 40% of the prison population at Strangeways at the time of the riots was on remand (Woolf, 1991, p. 45).
12. Address to the Gloucestershire branch of the Magistrates' Association, 11 September 1971.
13. *R. v. Rose* (1898) 78 LT 119.
14. Pltry. Debs. 912, 25 July 1976, 475.
15. *R. v. Nottingham Justices (ex parte Davies)* [1980] 2 All ER 775.
16. Criminal Justice Act 1988, s.155.
17. There is a further right of appeal to a judge in chambers in the Crown Court under s.59 of the Criminal Justice Act 1982.
18. Home Office Criminal Statistics (1979) Table 8:9.
19. NACRO (1988) *Briefing Paper*.
20. *New Law Journal* 17 February 1989, p. 209.
21. French remand facilities have an occupancy rate of 164% overall

compared with 100% in non-remand prisons (Council of Europe,
Prison Information Bulletin, June 1990, p. 20).
22. *The Times*, 18 July, 1990, p. 5. See also *Guardian*, 10 January 1990,
p. 10.
23. *The Times*, 5 March 1991, p. 10.
24. *Guardian*, 15 March 1991, p. 1.

References

Casale, S. and Plotnikoff, J. (1990). *Regimes for Remand Prisoners*.
London, Prison Reform Trust.
Farrar, J. H. and Dugdale, A. M. (1990). *An Introduction to Legal
Method*, London, Sweet and Maxwell.
Hayes, M. (1981). 'Where now the Right to Bail?', *Criminal Law Review*,
pp. 20–4.
Ingham, T. (1990). *The English Legal Process*, London, Blackstone Press.
Kattau, T. F. (1990). '*1992 – Europe Without Frontiers*'. *New Security
Concepts as a Consequence of diminishing Borders in Europe?*, London,
Unpublished Conference Paper.
Levasseur, G., Chavanne, A. and Montreuil, J. (1988). *Droit Pénal et
Procédure Pénale*, Paris, Editions Sirey.
Merryman, J. H. (1969), *The Civil Law Tradition*, Stanford, Stanford UP.
Morgan, R. and King, R. (1977). 'A trying time for the untried', *The
Howard Journal*, vol. 15, pp. 32–43.
Plotnikoff, J. (1986). *Prison Rules, A Working Guide*, London, Prison
Reform Trust.
Prison Reform Trust (1985). *Remand Project Report No. 7*, London,
Prison Reform Trust.
Smith, P. F. and Bailey, S. H. (1984). *The Modern English Legal System*,
London, Sweet and Maxwell.
Spencer, J.R. (1989). *The Machinery of Justice in England*, Cambridge,
CUP.
Spencer, M. (1990). *1992 and All That. Civil Liberties in the Balance*,
London, The Civil Liberties Trust.
Stein, P. (1984). *Legal Institutions. The Development of Dispute Settlement*,
London, Stevens and Sons.
Stern, V. (1987). *Bricks of Shame. Britain's Prisons*, Harmondsworth,
Penguin.
Treverton-Jones, G. D. (1989). *Imprisonment: The Legal Status and
Rights of Prisoners*, London, Sweet and Maxwell.
Vogler, R. K. (1983). 'The Changing Nature of Bail', *LAG Bulletin*,
February, pp. 11–15.
Winfield, M. (1984). *Lacking Conviction. The Remand System in England
and Wales*, London, Prison Reform Trust.
Woolf, The Rt. Hon., the Lord Justice (1991). *Prison Disturbances April
1990, Report of an Inquiry*, London, HMSO, Cm 1456.

Index